MW00445288

The cover photograph is by Leslie Roberts, council trainer and land steward at the Ojai Foundation for many years. The circle is made up of seniors from New Roads High School in Santa Monica and their youth retreat leaders, gathering during a rite of passage experience at the Foundation.

Graphics by Virginia Coyle and Leslie Roberts

After many years of dreaming, planning and fund-raising, the Ojai Foundation opened its Council House in October of 2008. The Council House is a thoroughly green indoor gathering space—and a "tent of meeting." It is a place for learning and confirmation, reconciliation and celebration, healing and transformation—and a home for listening.

THE WAY OF COUNCIL

2ND EDITION

JACK ZIMMERMAN
VIRGINIA COYLE

BRAMBLE BOOKS

For information contact Bramble Books,
email: info@bramblebooks.com, or visit our website, www.bramblebooks.com

---

Library of Congress has cataloged the 1st Edition as follows:

Zimmerman, Jack M.
    The way of council / Jack M. Zimmerman, in collaboration with
Virginia Coyle.
        p.   cm.
    ISBN 1-883647-05-3 (pbk.)
        1. Communication in small groups. 2. Interpersonal
communication. 3. Decision-making. 4. Listening. 5. Indian
councils. 1. Coyle, Virginia. II. Title.
    HM133.Z55 1996
        302.3'4—dc20   96-21974
                    CIP

2nd Edition ISBN: 978-1-883647-18-6

First Printing (1st Edition) 1996
First Printing (2st Edition) 2009

Printed in USA

The paper used in this publication meets the minimum requirements of
American National Standard for Information Sciences—Permanence of Paper
for Printed Library Materials, ANSI Z39.48-1984.

ACKNOWLEDGMENTS

The woman who told me the Pueblo story that opens the book was Marian Bayes, who survived being my eleventh-grade English teacher to introduce me to analytic psychology and other revelations of the human condition during my early adult years.

My first formal council was led by Elizabeth Cogburn on an Ojai Foundation backpacking trip to the Sespe Wilderness in 1980. She and her husband Bob had been using council for years as part of their New Song Sun Dance ceremonials. From 1980 through 1984, my life partner Jaquelyn McCandless, longtime colleague Ruthann Saphier, and many other teachers, parents, and children contributed their skills and enthusiasm to the development of the daily practice of council at the experimental Heartlight School in Los Angeles.

In response to an invitation from Paul Cummins, then headmaster of Crossroads School in Santa Monica, Ruthann, Maureen Murdock, and I launched the council-based "Mysteries Program" in 1983 at the school. Since then many have made substantial contributions to the Crossroads Program, including Rachael Kessler, Tom Nolan, Peggy O'Brien, David Bryan, Bonnie Tamblyn, Adam Behrman and its current leader, Sheila Bloch. In recent years, Mysteries Programs have been implemented in a variety of schools in California and other parts of the country. In 1992 Tom and I started the first formal council program in the Los Angeles Unified School District at the Palms Middle School with the support of Lana Brody and Hugh Gottfried, one of its assistant-principals and principal, respectively. Joe Provisor, then a Palms English teacher and Impact Coordinator, played a major role in the evolution of the Palms Council Program.

Council was first introduced to the Ojai Foundation in 1980 by Joan Halifax, who had encountered it many years earlier in her experience with native cultures. Council now flourishes at the Foundation as an integral part of student retreats, adult programs, leadership trainings, and the community's way of self-governance.

Council leadership trainings for educators, community members, therapists, and others came of age when Gigi and I began co-leading them at the Ojai Foundation in the mid-eighties. Gigi brought many years of circle experience with women's and wilderness groups to these three-day intensives. In particular, she introduced the teachings and practice of council in the creation of "The Box: Remembering the Gift," a unique collection of educational materials developed by the Terma Company of Santa Fe, New Mexico, designed to assist individuals and groups along their spiritual journey. In addition, Gigi has been instrumental in implementing council practice in cross-cultural communities and networks, and non-profit service and business organizations in the US and abroad.

Since 1980, I have sat in thousands of councils with primary and secondary school students, teachers, community members, business men, and women—and members of my own family. During this same period, Jaquelyn and I began using council as a primary process in our own relationship and in our counseling practices. "Dyadic council" turned out to be a major ally in developing better communication and realizing our shared vision of relationship as a spiritual path. Many couples who participate in our "Mysteries of Eros" (now called "Flesh and Spirit") workshops in Ojai, or with whom we work privately, have also found council to be an invaluable tool in building a more conscious and spirited life together.

In closing, Gigi and I want to acknowledge those who have made substantial contributions to the material in these pages, notably: Jaquelyn throughout—particularly in Chapter 9, Tom Nolan in Chapter 7, Sharon Gonzales in Chapter 8, and Elissa Zimmerman in Chapter 11. The graphic symbols used in each chapter were created by

Gigi and our friend and colleague Leslie Roberts. I am further grateful to Jaquelyn for originally encouraging me to write the book and unselfishly keeping my nose to the grindstone. Similarly, Gigi wants to thank her partner, Win, for his unwavering support in all ways and her dear friend, Meredith Little, for her edits on every level. These individuals and many others make up the circle that is the true source of our writings.

My friend and colleague Aaron Kipnis read the entire original manuscript and suggested many ways for making the material more accessible. Margaret Ryan's painstaking editorial scrutiny and enthusiastic support throughout the final stages of the writing significantly improved the book's organization, clarity, and grammatical integrity. We owe a great deal of our sense of satisfaction in completing *The Way of Council*, to Margaret's expertise, good humor, and unerring eye for "fuzzy" prose.

We honor all the native peoples whose roots are intertwined with the practice of council and sit in gratitude for the circle way that has been carried by our ancestors around the world. It is because of you that council is embedded in our bones. It is no small irony that the call to circle is so strong now, particularly from schools, where it was first banned in an attempt to eradicate native cultures.

Finally, to our teachers, in person and in nature, whose lessons surface in council when least expected, to all the many schools and organizations exploring council-like ways of communicating that help free us from old hierarchical authority patterns, and, in particular, to members of the Ojai Foundation Community, the several thousand students and many other friends with whom we have sat in council these past thirty years, our warmest appreciation for your stories and your listening. This book, our work, and our lives have been greatly nourished by the wisdom of this larger circle.

CONTENTS

PREFACE

In the 60's, I found myself longing for those Kindergarten circles when everybody held hands and was quiet for a minute. I had a hard time with the borderline-violent communication within our radical student movement. I yearned for those days of simple "show and tell" when each of us—boys and girls together—shared a special experience or object from home, and everyone watched and listened with full attention.

In the 70's, after emerging from twenty years of all-women's schools, I initiated women's circles and councils in the political arenas where I was so passionately drawn. When being the only woman in an international graduate school of U.S. and foreign students became overwhelming for me, I fantasized about a culture in which wisdom was drawn from the magic of silence and the circle. I began spending more and more time in nature, my place of refuge in childhood. There I sat in council with the animals and trees, the sun and moon, the wind and fire—elements of life that had unending patience, freedom, beauty, and fortitude. There I developed a connection with dolphins that inspired me to seek a similar communion between humans. I began a pilgrimage to discover others so committed.

In the early 80's I arrived at the Ojai Foundation, where I met Joan Halifax and, soon after, Jack Zimmerman. In Joan I found the sister I longed for who knew the power of silence and the medicine of bringing together teachers from different spiritual traditions and cultures. What I found at Ojai was familiar; the community's circle was embedded in the land in a way of life that embodied the wisdom of elders and a knowing that comes from living close to the earth. All seemed natural and on track at last. The pilgrim had found a spiritual home.

Although our early attempts were far from perfect, the practice of listening was seeded strongly in the councils at Ojai. I had sat in many circles of women and in a few with men. In Jack I was surprised and delighted to discover a white, mainstream male with a deep commitment and care for what we now call "the way of council." I already knew that it was essential for women to bring forth ways of leading and communicating that were not empowered primarily by societal position and gender. But I didn't expect to meet such a devotee of change among successful men who had a stake in the status quo.

In those days Jack sat in council with families, children, teachers, school administrators—virtually anyone who would join him. As the complex issues of living in community surfaced at the Foundation, he encouraged the practice of council as a way of governance. We came to appreciate the prospects for resolving immediate disturbances through council. More important, we began to recognize how the circle helped us to open our hearts and touch the "soul of the community" on a regular basis.

In the years that followed, I witnessed Jack bring council more strongly into his life, not only professionally as an educator and counselor, but also personally as a father and intimate partner with his wife Jaquelyn. Gradually I stepped forward myself offering some of what I had learned walking the road of listening and caring for "the whole." Jack's and my mutual commitment to council blossomed into a productive friendship that included co-facilitating council trainings, being co-directors (along with Marlow Hotchkiss) of the Ojai Foundation, co-chairing the Foundation's Board of Directors, and, ultimately, collaborating on the writing of this book.

Over the years I have remained respectful and a bit in awe of the dedication to the heartful way of council that Jack embodies. He is rightfully renowned for sitting through the longest, wildest circles in the Foundation's history. He has been recognized as a catalyst and visionary by taking council into independent and public schools, intentional communities, and business organizations as seemingly far afield as an automobile dealership. I am often touched by a wave of gratitude that I met Jack and acted upon the opportunity to sit, listen, and create with such a strong "carrier of council." It gives me faith and hope to work closely with a professional man at home in western society who also has the insight and devotion to bring forward the way of council in our times.

When Jack began collating stories and experiences for the first draft of this book, I questioned both his call to write and his invitation to collaborate. I worried about the time it would take us away from working directly with people and holding the spirit of the circle in our daily lives. Yet, as so many times in the past, Jack's determination won me over. As you read these pages, filled with pearls from many years of sitting in council, I am sure you will discover the value of the gift this man has brought to the medicine of council.

But I hope gratitude will be only part of your response. I also invite you to express whatever questions, challenges, and need for "tuning" this book stirs in you—as I have done over the years of our working relationship. Even when I strongly questioned Jack's way of expressing cherished ideas about council, he listened. By entering into such a dialogue you will meet Jack and join in the spirit of council to which our lives are dedicated. If we continue to question and listen, to speak and be heard, we can together create an offering for the benefit of all beings.

February, 1996

And now it is 2009 . . .

Jack and I continue to initiate and sit in many councils; we lead some alone, fortunately still a few together, and many with other carriers. For some people council remains a technique, but for us and many others we meet today, it is a way of life. Jack's focus in the area of education has become more as mentor and elder. A large emphasis for him now is in bringing council beyond the borders of the US, notably to Israel and Africa. His deepest passion remains in the relational world. He and his life partner, Jaquelyn, have most recently expanded their couples' council work in Israel. They have come to believe that the healing between men and women is at the core of co-existence, social and environmental justice, the exploration of true peace between humans and all our relations. I continue to go where and when the call comes—to Israel, to a prison, to Zen centers, to the wilderness, to indigenous elders, to the young people...As always, I continue to learn more as I sit myself down on the ground in the round.

Over the past ten years the network of council carriers—those who remember the council way in their bones, as well as those who discover it for the first time—is growing worldwide. After publishing this book In Hebrew in 2006, we are now responding to an offer to release a German Edition. It seems telling that we are often called back along our own ancestral lines to share the gift. Motivated by the interest and dedication of many council leaders in Europe, we have taken the time to update some of the material in the first edition. As we re-read the book, it was exciting for us to see how much of it stands up to time. We feel this is just a small reflection of how the spirit of council has weathered centuries, appearing and reappearing with new cultures and new generations. We have never doubted that the council way is beyond any "new age," as we offer it humbly and simply, as people of our own time.

What we have done for this second edition of *The Way of Council* is to make the necessary changes that reflect the passage of thirteen years, as well as adding a few new stories that explore the mystery of the practice. The major additions are two new chapters towards the end of the book which give Jack and I an opportunity to share some of our more recent work and reflections about council, and a new appendix about starting council programs in schools.

We offer this second edition particularly in gratitude for those who carry council beyond the US borders—those we know in South Africa, Mali, Ghana, Israel, Palestine, Germany, Austria, Switzerland, Italy, Wales, England, Australia, Canada and Mexico—and those we have never met in places we have not been. To you—and to all those who share the call for deeper listening, we offer the book as an ally, as we move into the cycle of healing among all peoples and with the planet that is so needed at this time.

Virginia (Gigi) Coyle
January, 2009

INTRODUCTION

It's the blood of the Ancients
That flows through our veins
The forms change
But the circle of life remains

—Chant attributed to Charlie Murphy[1]

I think his name was Joe—or something equally simple. He was part Hispanic and part Native American. His grandfather, his father's father, was full-blooded and a member of the Pueblo's Council of Elders. Joe had left the Pueblo as a child with his Hispanic mother and had come back during the Depression, when he was twenty, to further his education in the old ways.

---

[1] Since council is often initiated with a song or chant, we follow this practice by beginning most chapters with a chant that has been sung in many of our circles. Some of these chants were adapted from traditional cultures; some were created by contemporary communities or individuals. Where we have been able to trace the origin of the chant, we will acknowledge the individual, community, or culture from which it arose. However, in our experience, when a circle embraces a chant as part of its group practice, the chant's origins can be lost in the familiarity of repeated singing. In one sense this can be seen as disrespectful of the source—particularly when it is traditional. But it is also true that taking on a chant honors the culture, community or individual from which it sprang. We offer these chants respectfully, in the spirit of this second perspective.

Shortly after Joe's return, the Federal Government made an important proposal to the Pueblo People concerning a land trade and mineral rights. The elders called a council to decide what to do and Joe's grandfather invited him to join the circle as a witness.

Joe waited for the men to enter the kiva before he climbed down the ladder, carrying his rolled-up blanket. He found a place behind his grandfather near the ledge cut into the curved adobe wall that supported clay pots, drums, and bundles of dried blue corn. A fire burned in the pit at the center of the hard dirt floor. The traditional large reflecting stone sat on one side of the fire opposite the *sipapu*, which represented the opening in the earth through which the First People arrived from the Underworld.

The elders sat quietly for several minutes, while Joe listened expectantly for the start of the discussion. Then the Pueblo leader unwrapped a blue and white bundle and took out what looked like a pipe stem. It was about a foot and a half long and had feathers and strands of turquoise tied to one end; the other end was wrapped in leather. Although he had never actually seen it before, Joe knew it was the tribal "talking stick" that was used only for important councils. The leader held the stick gently in his hands for a moment and then told the story of how Deer learned to run like tumbleweed chased by the dry desert wind. Joe dimly remembered the story from his childhood in the Pueblo.

When the leader finished, he passed the talking stick to the elder on his left, who told a story Joe had never heard before about the ancestors who had built the Pueblo. And so it went, each of the old men adding his tale to the circle, as if he were placing a precious log on the ceremonial fire. Part of Joe became a child again, enthralled with the stories that had defined and sustained his people for generations. The other part grew increasingly confused and restless. *When are they going to start discussing the Government's proposal*, this part of Joe wondered. Although the stories touched something deep in him, four hours had passed and the proposal had not been mentioned even once.

When the talking stick returned to the leader, Joe sat up very straight in order not to miss a word of the discussion he assumed would follow. But the leader slowly laid the stick down on the blue and white cloth and closed his eyes. All the others did the same. The only sound was the soft crackling of the fire.

In the quiet of the kiva with the elders, Joe remembered the sounds of drumming and singing from his childhood—and he continued to wonder when they would start debating the proposal. After a very long half hour, all the elders stirred at once, as if by silent prearrangement, and looked into each other's eyes, slowly and deliberately. No words were exchanged. There was no debate. Then to Joe's amazement, the men stretched their limbs, immobile all those hours, got to their feet, and filed out of the kiva without saying a word. Joe waited until everyone had left and then hurried to catch up with his grandfather.

"What's going on?" he blurted out, a little out of breath. The old man stifled a smile and kept on walking. "I thought the council was going to take up the proposal," Joe continued in confusion.

"We did," his grandfather said in a quiet voice.

"I didn't hear any debate—and I certainly didn't hear any decision," Joe responded, still mystified.

"Then you weren't listening," his grandfather answered, and lost his battle with the smile. "In council one listens in the silences between the words with the ears of a rabbit."

"You mean the council actually took up the proposal and reached a decision?"

"Yes."

"In the silence?"

"And in the stories," his grandfather added, laughing. Joe suddenly understood what had happened. At that moment he glimpsed the magic of council and felt his connection to what had happened in the kiva. The way the men listened and spoke, each contributing their part to the truth of the whole circle, struck him as nothing short of miraculous.

Does this story seem unreal to you? Is it hard to believe that a group of people could communicate with each other so deeply and effectively about a complex, critical issue without ever once *directly* discussing it? Those were my initial reactions when I first heard the story more than forty-five years ago. The story was told to me by a friend of Joe's who visited him regularly in the Pueblo over a span of many years. (In case you're wondering, the council of elders rejected the Government's offer.)

Although I had heard the tale secondhand, the meeting in the kiva nestled quietly in a corner of my mind, until fifteen years later, the moment came for it to emerge and redirect my life's work. Such is the power of story. The Council of Elders became my inspiration for offering children and adults an opportunity to touch the ancient wisdom of the circle in meeting the formidable challenges of contemporary life.

Over the years council became an increasingly strong presence in my life. As its power to support individual growth, family, relationships, and community became increasingly visible, those of us who had come together to explore the process became more curious about its roots.

The tradition of council is ancient. On this continent, it can be traced to the League of the Iroquois (who had a great influence on shaping our form of government) and the native peoples of the Plains and Southwestern Pueblos. The traditional practice of council has also emerged in contemporary form in the Native American Church. In the traditional Hawaiian Culture council arises in the form of the "ho'o pono pono" practice now being revived on the Islands. References to council can be found in classical Greek literature in no less a

prominent source than Homer's Iliad.[2] The spirit of council is strongly present in the Islamic world as well. On the day of prayers, a person
is chosen to hold the staff, representing the one who speaks to the
gathering, as did Mohammed on the mountain.

Our exploration of council was inspired only in part by Native
American traditions. Other influences include the wisdom of the
Quaker meeting, extended family gatherings, and many contemporary techniques of group dynamics. The Ojai Foundation and other
organizations that seek to embrace cultural differences and honor the
sacred in all spiritual traditions, embody the essence of council and
support its practice. The simple teachings that arise from living close
to the land in places of power and beauty, such as the Foundation,
have probably had the greatest influence of all.

In implementing council in contemporary settings, we have shared
the concern of many people, Native American and others, about the
appropriation of one culture's sacred ceremonies by another. Our aim
has always been to practice a form of council that honors the spirit of
the ancient ceremonies without the pretense of being traditional. *We
believe that the many forms of council belong to all people who gather in the
circle to embrace the challenge of listening and speaking from the heart.*

One of our intentions in writing about council is to provide a
practical guide for conducting council in a variety of settings and
situations. However, since council is not simply a technique to be
acquired, we have also included numerous stories and personal experiences in the hope of conveying the spirit of the process as well.
Indeed, many of us who sit in circle regularly have come to see council
as a spiritual practice, whether the circle is comprised of many dealing
with community concerns or just two people exploring the mysteries of intimate relationship. By spiritual we do not mean to suggest
a connection to any particular tradition or doxology. For us, a
spiritual practice is any activity that both awakens the desire for, and

---

[2] For example, see *The Anger of Achilles: Homer's Iliad*, translated by Robert Graves, Doubleday, 1959. The opening scene (p. 44) of Graves' retelling of the story includes a council in
which a "gold-studded wand" was used in an attempt to resolve a bitter dispute between
Achilles and Agamemnon.

provides the means to expand consciousness of Self, Other, and the Larger Mystery.

In council the gateway to the Mystery is *listening*. We listen in council with more than our ears. We listen with the same awareness a mountain person gives to the wind in the alders or a mother gives to her young child learning to speak. As we practice the way of council, we listen increasingly without reaction, without being influenced by long-held thoughts or associations—as a five-year-old would listen to a favorite bedtime story. When we listen this way, and the person speaking is able to do so authentically, we can see his or her story unfolding in front of us.

Participating in council teaches us how to let go of personal expectations and become fully attentive to others. The practice fosters compassionate response and provides a continuing source of wisdom. Compassion arises naturally when we listen with respect and express ourselves honestly with an open heart, whether it be in words, song, movement, or silence. Wisdom flows from the wholeness of the circle and reveals itself as the "truth of council." The expression of this truth can come through anyone in the circle or through the silence. Listening to the voice of council teaches us that the circle's knowledge is greater than the totality of its members' individual knowing.

In this state of collective awareness, diversity and disagreement do not lead as readily to polarization and hostility. Learning to hear the voice of council can help people transcend even the most deeply ensconced cultural, racial, and personal identifications. Feeling part of the circle's wholeness reduces the fear and despair of isolation, which allows disagreement to become the bridge to greater mutual understanding. Witnessing the truth of the circle emerge from a cacophony of diverse views can be a remarkable experience. Some have described it as a feeling of unseen voices supporting the group— a spirit circle that meets concentrically with its earthly counterpart, guiding it towards greater mutual understanding and right action.

This feeling dispels the illusion that we are separate individuals living inside the boundaries of our skins. The sense of wholeness during council can be astounding, probably because most of us have rarely *felt* the reality of interdependence in such a tangible way. Most religions teach the importance of treating others as you would have them treat you. In recent years, awareness of the interconnectedness of all life forms with the earth itself has spread around the globe with increasing urgency. From the general public's growing focus on global warming to the current interest in self-organizing and co-arising fields on the part of both spiritual teachers and academicians, the notion of interdependence has become a part of mainstream life. This is the territory of council —now being given insightful descriptions and formulations in contemporary terms. We hope part of our contribution is to remember the roots of these ideas and see them as evidence that the way of council is continuously evolving. To *feel* interdependence in a council circle anchors these primal teachings in the personal realm of direct experience.

1

CALLING
THE COUNCIL

Where I sit is holy
Holy is the ground
Forest, mountain, river
Listen to the sound
Great Spirit circling
All around me

—Native-American Chant

Several years ago I was asked to speak about council to a group of seventy-five teachers and storytellers who were participating in a conference on the power of story. Mid-morning of the first day, I found myself standing behind a traditional lectern, looking out over very straight rows of expectant faces. The incongruity of the situation stopped me cold. Rather than talking at them about council, I wanted to provide an experience of participating in one directly. But I had less than two hours and there weren't enough experienced council leaders at the conference to create smaller, more manageable groups. Introducing council for the first time to more than twenty people is a challenge. A council of seventy-five felt overwhelming!

In my moment of indecision, I remembered that a council leader's overriding commitment is to respond creatively to the moment. The situation may demand relinquishing familiar patterns in order to work with current realities in a productive way. So, throwing caution to the wind, I asked my audience to rearrange themselves in a large circle. The sound of scraping chairs dominated the next few minutes as I tried to come up with a plan that would allow seventy-five people the option to speak in the time allotted. Some might choose to be silent, but I needed a focus that would allow those who wanted to speak to do so—briefly but in a satisfying way.

Sitting in the large circle brought me home. Immediately a workable plan and a suitable theme popped into my head. Unwrapping the carob pod talking stick I usually brought to such gatherings, I began:

> "We're going to pass this large carob pod around the circle in a clockwise direction from person to person. Only the person holding the pod is allowed to talk. The rest of us listen as attentively as we can. You may choose not to speak. Silence can make an important contribution to the circle. For this council I'd like you to tell a very short story about a shameful or embarrassing moment in your childhood—a story you haven't shared with many people, perhaps not even your immediate family or closest friends. Our circle is large, so choose your words carefully and relate just the essence of the story."

I decided to begin.

> "Although my grandmother intimidated many people in our family, I was her favorite, which is probably one of the reasons I loved her so much. In my earliest memories, she already

had a full head of white hair and the caustic sense of humor she took to the grave. Towards the end of her life we played hilarious games of gin rummy in the living room of her Atlantic City boarding house. When Nellie died, I experienced penetrating grief for the first time in my life.

"One of my greatest joys in those teenage years was playing a favorite piece of classical music on the phonograph while I 'conducted' the orchestra. After my mother told me the news of my grandmother's death, I closed the door of my bedroom and put on the slow movement of Beethoven's *Seventh Symphony*, a piece I knew would embrace my sadness. I was passionately drawing out the best from the New York Philharmonic, when my mother burst into the room. 'Shut it off!' she shouted over the music. 'In the Jewish tradition, you're not supposed to do anything joyous when a family member dies!' I thought playing a melancholy piece I loved dearly honored my grandmother, so the intensity of the rebuke left me confused and ashamed. I didn't know about the tradition and, besides, we could hardly be called observant Jews. I smoldered with injustice for days. My mother and I didn't have a chance to clear the air between us until a week after the funeral."

My story took less than a minute. Others followed in turn with their anecdotes, some funny, some sad, some mundane, some bizarre. A mood of relaxed attentiveness prevailed, which soon created a feeling of intimacy in the circle. One man took a few minutes to share something he had never told anyone. His tears were contagious. As it turned out, only one person passed the talking piece without speaking. When I finally took the large carob pod from the person on my right, I glanced at my watch. We had gone around the circle in one hour and twenty minutes. There was still time to have a discussion with a group of people who now felt at ease with each other and touched by the magic of council.

SETTING THE SCENE

The Size of the Circle

There are different forms of council for working with "groups" of two to groups of a hundred or more. The most appropriate size for a circle depends on the time allotted for the council, the agenda or theme chosen, and the attention span of the participants. If building intimacy within the group is a high priority, then everyone in the circle needs to have the chance to express themselves at least once. We have found that most adults can remain attentive for two or three hours. For young children, an hour can be a long time to listen carefully to others. Generally (but not always), the more experienced the participants, the longer their attention span.

Councils of ten to fifteen generally provide a comfortable balance between the number of voices and the demands on participants' attentiveness. Above twenty, councils can get unwieldy, so that special forms or time restrictions may be necessary. Smaller councils of four, five, or six (family councils, for example) usually allow ample time to explore the issues. When the group is unavoidably large and the time limited, the leader can reduce unfocused meandering by asking for attentiveness to the situation so that everyone has an opportunity to share. If long-winded sharing and a lack of focus become an issue in an ongoing group, it may be helpful to conduct a "time awareness" council, in which conciseness is made a high priority.

Sometimes size is not as influential a factor as one might expect. Gigi has led successful councils in circles of 150. I have participated in councils of ninety teenagers who worked together smoothly—and fifteen young people who were fragmented and unfocused. I once survived an eight-hour council with a group of adults who knew each other well and shared a common vision. Gigi has sat in council with an adult group continuously from sunrise to sunset, over a three-day period, with the understanding that individuals could come and go quietly from the circle to take care of personal business.

In leading councils we usually advise participants to take the time they need and also be aware of the needs of the whole circle. One person may hold the talking piece for quite a while, which may well serve the circle. The few minutes remaining for another might inspire that person to sing a song or make a few gestures that "say it all." Learning to trust that such apparent unbalance can be consistent with a productive circle is part of the magic of council.

Shaping the Circle

The configuration and comfort of the circle are important. Start by arranging the seating so that participants can see one another without straining. A square or lumpy configuration diminishes the power that a cohesive, circular shape transmits. Some groups place an extra pillow in the circle to represent a regular participant who is absent. An empty pillow can also be reserved for the unexpected or "sacred guest" (as in the tradition of the Jewish Seder). When we were struggling to meet county building requirements at the Ojai Foundation, we often included a pillow, named the "Ventura County Seat," as a reminder that the county bureaucracy was an influential part of our council, whether we liked it or not!

When possible, have everybody sit on the floor with pillows and backrests for those who need them. Sitting closer to the ground supports council's strong earth-based tradition and helps to "ground" the group. However, if a few individuals want or need a chair, accommodate them without judgment. Even a whole circle of chairs may be the best approach for some groups. Sitting in council is not supposed to become a heroic physical feat! When people are comfortable, they have an easier time giving undivided attention to the person holding the talking piece. On the other hand, excessive lounging or lying down in council may not be consistent with creating a strong "container." As in meditation, maintaining one's spine in a vertical position usually increases attentiveness and can also help the body release aches and pains.

Long sessions can produce back strain or "council knee" (achy knee joints that yearn to be stretched), so pausing for a moment halfway around the circle to give everyone a chance to stand and take a number of deep breaths is often a good idea. The circle can make an agreement beforehand about taking regular bathroom breaks or allowing people to slip out briefly as needed. Being sensitive to the body's needs is not only the responsibility of the leader. When the talking piece comes around, anyone in the circle can suggest a stretch or a few moments of movement.

Being in council requires a commitment to participate in the creation of "sacred time and space," in which the business of the circle is given full and openhearted attention. In particular, this means being present at the beginning of the council, leaving only at the breaks, and remaining to the very end. Interruptions, such as making phone calls or receiving messages, should be limited to emergency situations.

Naturally, there may be exceptions to this policy for elders and young children—particularly during long ceremonial councils. Children can be allowed to come and go from the circle, as long as parents (or guardians) are willing to help them abide by the rules of council when they are present. A parent with an infant usually works out fine and is an excellent way of including children in spirit work. If another member of the circle finds the baby's presence distracting, the matter can be discussed and a compromise found. We have been told that in some Native American traditions, pregnant women attended council to begin the training of their children while still in the womb.

Connecting With Place

"Welcome to Calabasas," I began in the silence before the dedication. "This house is an appropriate place to have the first of these 'New Visions of Education' meetings. When our work with children began many years ago as part of Heartlight School, we started each day with a council in this room. So we begin this circle of educators in a room where hundreds of councils of young people have taken place, not to mention the many circles of friends and family that have gathered here as well."

Attention to place is an important part of setting a council, particularly when the location of the gathering is directly related to the group's focus or agenda, as in the above example. In some instances the history of a place can give direction and a context for the ensuing council. In any event, place exerts its influence on participants, even when they are not aware of it, and should be acknowledged as part of the opening of council.

Sometimes the importance of place is revealed in a surprising or synchronistic way. I remember a magical campfire in the wilderness, at which everyone became a master storyteller for an evening. On returning to the nearby town we were told by a long-term resident that the same spot was used by native peoples for their councils many years before.

It is worth taking the trouble to honor place by describing how its history might relate to the present moment. Long after the first New Visions meeting, educators who came to Calabasas, even for the first time, talked about a feeling of "coming home" or being inspired to speak their real voice in the circle. They had entered a house with a tradition—even if a relatively new one—of welcoming those who work with children.

Choosing between an indoor and outdoor site for council is also important. Holding the council outdoors and making close contact with the earth can add to the experience in many ways. When the group is in a natural setting, factors that can influence council—such as the weather, time of day, season, and visits from animals—can be noticed and honored more directly. For example, in working with a business group, Gigi utilized the nearby park rather than the familiar boardroom in order to bring new energy into the council.

If, however, the primary intention of the council is to improve communication within the group, it may be important to utilize the "container" that an indoor environment offers. With an ongoing group, moving back and forth between indoors and outdoors allows the wisdom gained from connecting directly with the earth, and the quiet and comfort of the indoors, to both be embraced.

Creating a Ceremonial Environment

Council flourishes in a ceremonial environment, which includes acknowledging the physical location and its connection with the council, creatively arranging the setting, and using ceremonial objects appropriately. When people feel welcomed into the setting, they are more likely to participate in the council with greater sensitivity and attention.

Although successful councils can be held under a variety of adverse conditions, it helps for the council room to be clean and spacious. Bringing an offering or gift to the circle, or shifting the furniture in the room to activate awareness of place, can help to increase the sense of sacred space. Council is akin to meditation and prayer, and most of us are more comfortable meditating or praying when the surroundings are simple and orderly.

Arrange the center of the circle in the "beauty way"—that is, with flowers, candles, and objects that are meaningful to the circle or reflect the particular season. Placing musical instruments in the center, for use before or during the council, reminds participants they can also play and sing their stories in the circle.

If the group is associated with a particular tradition or culture, its customs can be honored when creating the council environment. For example, with a Buddhist group, a simple, uncluttered setting incorporating zafus and a Buddha figure would probably help participants feel at home. In contrast, a business group is likely to feel more comfortable meeting around their boardroom table for their first few councils.

Lighting a candle in the center before beginning invariably evokes a sense of ceremony, because fire has been the center of tribal and community circles throughout the world since ancient times. According to the teachings brought to the Ojai Foundation by Hyemeyohsts Storm, the central candle in a circle represents the "Children's Fire." This is both the nurturing source of warmth that is maintained in the center of the traditional Native American dwelling and also symbol-izes the transforming power of fire. It is called the Children's Fire as a reminder that what we do now is "for the children"—that is, for those who will follow—and as a challenge to be present in council in the open, trusting way associated with children.

In a group meeting for the first time, asking participants how they feel about this practice before starting the council avoids unspoken and possibly distracting associations with particular religious prac-tices. Usually we ask for a volunteer to offer a "dedication" when the candle is lit. The dedication can be offered in silence or in the form of a prayer for a meaningful council, for the healing of an ill member of the circle, for the group's shared vision, or simply in appreciation for being able to meet in a sacred way.

THE TALKING PIECE

The central ceremonial object in council is the talking piece, which can evoke the intentions of council even when a carefully prepared setting is impossible. The talking piece represents the organizing principle of council and powerfully communicates the spirit of the circle. Its pres-ence reminds everyone of their commitment to the form and inten-tions of the process. Holding the piece empowers expression. Watching it move around the circle supports attentive listening.

Sometimes the talking piece "carries" stories of shared experi-ences, which are represented by objects added to the piece over a period of time. Often the piece becomes closely associated with the circle's commonly held vision and identity. Talking pieces that helped to build community in this way often have an auspicious beginning and a long history.

I found what was to become my first talking piece thirty years ago, under a majestic Carob tree in central Mexico. The unusually large size of the dark brown pod and its gentle S-shape immediately caught my attention. I was delighted with the resonant rattle sound it made when shaken, and knew immediately that this seed carrier would return home with me, even though I had not the slightest idea what I would do with it!

The pod remained on a bookshelf near the front door of our house for more than five years, peacefully gathering dust, until we started Heartlight School in September of 1980. We had planned a field trip the second day of school with the hope that our small band of thirteen kids (ages five through seventeen) and three adults would be able to come together in a cohesive way that had been lacking the preceding day.

As I was leaving the house, the pod caught my attention. Surprisingly it triggered thoughts of the Pueblo's council of elders and my first council six months earlier in the Sespe Wilderness near Ojai. Suddenly I realized we would have a council that morning, using the pod as a talking stick. An hour later, the sixteen of us were sitting around a large picnic table in the park, passing the pod around our circle and sharing how we felt about starting a new school.

We met in council every morning thereafter for the four years the school existed. As the circle grew, we added feathers from a farm we visited, shells from a day at the beach, strings of dried manzanita berries from our home in Calabasas—and a bandage around the pod's middle (but that's another story). The talking piece soon became a silent carrier of our circle's history and a strong reminder of our commitment to communicate authentically with each other.

Choosing a Talking Piece

Creating a talking piece together gives new life to a circle. I remember a third-grade class that had struggled for weeks trying to establish a council environment in which the students felt safe enough to speak openly. At the time the teacher asked me for assistance, the class was using a talking piece she had provided. The teacher said she was committed to the program, but, as we talked, her fears and doubts about leading council became apparent. I wondered if the object she had chosen had come to represent her uncertainty about the process. Perhaps the talking stick reminded the children that their teacher was uncomfortable in council, which in turn prevented them from feeling safe enough to speak honestly.

I suggested the class go to the beach, search for a piece of driftwood, and make a talking stick by attaching objects that everyone brought to school. The piece that emerged might not have appealed to everyone (an old earring, a small plastic animal, a feather from a pet parrot, etc., all tied to the pale gray piece of driftwood), but each person in the circle was represented in its creation, including the teacher. The new talking stick "worked." With its inauguration, the students started talking about what really mattered to them—and the third-grade councils came to life.

Sometimes one member of the group will bring a piece that has both personal meaning as well as relevance for the group. For example, for many years the Ojai Foundation Board has used a beautiful doughnut-shaped African stone that had been a valuable coin in its native land. Gigi introduced the piece because of the stone's shape and history. She hoped it might assist the Board in developing a more enlightened relationship to wealth and abundance by reminding the circle that the earth is the ultimate source of all our resources.

Objects that are frequently used as talking pieces include old Bibles or other family heirlooms, traditional and contemporary rattles, stones, shells, rain sticks, and particular ceremonial objects that honor the council location or the traditions of the group. We hasten to add that the talking piece needn't convey solemnity. Sometimes lighthearted or whimsical objects are appropriate, particularly if the circle has been taking itself too seriously. I remember a tense community meeting in Ojai, for which the council leader wisely chose a small bunch of wild flowers as the talking piece. In one third-grade council I joined for a while, the students chose a pinwheel for their talking object. Sometimes they would blow on the plastic vanes and watch the wheel spin while they thought about what to say.

And then there was the apple that a group of Xerox managers chose . . . and the whistle that a group of correction officers selected for a prison council.

Imaginative selection of the talking piece can help bring the group together, as the following suggestions and anecdotes illustrate.

If a group is meeting in council for the first time, the leader may want to choose a familiar object as a talking piece. Once, ten minutes into introducing council to a rather formidable collection of school administrators, counselors, and parents, it became clear to me that the ceremonial rattle I had brought would be a poor choice of talking piece for the occasion! During my opening remarks, the principal received a message on his walkie-talkie, which consumed his entire attention for several minutes. He then placed the instrument on the table in front of him, leaned back, and rejoined the circle. When it came time to start the council, I asked him if he would like to use the walkie-talkie as our talking piece. The irony of my suggestion brought an appreciative smile.

In an ongoing group, involving each member of the council in choosing a talking piece is an excellent way to share the creation of sacred space. This approach can bring a new talking piece and its story into the circle for each meeting. For example, one New Visions Group of principals used to meet in a different school each session and it had become the custom for the hosting administrator to provide the talking instrument. Each council began with comments about the piece, which was usually of personal significance to the particular educator.

In councils with an ongoing group, having a few talking pieces from which to choose allows the leader or the circle to make a choice just before the council starts. In such situations it is customary to display all the pieces in the center of the circle, along with the candle and other objects. Varying the talking piece can be a subtle way of honoring the particular intention or agenda of the council.

When a new talking piece is being introduced to the circle, a playful option is to keep its previous history and significance a mystery until the end of the council. Then the piece itself carries its story silently, creating reactions and associations for each member of the circle as they hold it for the first time.

Objects that can produce simple sounds, such as rattles, make excellent talking pieces, particularly for children's councils. Being able to conclude one's remarks with a good shake is personally satisfying and provides musical punctuation between speakers.

Weaving the Web

Using a talking piece in the circle calls forth the creative power of story. I have often imagined that the circle is a loom and the talking piece a shuttle that moves around it, weaving the threads of the people's stories together in unpredictable ways. The resulting tapestry may be obscure at first, but if the magic of council is awakened, its design will eventually become clear to many in the circle. There is a chant we sing at the Ojai Foundation about "Spider Woman," the creatrix and weaver in Northwest Native American mythology, which includes the lines, "She is the weaver and we are the web. She is the needle and we are the thread." The piece calls forth the presence of this spirit weaver, inviting her to work her magic in shaping and unifying the council.

When it becomes an integral part of the circle, a talking piece can give rise to spontaneous teachings that are of great value to the group. Relationships may shift suddenly and solidify or a member of the circle might become present in an entirely new way. The story of how the Heartlight School talking stick acquired its bandage is a good example.

Bo and Billy had been getting on each other's nerves since Heartlight's opening day. Even though he was five years younger, Billy had the ability to push Bo's buttons and penetrate his seventeen-year-old "cool" exterior. At one of our morning councils, Billy could hardly wait to get his hands on the carob pod—he had a lot to say about the mean way Bo had treated him the previous day. When it was his turn, Billy laid the talking piece down in front of him and told his side of the story in passionate detail, moving his arms about for emphasis. Bo's face turned a vivid pink color. Suddenly he leapt to his feet and, breaking council form, lunged across the circle, apparently bent on wringing Billy's neck. A loud snap stopped him in his tracks. Bo looked down at his feet, one of which had landed squarely on the pod and cracked it. No one made a sound. In shock, he slowly picked up the damaged pod and bent it back and forth at the break a few times. Then he put it down in front of Billy, and slunk back to his seat.

Everyone waited to see what I would do. I felt angry at Bo but grateful that our talking piece had stopped him from physical violence. "I've ruined the stick," Bo groaned. "Now I've really blown it."

"We can get a splint and bandage the wound," I began in a shaky voice. "The pod is wounded, but not ruined . . . Our talking stick has been initiated." Then I told the circle about the shamanic tradition of the wounded healer.[1] Bo listened intently and then asked permission to leave the circle to find a splint. Someone found an attractive strip of orange cloth to use as the wrapping. I asked Billy to get the glue. We all gathered around the wounded pod as Bo, Billy, and I set the break. When we reconvened the council, Billy picked up the stick with new respect. He apologized to Bo for his teasing, shook the pod gently, and passed it on. A new friendship began to flourish between the boys after that council.

---

[1] For example, see *Shaman: The Wounded Healer*, Joan Halifax. London: Thames & Hudson Ltd. 1982.

It is not unusual for a council leader or an entire circle to become attached to a talking piece that has been used by the group for a long time. This very attachment may call in the wisdom of non-attachment, with the piece itself playing a central role in communicating this teaching.

I had been using a ceremonial gourd from Peru as the talking piece with a circle of twelfth-graders from Crossroads School. The gourd was delicately carved with many figures from Incan mythology; the smooth curved handle fit the hand comfortably. The group was becoming more trusting, except for a bright, dark-haired boy named Steve, who took an instant aversion to council and to me as well. No matter what the theme, he used his turn to denigrate the council process, my leadership, and the whole class.

"It's just New Age bull shit," he said one day. "Like we're playing Indian. Who do we think we're kidding?"

His classmates often told him what a pain he was or invited him to contribute positively to the circle, to no avail. For weeks I gave him a lot of room. I had the feeling that council threatened him precisely because he recognized the potential of the process but wasn't ready to get involved.

One day about six weeks into the program, Steve arrived in class with a scowl on his face that persevered through the lighting of the candle and the beginning of council. As others spoke, I could feel the storm clouds gathering. When Steve was passed the gourd, his dark brown eyes flashed with anger. Suddenly he was on his feet, leaping around the circle, our talking piece held high over his head in a threatening way. A moment later he stopped and brought his hand down forcefully, as if to smash the gourd on the hardwood floor. My heart leapt into my throat. He stopped his arm just in time, held the gourd a few inches off the floor for a moment, returned to his seat, smiled sardonically, and passed it on.

The circle sat in stunned silence expecting a reaction from me, but I maintained council decorum and waited my turn. Others took Steve to task and suggested he "shape up." A few acknowledged the courage it took to express his point of view so dramatically. When the gourd had made the full circle and returned to me, I held it silently a moment while my fingers explored the intricate carvings.

"I get the point, Steve," I began. "Obviously the source of power is not in this gourd, but in the intentions of council. But I have to confess I almost lost it!" I took a deep breath. "I've grown attached to this piece. You showed me that in a creative way."

My acknowledgment of Steve and what I had to learn broke the ice. He saw that I was willing to be part of the circle and not hold myself above it. Seeing that council could be authentic gave him courage. By the end of the semester, Steve had become one of the circle's more active participants.

These stories reveal the interactive role a talking piece can play in the council process. When, years after leaving Heartlight, a student or parent would join a council in which the carob pod was being used, they would often hold their "old friend" with great affection and comment on some of the insights previous councils had brought them. In such moments the pod became a link with the past and a silent witness to the power of council.

To explore the role the talking piece is playing and whether there is too strong an attachment to it—particularly in an ongoing group—it is a good idea occasionally to meet in circle without one. Then the group can see their relationship to the piece more clearly. Sometimes the use of a talking piece can be a strong challenge for a group unaccustomed to ceremony or for whom using a strange "medicine object" is counter-cultural. The latter situation arose in recent years introducing council to a professional group in Mali. In such circumstances, the leader faces what can be an important judgment call. Using the piece might be just what is needed to overcome sources of resistance in the group. On the other hand, if the leader is so attached to using a talking piece for his or her own comfort, then insisting on its use can be counter-productive to eliciting the spirit of council.

CROSSING THE BORDER

Trying to plunge directly into council, fresh from the stresses of work and family life, or even from the "small talk" of casual conversation, can be difficult. To help enter the heightened awareness of Self and Other that council fosters, we suggest creating a transition period of a few minutes or more, depending on the group and the total time available for the gathering.

Transition can be achieved through a combination of silent meditation, singing, and drumming. If the group regularly meditates together, sitting can serve as a natural bridge to council. When the group is diverse and members have no common practice, several minutes of silent reflection and a simple slowing of the breath can help everyone get "off the road" and into the circle. If the group has been inactive for a long time, a slow, silent walking meditation can provide an excellent means of making the transition.[2]

Voice is another vehicle of transition. A few favorite songs or chants, possibly related to the topic of the council, awaken the expressive mode in the circle before the talking piece begins making its rounds.

Drumming is one of the most potent transitions into council, particularly in groups that have a special affinity for making music together. Drumming is itself a form of nonverbal council in which each drummer's contribution ideally becomes part of a unified field of sound. Rattles and other simple percussion instruments can be used in addition to drums.

---

[2] See A Guide to Walking Meditation, Thich Nhat Hanh. Fellowship Publications. 1985.

When the group is not accustomed to making music together, a little conversation about attentiveness may be helpful before plunging into drumming. (I've sat through some ghastly sessions of fragmented drumming that, at best, could have been described as "noisy.") Experienced music-makers speak of three important levels of listening when drumming and rattling. First, listen to your own sound and become more conscious of its beat, intonation, and dynamics. Second, listen to all the other instrumental voices in the circle. Finally, sense the "rhythm of the group" that emerges, often dramatically, when the circle starts making music as a true ensemble. Once established, this beat serves as a foundation for individual riffs and rhythmic variations without the need of direct leadership. To reach this point, it is advisable for one or more drummers to take on the role of holding the basic beat when beginning the music-making.

Marking the transition *out of council* consciousness is also important. Closings can be as simple as a song, a circle of hands, or blowing out the candle. Sometimes a more elaborate ceremony is needed when the council has been long, intense, or clearly incomplete. An expanded closing might include acknowledging the lack of resolution, going around the circle with brief gestures of appreciation, or several minutes of silence followed by an appeal for the spirit of council to continue working through each member of the circle until the next gathering. Sometimes in can be quite rewarding for the leader to ask the circle to co-create a closing in which other members of the council take the lead.

2
BEGINNING
THE JOURNEY

Follow the light within
You've got to follow the light within
It's your heart that's telling you
Where is your freedom
Follow the light within

—Adapted from an
African-American spiritual

N ow that we've set the council and chosen the talking piece, we're ready to light the candle and begin. The basic ground rule is already clear: Only the person holding the talking piece is empowered to speak. Apart from emergencies or indications of not being able to hear the speaker, the only exception to this rule is the use of a chosen word, sound, or gesture of acknowledgment, such as "*Ho.*" Borrowed from the traditional peoples, *Ho* or *Aho* are expressions of agreement or appreciation that someone has spoken or expressed themselves silently. In the Lakota Tradition, Ah-ho is an abbreviated form of the phrase, "Aho Mitakuye Oyasin, "which translates as, "To all my relations" and is called, "the shortest prayer." In some circles, as a sign of respect, a chorus of *Ho's* is spoken after each member is finished, more or less independent of approval or concurrence. Cognates used by some groups for Ho include, "Amen," "right on," three claps, or a silent bow with hands together. A group of women Gigi sat with recently touch the earth after each sharing. On occasion, an exuberant member of a teenage council has been known to stretch the customary *Ho* to "a million *Ho's*" and "No-*Ho*."

In the simplest form of council the stick is passed around in a clockwise direction (the "sun" direction in most traditional councils). Passing the stick the other way (the "earth" direction) may signify a "coyote council," in which the "inner trickster" is specifically invited to appear. However, the earth direction is commonly emphasized in ceremonies by some traditional people (the Hopi, for example).

Every member of the circle always has the option of holding the talking piece in silence for a moment, leading the circle in a song or offering a simple gesture, and/or passing it on without speaking. Silence may be appropriate when there is no inner indication of a need for expression or if one prefers to hear more of the other voices before speaking during a subsequent round. Sometimes silence reveals a resistance to sharing or a feeling of separation from the group. In a perceptive circle this kind of silence becomes an eloquent part of the truth of the circle. Letting go of the expectation that people will speak is an essential part of the practice of council. Whatever the reason, *expressing oneself through silence* is always acceptable.

THE FOUR INTENTIONS OF COUNCIL

Although introducing council to newcomers in the circle is ultimately best accomplished by each group in its own way, we offer four basic intentions as a way to begin. The first three evolved at Heartlight School as a way of instructing guests participating in the morning circles who had never sat in council before. The kids wanted a simple and shorthand way to describe the process, so we came up with a set of guidelines that is both poetic and practical. The fourth intention was added later in recognition of its importance and difficulty of achievement, even in an experienced circle. In recent years we have heard similar goals expressed by a variety of groups with whom we have had no historical connection.

Speaking From the Heart

The expression, "speaking from the heart," has come to represent the essence of council to a great number of adults and young people in families, schools, and communities. I have suggested it be taken quite literally by newcomers to the circle as part of an exercise in which they imagine their words emerging from the mid-chest region rather than the mouth. Now and then, it is a good idea for all council participants to return to this image when speaking in the circle in order to renew this intention. When our words, or silence for that matter, come from the heart, there is usually a tangible feeling of expansion and a sense of greater connectedness to others in the circle. We are more likely to feel non-attached to personal positions, non-defensive, and committed to recognizing the truth of the circle as a *whole*.

Of course, speaking from the heart doesn't necessarily mean saying something nice about oneself or somebody else. As the kids say, being "loving" and being "lovey-dovey" are not the same thing. Speaking from the heart means being as honest as one's feeling of safety in the circle permits. In a council that has built a substantial degree of trust, participants can be remarkably honest about themselves and each other, relative to their ability in ordinary conversation. Council can also be a safe place for "tough love."

Speaking from the heart also means saying something that really matters. Ideally, the entire circle is giving the speaker its undivided attention. The opportunity should be used wisely. *Simplicity* and *passion* are two attributes that support heartfelt expression. Long, rambling stories about people unknown to members of the circle, or getting lost in topics tangential to the issue at hand, place a strain on the circle's patience. Authenticity and a focus on *personal revelation* rather than philosophical reflection helps everyone stay attentive and honors the circle further by showing a willingness to take risks.

Listening From the Heart

As rare as speaking from the heart may be in our ordinary lives, *attentive listening* is probably even rarer. When the topic of an ordinary conversation is engaging, most of us listen until we sense the direction of what's being said, and then we begin preparing our response before the other person has finished. This is particularly true when strong emotion enters the interaction. On the other hand, when we're not engaged, disinterest leads to intermittent listening, which leads to misunderstanding and irritation for all parties involved. The frustration of talking to someone who is distracted and not really present is familiar to all of us.

The success of council is largely determined by the quality of listening in the circle. When it is "devout" (as the Quakers would say), the speaker feels empowered and is more likely to rise to the occasion:

> "Sometimes I feel awkward and nervous, so it's amazing to feel the words come through me like this. I don't consider myself eloquent, but when the circle is really listening, I can speak in a way I never thought possible."

Conversely, listening devoutly invariably helps the listener feel more connected to the speaker, even if there's strong disagreement with what is being said:

> "I used to really get irritated listening to you, but in council I can't react so quickly. By the time the talking piece comes to me, I've had the chance to listen to others as well as to you. I may still disagree with what you say, but I don't feel the same kind of charge."

> "Once in meditation, I asked the Powers-That-Be to explain the sense of communion and wholeness I had felt in a recent council, during which we had exchanged stories about our mothers and fathers. The response was simple: *When people sit in council and listen heartfully to each other's stories, God listens also.*"

The basic form of council creates the framework for attentive listening, because the option to interrupt has been removed. But that's only the first step. Ultimately, developing the ability to listen devoutly in council depends on training the whole body to listen more consciously through the practice of "persistent self-witnessing."

As with speaking heartfully, one way to witness the quality of one's listening is to shift focus, as in the following exercise:

> Imagine that the speaker's words are entering your mid-chest area rather than your ears. Take a few deep breaths while holding the image of listening from the heart. Do you feel a shift in perception? Are you more present?

After doing this simple exercise for a little while, the listener may experience an expanded understanding of what the person is saying or a greater personal connection to the speaker. The feeling of a "heart connection" with the speaker that follows the shift into devout listening can be remarkable. One circle member described such a shift to me:

"I was trying to keep from nodding off as she droned on and on. I'd heard her talk like this a hundred times before. I tried pretending my ears had moved down to my chest. That helped a little. Then I took several deep breaths...Something shifted...I entered the mystery of sitting quietly, listening, knowing that everything she was saying was important and had to be said. My body felt noticeably warmer. I heard the fear in her voice and was surprised by how close I suddenly felt to her."

If you find yourself growing restless and bored in council, you're probably not listening devoutly. Listening from the heart is energizing, even if the speaker is inarticulate, dull, or the topic or story is not your "cup of tea." If you can shift into devout listening, you will become more conscious that you're bored and begin to wonder why. Curiosity may be followed by some insight (about your resistance to what's being said or to the speaker, for example), but in any event, the shift reduces the actual feeling of boredom and may even make you feel closer to the speaker. People often express amazement at feeling affection for individuals they thought boring or objectionable by listening more attentively to them in council.

If the council room is poorly ventilated (or too hot or cold), devout listening suffers. The leader needs to share responsibility for dealing with this situation by reminding the circle at the start that anyone can ask for a stretch, song, or whatever change-of-pace is needed when he or she has the talking piece.

Obviously, a necessary condition for devout listening is the ability to actually hear the speaker or, in the case of a person with hearing loss, read his or her lips. A well-formed circle ensures a direct line of sight for everyone and reminders to talk louder usually solve this problem. One of the few acceptable interruptions in council is, "Can you please speak up." If a circle has one or more individuals with hearing problems, it is essential for everyone to remember to project their voices distinctly. A person with such loss may only remind people once or twice of their difficulty before retreating into isolation. Personally, I have never sat in a council in which signing is an integral part of the process, but I see no reason why such circles would not work effectively.

Being of "Lean Expression"

The third intention in council is a practical one. "Be brief" is the way the kids say it, since the length of school councils is usually limited by a rigid schedule. As a general rule, everyone should receive their fair share of the council's attention. When the council has the space to develop more slowly, I usually suggest that everyone express themselves in a "lean" way, but also emphasize that some individuals may need more time if their stories are truly longer or they have more going on at the moment. The question of how long to speak reminds me of Lincoln's response to a curious admirer, who commented on the unusual length of the President's legs. "They're not so long," he's supposed to have said. "Just long enough to reach the ground."

Being lean is an art. Great storytellers and poets have the skill to prune their stories and poems so that every word spoken keeps the narrative, characterizations, and images moving at just the right pace. Perhaps only a few of us can approach this level, but council is an excellent arena in which to improve one's ability to be concise and to find words and images that enliven our stories and statements —and so allow them to be heard.

Of course, some stories are meant to meander for a long time, perhaps even without a clear sense of beginning, middle, and end. The teller may get lost in the story and draw the whole circle into his or her web. Sometimes this shared surrender may produce a new understanding of the story's meaning or bring about a new ending for the teller.

I remember a fifty-year-old man who, during a relationship weekend, started out describing how happy he and his wife had been for "as long as he could remember." He gave detail after detail of their connubial bliss—as one could imagine he had done on many social occasions. Normally this would have engulfed the circle in boredom, but most of us soon began to hear the mutual isolation and stagnation that shaped his relationship. We waited attentively for him to hear his true story. After fifteen minutes, the quality of our listening finally forced him to abandon his familiar patter. Within a few minutes, his mood shifted, fear and sadness crept into his voice, and he began to falter. He ended his story in tears and with a new recognition that he and his wife were adrift in a marriage that lacked vitality and genuine intimacy.

The purpose of sharing stories in council is not to become professional storytellers or charismatic orators. Speaking from the heart creates its own eloquence and vitality that is invariably engaging. In storytelling, the underlying challenge is to find a means of expression that serves both the teller and the circle.

One way to avoid unfocused stories and rambling statements that are not likely to serve the group is for the leader to make the theme of the council "crystal-clear" at the outset. When it is important to stay strongly focused on the issue at hand, an experienced council leader I know asks each person to restate the theme as a question to the person on his or her left as the talking stick is passed. However, when the theme is set strongly at the outset and shifts still occur during the council, the leader can usually trust that the circle is searching for its true agenda.

Another ally in the quest for leanness is the willingness to give honest reflection to those who ramble. If anyone in the circle feels someone has gone on too long, been repetitive or unclear, they always have the option of saying something about it when they get the talking piece. A circle in which people can be that open with each other usually improves everyone's capacity to make their story "just long enough to reach the ground."

Spontaneity

The fourth intention of council evokes the principle of spontaneity. As the talking piece moves around the circle, a flood of memories and thoughts may be triggered, each one of which is a candidate for sharing. Trying to hold on to these while waiting to speak can be overwhelming. To counteract this tendency, *set the intention not to rehearse what is to be said.* The importance of this in regard to listening is obvious: preparing an agenda while others are speaking limits the ability to listen attentively.

Rehearsing may also limit the ability to speak from the heart. Freed from the need to prepare, the ordinary mind is more likely to step out of the way and let the more intuitive voice speak. Holding the stick silently for a short while and letting the presence of the circle and the moment evoke what needs to be said, often dissolves habitual reactions and attachment to long-held positions. Perseverance with this practice leads to the realization that *everything* that feels important at the time doesn't have to be spoken. Council teaches us that, often what we forget to say is either not essential or will be brought to the circle by someone else.

Ultimately, we learn that each voice in the circle, including one's own, is part of the larger "voice of the circle." We speak personally and, simultaneously, as an aspect of this composite voice. In order for this transpersonal quality to fully emerge, the I-better-prepare-because-I'm-nervous part of us needs to get out of the way. Veteran members of a circle come to trust that when they are handed the talking piece, everything they have already heard in the circle will have been internalized and integrated with their personal associations and memories in just the appropriate way. They come to trust that they will say exactly and uniquely what the circle needs to hear from them in that moment.

Developing this trust can be supported by a few simple practices.

As you listen to others, acknowledge your associations, memories, and insights with affection—and then let them go. Take a breath as the stick is being passed from one person to the next and prepare yourself as if each new speaker were the first in the circle. Wipe the slate clean each time. Remind yourself that you are an integral part of the circle and, as such, will find the voice that is uniquely yours to speak. When you receive the talking piece, hold it for a moment, take a few more breaths, clear your mind and ask, "What is to be spoken now?" Wait for a response. If, after a while, your mind remains blank, scan the sensations occurring in your body. Identify their locations and note their qualities. Generally this will help initiate spontaneous mental activity. As each image, story, or statement arises in your mind, note your willingness to put it out in the circle. If the feeling is yes, then go for it. If you have doubts or fears, silently ask yourself the following three questions:

Will speaking this serve me?

Will speaking this serve the circle?

Will speaking this serve the greater good?

By the "greater good" we mean the largest community or spiritual presence with which you identify in the moment. For example, in the moment this community might consist of your extended family, school community, neighborhood or city, business organization, racial or cultural identity, gender, the human family, the earth and all its sentient beings, God, Great Spirit, Buddha...

Definitive answers to the three questions are not necessary. Just asking them usually brings forth the clarity and courage needed to give voice to the thought or let it go. What you finally choose to do also provides insight about your long-term relationship to the circle. For example, if you find yourself often censoring what serves you because you don't think it will serve the circle, you may begin to wonder whether the group is an appropriate place for you. Sharing this feeling with the circle is essential to keeping your relationship with its members current and productive.

We don't want to imply that completely satisfying the fourth intention is a necessary condition for having a good council. Most of us do collect comments or stories we want to share as the talking piece moves around the circle. Then, if we feel safe and our intuition says these comments are appropriate, we go ahead and share them. Usually this approach serves us and the circle well. The fourth intention—and the first three as well—are offered, not as prerequisites for success, but rather as guiding principles for expanding and deepening the rewards of council.

CONFIDENTIALITY

After the candle is lit, I sometimes find myself looking around the group, making eye contact, and wondering how good a container the circle will be. Starting a council is like beginning an uncertain voyage. One wants to know who is on board and how much they can be trusted if the weather turns rough. Since there is only one vessel, everyone will sink or swim together.

When confidences are broken, people feel betrayed and trust erodes. If an appropriate level of confidentiality is not maintained, everyone has to spend a lot of time repairing damaged feelings and getting the council going again. With repeated violations of confidence, the circle loses heart, becomes dysfunctional, and eventually the vessel flounders altogether.

For these reasons it is important to give attention to the issue of confidentiality. Even in a group of mature adults, it is unwise to assume people will know how to maintain the integrity of the circle. Everyone in the group may not have the same tolerance for hearing what they shared in council repeated by someone outside the circle! A discussion about confidentiality needs to take place early in the life of the circle and renewed regularly as intimacy deepens. Agreements about confidentiality made at the launching of an ongoing council may be obsolete six months later.

"How do I know people will keep my secrets?" Jenny asked plaintively after we discussed the power of honest self-revelation.

"You don't, for sure," I responded. "But that's the point. We're setting out to build trust."

"But if I don't feel trust yet, how can I be honest?"

"By taking a few risks. Otherwise, it's a vicious circle rather than a trusting one, and we never get anywhere."

"Sounds scary."

"It is, but our agreement about confidentiality and practicing the four intentions of council help a lot. Without the agreement, it would be hard. Of course, we have to keep our agreement. Let's go over it again to see if everyone is still clear."

Honoring the Integrity of the Circle

The maturity of the group, its intentions, the frequency of meeting, and the human environment in which it functions are all important in determining an appropriate confidentiality agreement. Here are a few general guidelines.

1. *Determine the need to know.* If a person outside the circle asks you questions about council business, ask yourself if he has a need to know. Perhaps he is a member of the community in which the council functions or the results of the circle's deliberations affect what he does. If the person has an authentic need to know, talk about the general conclusions the council reached. If there is no need to know, be direct and tell the questioner that the council has an agreement about confidentiality and you'd prefer not to talk about its proceedings. Explain the difference between secrecy and confidentiality, if that issue arises.

2. *Examine your motivations.* If you find yourself telling some-one, who has no clear need to know, about a recent coun-cil, ask yourself, why am I talking? Am I motivated by self-importance? Am I gossiping? Is my integrity intact?

3. *Talk about topics*, not personal stories. Identifying the topics and issues that have been discussed in a council is rarely a problem. However, if you suspect it may be, follow the first two guidelines. Retelling specific stories or comments and identifying the source is almost always a breach of confi-dence.

4. *Stick to your own experience.* If someone with a need to know asks you about a council, summarize *your own* experience, not another member's. If you have a desire to describe a council to a nonmember, stick to your own stories and comments.

5. *Invite the curious.* If a person expresses a lot of interest in the council, invite her to witness the next session, as long as that is appropriate and the rest of the group agrees. Don't get into the habit of being someone's source of informa-tion, even if she has a legitimate need to know.

6. *Avoid leaks within the council between sessions.* People who council together naturally feel free to talk about the sessions with each other in-between times. But damaging leaks can arise from this situation as well. At the Ojai Foundation, we call it "talking in the bushes." Intimate conversations by and about people in the circle may rob the council of an opportunity to work through important material *together.* (This is often the case when "talking in the bushes" is used as a way of avoiding a face-to-face confrontation in front of the whole circle. If you find yourself talking about someone outside of the circle, a good question to ask is, "Am I will-

ing to say this directly to the person?") On the other hand, the council may ask two or more individuals to work out some personal issues before the next meeting and report to the whole circle. This approach is a common one in business, family, and community councils.

7. *Make clear agreements.* When your council begins to formulate a confidentiality agreement, stress the importance of making it simple and clear. Misunderstandings about confidentiality are not uncommon, particularly in circles of school children. In many situations writing out the agreement can be helpful. In an ongoing council, be sure to strongly discourage "talking in the bushes" as part of the confidentiality agreement.

8. *Deal with broken agreements quickly.* Everyone in the circle (not just the leader) is responsible for bringing breaches of confidence to the attention of all the members. Trying to find out who broke the agreement is less important than acknowledging the breach, processing the feelings, and re-evaluating the confidentiality agreement. The violation may seriously diminish trust in the group for a while and the circle may have to go through a painful process of rebuilding. As well as signaling the need to renegotiate the confidentiality agreement, broken agreements are sometimes a sign of the need to reassess the group's vision or way of working together.

9. *Encourage transparency.* Whatever the agreement about confidentiality, remember that the nature of council is essentially non-secretive. Most of us feel unsafe in the world unless we have ready access to information and people that affect our lives, either directly or indirectly. More than creating a protective or defensive environment, council seeks to create freedom of communication while encouraging awareness

and care for self and others. Although a confidentiality agreement is recommended for circles of children, many organizations and communities find that formalizing this precaution is unnecessary. Ultimately, the way of council challenges each of us to take responsibility for what we share outside, as well as inside, the circle. When the spirit of council is well grounded in a group, confidentiality issues are rarely a problem. Ultimately, a safe container is achieved through circle members staying open and current with each other more than through confidentiality agreements.

Limits and Legal Obligations

When council is being conducted in an educational setting, confidentiality can involve important legal issues.

"I'm a teacher and there are specific situations that can't be kept confidential. My primary concern is the physical and emotional well-being of my children. I'm also legally obligated to report any strong suspicion of child abuse or life-threatening statements to the appropriate authorities. The intentions of council are important *but secondary* to these responsibilities. How do I draw the line?"

Therapists have similar concerns.

"As a therapist, I have legal and ethical obligations to my clients and my profession. When I'm working in council with clients and one of them talks about taking his own or someone else's life in a definitive way, I have to report the situation to the authorities. I work with groups of teenagers, too. What information can I legitimately hold back from their parents?"

These questions are difficult, indeed! Such legal, professional, and strongly felt personal obligations must be honored along with confidentiality. If the council leader is clear and direct, this can be achieved without compromising the integrity of the circle. In all the years I have participated in school and therapeutic councils, there have been only a few situations that required breaking the circle's confidentiality. Some guidelines for council leaders are:

- Tell the group "up front" what your personal and legal obligations are as leader, teacher, therapist, parent, etc. Make clear that the confidentiality agreements have to be consistent with these restrictions. Your obligations as leader may inhibit the group somewhat, but that's the way it has to be.

- If a situation arises that has legal overtones, talk to the individual involved outside of council as soon as possible and reiterate your obligations. In a school situation, for example, strongly urge the student to speak to a counselor, school administrator, or parent (as appropriate). If you feel an ethical obligation to inform parents about a child who seems to be in serious trouble, tell the child of your intent to do so before you speak to his or her parents. Propose that the two of you, or the child and a counselor, speak to the parents together.

- When it has been necessary to take action outside of council, tell the circle as many, or as few, of the details as is comfortable for the person(s) involved. Minimally, the council leader need only acknowledge in the circle that the situation was handled outside the council in accordance with the confidentiality agreement.

FOCUSING THE COUNCIL

The circle is set, the talking piece chosen, the four basic intentions of council have been reviewed, and a confidentiality agreement is now in place. The next challenge is whether to set a theme for the council and, if so, how. To what extent can a council be given a specific focus? Can councils be shaped by establishing an agenda?

Yes and No!

Yes, you can set your course to investigate a chosen issue, make a decision, resolve a particular conflict, or deepen the feeling of community through council. But unlike meetings conducted in a hierarchical context (e.g., a board meeting run by the CEO or a faculty meeting led by the principal or department chair), the process of council has a way of refocusing or shifting a stated purpose by revealing hidden agendas. Specifying a direction for council is a little like two lovers attempting to set particular goals in their intimate relationship. Some movement in the desired direction may indeed take place, but the relationship has a life of its own, and the process of achieving their goals may only partially resemble what the partners originally envisioned.

Similarly, every council has its own shape and feeling tone, its own rhythm and pace. Since it is a ceremony, every council also reveals its own quality of spirit. As the talking piece makes its rounds, themes and feelings often emerge that augment or alter those offered at the outset. An effective council leader can pull the group back to a preset direction if the circle gets too far afield, but sometimes the spontaneous "will of the circle" cannot, or need not, be denied. It is not so much that the council leader loses control (as might happen in a conventional meeting), but rather that the council itself moves organically in a direction that is undeniably *right*. A sensitive council leader recognizes and supports this movement, even if it seems at odds with the original intention. Indeed, part of the power of council is to uncover the real agenda for the group, even when no one in the circle (including the leader) was in touch with it at the outset.

I remember an early Heartlight council, for which the teachers had set the theme: How can the students take greater responsibility for the upkeep of the school? A few of the children who spoke initially did their best to respond to what was clearly not a compelling topic for them. Instead their comments consistently revealed a feeling of not being empowered to make decisions that significantly affected their school life. For a while I resisted shifting the focus, since I didn't want them to sidestep their responsibilities, but it soon became apparent that the real agenda was: Who has the power in this school? I interrupted the council, acknowledged that the theme had shifted—appropriately so—and we proceeded to discuss the deeper issue productively. As a result of that council, the teachers and I brought the students into our decision-making process in a more active manner. Once the power issue had been explored, taking care of the school grounds no longer remained the thorny problem it had been before.

The feeling of *right movement* in council is akin to an orchestra willing to be directed by an unseen conductor who has a far clearer grasp of the music being played than any of the orchestra members. When right movement reveals the presence of this conductor, a good council leader and responsive circle are willing to follow and bring the music into fruition. Skilled classroom teachers have a similar experience. They prepare their classes carefully, but are willing to alter or even abandon the lesson plan if a more compelling issue emerges spontaneously in the classroom.

Having acknowledged that the council's actual agenda may not be what you had in mind, you can now explore the choice of themes with humility and realistic expectations. *Many council themes are best presented in the form of a question or request for a particular kind of story, which will shed light on the underlying agenda.*

Ways of Beginning

At last, your circle is coming together for the first time. Perhaps it is the start of a workshop, the first of a series of project planning meetings, or the initial council of a group of older students. As one of the council leaders, you have talked about the group's basic intentions, told a story or two, and introduced the process of council. Now you want to help everyone get to know each other and begin to explore the group's dynamics. Here are various questions you can ask, starting with the least demanding from the point of view of personal risk:

- What are your expectations of our time together?

- What do you see as the agenda for this group right now?

- What intentions brought you to this circle?

- What is your given name? Who gave it to you and why? What does it mean in its original language? Do you like your name? If you have a nickname, how did you get it? (This is a particularly effective way to begin a multicultural group.)

- Who are your ancestors? Share something of your lineage.

- How would you describe the "tribe" or "tribes" to which you belong—racially, culturally, ethnically, and/or spiritually? (For adults and older children)

- What experience, skill, or aspect of yourself do you bring to this group as a gift right now?

- What's going on in your life right now? How does that connect with why we've come together?

- What is birthing, growing and alive in you right now? What is dying?

- Can you tell a story about one of your grandparents, aunts, uncles, or mentors—whoever comes to mind?

- Can you tell a story about something completely unexpected that happened to you recently?

When the group is mature and its members know each other or have met together in the past, more probing openings are possible. For example, if you sense uneasiness in the circle, the following kinds of questions might be useful:

- What feeling, pattern of behavior, or aspect of yourself do you want to let go of right now in order to be more present in this circle?

- Is there anything about this group or its purpose that makes you uneasy?

- What is the greatest obstacle to feeling good about yourself right now?

- What is your greatest fear right now?

Weather Reports

As a leader, it is often a good idea to check in with the circle to see how everyone is doing, uncover possible hidden difficulties in the group's dynamics, or set the agenda for a future council. In such situations you can set the theme in a straightforward manner:

"Tell us how you're feeling or what's on your mind right now. You may want to include comments you feel will serve our time together."

Another way to uncover feelings in the group is to ask for a "weather report": "How's your internal weather right now? Are you calm and sunny or is there a storm brewing? Give us a report."

Weather reports are effective when council time is limited or members of the group are still a little shy with each other. They are also particularly effective with young people when the group is still in the stage of building trust. The weather metaphor usually stimulates lighthearted, simple, and imaginative responses that are less threatening to share than direct revelations but still give members a "snapshot" of the circle's climate. (Obviously, strict adherence to weather vocabulary is not necessary.)

"Turning Into the Skid"

Strengthening trust is central to the viability of council. To build trust, members of the circle need to express their personal feelings as honestly as possible. A productive conversation in a circle of adults might sound something like this:

"I haven't been feeling comfortable in our last few councils. I ask myself why I should trust this group with my personal stuff. I don't feel safe, even though I'm getting to know everyone better. I don't know why it's so hard for me to feel trusting here."

"I've been struggling, too. I notice we've been staying on the surface lately. We seem to be protecting ourselves. I wonder if we've been breaking our agreement of confidentiality and talking about our councils with other people."

"It's good to get all this out in the open. At least we trust the circle enough to say when we *don't*! Maybe we're not really listening to each other the way we used to."

Fluctuations in trust are not unusual in an ongoing council. Often a loss of trust can be understood if the group is willing to explore the issue honestly. Common reasons for diminishing trust include:

- A clear confidentiality agreement has not been made.

- One or more people have violated the group's confidentiality agreement.

- There is conflict in the group that has not been addressed.

- Factions have developed, or personal animosities have arisen, which have not been confronted.

- The council leaders and/or participants are inattentive and unable to do their part in keeping the circle on track. As a consequence, the council does not feel like a "safe container."

- There are a few people in the circle who are uncomfortable (perhaps without realizing it) with a sensitive issue that is on the agenda. They may laugh nervously or change the subject whenever the topic arises and it is their turn to speak.

- The circle is made up of a group of experienced council facilitators that, instead of supporting those chosen to lead, are consciously or unconsciously thinking they know how to lead more effectively. As a consequence, they are caught in critical thinking and fail to fully meet the intentions of council.

Sometimes the sense of well-being in the circle diminishes for subtler reasons. It may be that enough trust has been built to break through to a deeper level of honest interaction, but the group hasn't made the leap, perhaps simply out of attachment to old patterns. People feel restless and grouchy; minds wander. The councils seem flat or stuck. Finally, somebody says, "We're not listening to each other. Maybe we're avoiding going deeper."

Crises of trust in an ongoing council offer opportunities for expanding and deepening the work of the council—if the group is willing to attend to the difficulties and speak truthfully to each other. We call this "turning into the skid." A council that avoids openly dealing with its unhealthy dynamics loses power to communicate in a trusting way and so misses the opportunity for greater intimacy. Eventually the councils become superficial and flounder.

The simplest way to explore the trust issue is to ask everyone to say how trusting they feel about the group process. If the circle has reached a level of intimacy that will support making comments about specific people, all the better. Sometimes the council leadership can support this process by speaking to those members of the circle outside of council who have concerns not being expressed to the whole group and inviting them to share their feelings at the next meeting.

If the group is fairly new or trust has become a problem, then one or more councils focused on the issue of trust may be useful. The theme for such meetings is often best expressed in the form of a question or request for a story:

- What does trusting someone mean to you?

- Whom do you trust a lot in your life?

- What is it about that person that allows you to trust him or her?

- How do you know when your trust is faltering?

- Do you feel you are a person who can be trusted? In what areas are you particularly trustworthy? Are there areas in which you are not?

- What is it about a group that makes you feel more trusting? Less trusting?

- Tell a story about a time when a group or individual you trusted betrayed you.

- Tell a story about a time you betrayed a trust.

"Turning into the skid" is an effective policy in many situations. Feelings of fear, confusion, discouragement, and loss of direction are other kinds of "skids" that arise frequently in ongoing circles. Each of these can be addressed by choosing a suitable question or request for a story as the focus for an exploratory council. If there is insufficient time for an additional council, then at least naming the "elephant in the circle" to determine if others see it as well can release the beast back to the wilds.

A while ago, the Ojai Foundation Board was facing a number of challenges due, in part, to unclear vision and attachment to old ways of doing business. We had planned a series of fund-raising evenings, the second of which had been poorly publicized. Not a single prospective donor showed up! After moping around for a while, we started poking fun at ourselves and wondering how we might use our experience productively. We then "turned into the skid" in an impromptu council. Our painful experience that night led to the choice of a theme for the opening council of the board meeting a few days later: "Imagine that we are going to close down the Ojai Foundation, disburse our assets, and bring all our projects to a close. Is there anything you haven't done or would regret not doing? What do you need to accomplish to feel complete? This is not merely a hypothetical exercise. Shutting down is a *real* possibility."

It was a startling and powerful council. Each of us, in our own way, let go of our attachments to the community in that moment. We mourned our loss, described an abundance of unfinished business, and reiterated our deep affection for each other, the Foundation land, and our service in the world. We went to bed that night without making any decisions about the future. The next morning we held a "visionary council" (see Chapter 4), from which the Foundation's purpose and direction emerged more clearly than ever before. Several bold new ideas were put forth for improving our programs and financial position. Later that afternoon we created a ceremony of "rebirth."

3

MATCHING
PURPOSE
AND FORM

Spiraling into the center
The center of the wheel
Spiraling into the center
The center of the wheel
I am the weaver
I am the woven one
I am the dreamer
I am the dream

—Chant by Lorna Kohler;
recorded by Acoustic Medicine

The discipline of council challenges even the most patient of us. Perhaps I forgot to say something important when I had the talking piece, or I passed the first time around and now I'm desperate to speak, or someone across the circle has just said something that demands my response, or I'm sure I could clear up the group's confusion if only . . . Perhaps there isn't time for another round, or the circle is too big for everyone to share their point of view, or a conflict between two people is dominating the council.

Even though the simplicity and wisdom of the traditional practice works well in many situations, there are times when the group's intentions are better served by other forms of council. Going around the circle, one person speaking at a time, is the steady drum beat of the process. But once that has been established the rhythm can be varied. The possibilities are unlimited, as long as the group understands the ground rules and agrees to follow them respectfully.

ALTERNATE FORMS

Many forms of council have proven useful over the years. Generally these have emerged through a natural process of evolution. The practices that endure are those that adapt well to a variety of situations.

Our explorations have been inspired by many sources, particularly the allied fields of mediation and conflict resolution. We have also learned from the way actors and musicians work together, from gifted teachers of children, and from such diverse traditions as the Quaker service and the early Hawaiian Culture.

Dialogue: The Web

Eavesdropping on a group of twelve-year-olds, who have been exploring council for ten weeks, a common predicament becomes apparent . . .

"I've got to speak again or I'll blow my stack!"

"Shush! Lynda has the stick. You've had your turn."

"But I can't let Sam spout all that stuff without—"

"We're in council, please!"

"I can't—"

"If you can just hold on until we've completed the round, we'll put the talking piece in the center. Then anyone who needs to speak again can pick it up."

"If I last that long!"

By putting the talking piece in the center of the circle after one or more traditional rounds, anyone wishing to speak can pick it up, have his or her say, and then return the piece to the center. We call this the "web format" because the talking piece moves back and forth across the circle in an orderly, yet irregular way, as the dialogue unfolds. The web is spun until time runs out or a sense of completion is achieved.

Placing the stick in the center is an excellent way to give people a chance to speak who passed originally, and for others to add postscripts and tie up loose ends. These closing statements can be particularly powerful, since it is often after hearing from everyone in the circle that understanding and insights emerge. The web format also makes it possible to integrate remarks and story fragments from different people and to respond directly to someone who has already spoken.

The web is particularly useful in time-limited situations, because the commitment to continue the council is made one speaker at a time. The only risk is that a few people will dominate the discussion, but should that occur (rare, in our experience) the leader, or anyone else in the circle, can pick up the talking piece and ameliorate the situation.

Finally, putting the talking piece in the center after it has gone around the circle is a good way to involve everyone in summarizing the proceedings and bringing the council to a close without over-relying on the leader.

A playful variation on this format is to allow the person who has just spoken to either put the talking piece back in the center or *give it to any other member of the circle*. This format is particularly well-suited to an ongoing group who is open to deepening their practice of spontaneity. As always, the person to whom the piece has been given has the option of responding with silence before returning it to the center or giving it to someone else in the group.

Personal Reflection: Response Councils

A council member can always ask for personal feedback when they have the talking piece, although in the usual council format anyone wanting to respond has to wait until they hold the talking piece. When a group is in an ongoing process together (for example, a weeklong training), providing the opportunity for members of the circle to directly ask for and receive responses from others can be extremely important.

The talking piece goes around the circle in the usual way, but whoever holds it has several options, depending on personal needs. For example, the speaker might start off by giving a deep weather report; maybe she is feeling isolated or angry about something. She might talk about how the training is going for her or how she is feeling about the group facilitators or the other trainees. Maybe she just wants to complain about the food! Then the speaker has the option of asking others in the circle to respond while she is still holding the stick. Others in the circle can give witness comments, offer advice, or respond to questions directed at them personally—whatever the person holding the talking piece solicits.

This kind of council can clear the air between people and give members of the circle the option of asking for as much feedback as they feel ready to receive. By offering each person the opportunity to act as his or her own council leader, a response council provides a structure that supports interactions similar to those that occur naturally in a functional family.

In particular, a response council is effective when . . .

- A small group of co-workers or peers wants to stay current with each other on a personal level.

- A family wants to expand the basic form of council.

- An individual or couple wants reflection from friends or family, perhaps to review a challenging situation prior to making an important decision.

Multilogue: The Fishbowl

Another alternative to the conventional council is the "fishbowl" or *double circle format*, in which the part of the group holding council forms an inner circle and the remaining individuals create an outer ring of witnesses. The fishbowl is often a suitable option when the group is too large to conduct a conventional council in the time allotted, yet everyone needs to be privy to the deliberations. We have used this configuration for a variety of purposes, some of which are described below.

- The inner circle consists of experienced council participants who are demonstrating council to the outer circle of less experienced witnesses.

- The inner circle consists of council trainees who decide, in the moment, what council format to use, what talking piece to choose, and who is to lead the council. The outer circle witnesses the process and offers reflection and guidance.

- The inner circle consists of elected members of the group; the outer circle is formed by those who want to observe their representatives in action. This particular use of the fishbowl format is similar to the traditional "wisdom council," in which the inner circle is formed by the elders of the community, who have been called together to share their insights with the others. A secondary school we know uses the fishbowl in this way when conducting its regular student-council meetings. Student officers and faculty advisers form the inner council, while the rest of the school is invited to make up the ring of witnesses. This format permits the student council to do its business efficiently and in full view of the entire faculty and student body.

• The inner circle is formed on the spot through self-selection or a lottery to represent the entire group in exploring an important situation. Witnessing the inner council's attempt to resolve a conflict, make a decision, or debate an issue can be quite illuminating to the circle of witnesses and even obviate the need for further deliberations involving the full group. The fishbowl can also be used to offer members who are particularly concerned the opportunity to debate an issue in front of the entire group.

• The inner and outer circles constitute a natural partitioning of the full group (women/men, children/adults, youth/elders, parents/teachers, full-time staff/board members, etc.) and the intention is to provide an opportunity for each part to learn more about how the other functions. Thus, after one group shares while the other witnesses, the roles are reversed and the groups change seats.

Gigi remembers one of the first men's and women's fishbowls she ever led.

". . . After twenty years in groups. I thought I probably had heard it all. But when I witnessed the men sharing their anguish over the suffering in the world, I found myself needing to lie down. I continued to listen in a state that was seemingly 'between the worlds.' Although I was concerned that others in the circle might feel I had disappeared and stopped witnessing, I stayed with the truth of my body. When it was my turn to witness, I sat up wide awake and realized that hearing the men's compassionate concern as never before had lifted a huge weight from my shoulders. I felt partnered and no longer alone. My sense of peace renewed me and generated a new level of trust in men that I felt had been missing since childhood."

Honing the Issue: The Spiral

Suppose there are thirty, fifty, or even a hundred or more people in your group, many of whom have a lot to say about a particular situation. A traditional council would probably be interminable and repetitive, yet every group member wants to be present for the exploration of the issue and have the option to speak.

A practice that works well in this situation is an adaptation of the fishbowl we call the "spiral."[1] Four to eight places are set in the center of the larger circle, depending on the size of the group. Then, after framing the topic, one of the council leaders introduces the process:

"We're going to use a spiral format to explore this issue. When we start, those of you who are ready to speak are invited to take one of the empty seats in the center. After the inner circle fills, the council is dedicated and anyone in the center can pick up the talking piece and begin. (To establish the base of the spiral, it is useful to pass the talking piece around the inner circle in the sun direction.) When the person who speaks *after you* has finished, you leave the inner circle and return to your place in the outer one. Then another person from the outer circle takes the empty seat. This practice breaks the pattern, so prevalent in our culture, of making a passionate statement without listening attentively

---

[1] Some facilitators refer to the spiral as a fishbowl, which seems inappropriate to us, because the spiral, unlike the fishbowl, creates a continuously changing and open container.

to the response it elicits. In this way individual voices spiral into the center and then return again to the outer circle, which acts as a continuously changing ring of witnesses. We'll stop when we run out of time or when we see that the process is ready to end."

People can be allowed to enter the inner circle more than once, unless the group is very large and/or a broad diversity of opinion is desired. In any case, sensitivity to the flow of the process is called for, as always, in deciding if and when to speak. It is a good idea to wait initially until all the seats in the inner circle are filled before a talking piece is chosen and the candle lit. However, once the spiral has started, it is usually better not to wait for all the seats to be filled, but continue to pass the talking piece around in the sun-wise direction, acknowledging any empty seats.

The council leaders can participate in the inner circle as well as guide the entire process from their places in the larger one. Alternatively, the leaders can decide to remain as witnesses throughout the spiral. When it is time to end, one of the leaders can suggest that by removing a seat from the inner circle and asking the remaining participants to close the council, however they choose. Then a few final witness comments can be invited to conclude the spiral.

There are innumerable variations in implementing the spiral. For example, the entire inner circle can remain in the center until each person has spoken. Then this group leaves together and a new inner circle constellates. This "serial fishbowl" format is less flowing than the spiral, but allows for considerable interaction among members of each group that forms.

Participating in a spiral can be a powerful experience. The movement back and forth between the participating and witnessing circles brings fresh insight to the issues being discussed. Listening to others express their views, without being continuously immersed in the debate, supports a balanced blend of detached witnessing and personal involvement. This integrated perspective helps reduce identification with long-held positions and so allows the discussion to flow more freely. The spiral offers an excellent format for the deep exploration of values and for helping each individual get in touch with their "nonnegotiable" assumptions. As we witness and participate in the spiral, the attitudes and positions of others can be heard free of the blocking that results from repeatedly insisting on our own point of view. When we can hear another's nonnegotiable assumptions without reaction, our own fundamental values and attitudes become more available for conscious exploration. In the spiral you may also have the liberating experience of making a strong statement about an issue and then letting go of the need to repeat yourself, as others reiterate the position in their own way. In the spiral we can be blessed by hearing another articulate what we had wanted to say in a fresh and clearer way than we would have spoken it ourselves.

The flowing movement of the spiral helps a group avoid polarization or factionalism, as participants begin to hear each voice express a different facet of the truth of the situation. Soon a "larger picture" emerges, encompassing all the views expressed with a clarity that is rare in ordinary discussion groups.

CONFLICT EXPLORATION

I remember one staff meeting at the Ojai Foundation, about the issue of job assignments that started to come apart at the seams. For a while nothing was accomplished, primarily because "Nancy" and "Merle" got into an argument about who should work the following Saturday. It soon became clear that their disagreement over work schedules was only the tip of the iceberg. After a few more minutes of frustrating exchanges, I had no choice but to break in and acknowledge the highly personal nature of their conflict.

> "The meeting is stuck and it seems the struggle isn't only about scheduling," I said. "If everybody is willing, we could take a look at whatever is going on between the two of you

right now. That would probably save time in the long run. We can move into council and use the fishbowl. Is everyone game? . . . Good.

"Nancy and Merle, we invite you two to sit in the center. Each of you can choose one of us as a witness. We'll need two more pillows . . . Let's use this stone as a talking piece and do two rounds with just Nancy and Merle addressing whatever is difficult about their relationship right now. That way, you have a chance to respond to each other. The more honest the two of you can be the better. Then the two witnesses can speak, not necessarily taking sides but rather reflecting, as dispassionately as possible, on what they have observed about the interaction. We can also ask for further witness comments from the full circle. This may not resolve what's going on between the two of you, but getting it out in the open should help us get on with the meeting."

It did. Forty-five minutes later we resumed the business meeting, which proceeded much more productively. Nancy and Merle continued their dialogue informally during the following week, both with and without another staff member present as a witness.

A variation of this format is to have the two people in conflict sit in the center alone, make their statements, and then respond to each other with the entire circle witnessing the interaction. This variation is appropriate when the group is small and its members are used to working together intimately.

DECISION-MAKING

The spiral is an excellent format for group decision-making. For example, if the challenge is to choose between two well-formulated alternatives, A and B, then the inner circle configuration can be set as follows:

Advocates of B

Advocates of A   *Advocates of A*

Advocates of B

As the spiral proceeds, others fill the seats appropriately, until one alternative dominates, a third possibility emerges, or it becomes clear that the group is not ready to make a decision. Particularly in the latter case, it is a good idea to follow the spiral with a round of witnessing. When the decision process involves the exploration of several alternatives, the regular spiral (without identified seats) can first be used to narrow down the various choices.

If the choice is between two broad alternatives, neither of which has been well-formulated, the fishbowl format can be used in a two-step process. First, the group divides into two subgroups corresponding to the two alternatives, one of which forms the inner circle and the other the outer circle. The inner circle members hold a regular council to clarify and refine their position while the outer circle members witness silently. Then the two circles reverse roles. Finally a combined circle is formed to hear witness comments and decide what to do next. This process offers each group the opportunity to clarify its point of view and hear the other's before trying to make a decision. The result is usually a greater understanding of the issues involved and less polarization.

In making important decisions, any group—be it an intentional community, school, or a business organization—can get stuck in disagreement over fundamental values, principles, or philosophical outlook.[2] Instead of members debating endlessly in the full group, the circle can call for a "wisdom council" to reflect on the underlying issues. The individuals invited to hold the "wisdom seats" might be outside specialists, the organization's elders, its children, or a handful of self-selected people. Often, it is not so much personal knowledge or even experience that makes a person effective in holding a wisdom seat, but more an

---

[2] The use of council to support organizational decision-making is explored further in chapters 10 and 11.

openness to the insight that can emerge during the council experience. We have found that witnessing a wisdom council helps members of the larger circle realign themselves, clarify the underlying issues, and then re-enter the decision-making process more effectively.

Sometimes members of a circle leave council without a decision being made but knowing that a process has been inaugurated that will lead to resolution in the near future, perhaps even without having to meet again. A night or two of "sleeping on it" may be all that is needed for everyone to reap the harvest of the council and reach a clear consensus on the matter. When people are strongly identified with their positions, it may take a little time and a period of quiet for them to let go enough to hear the "voice of council." Trusting this process can be a productive alternative to forcing a decision before there is sufficient understanding.

Deciding where on the community's land to locate the new bank of solar panels at The Ojai Foundation many years ago is a good example of how patient—and creative—a group has to be sometimes before a true consensus can be reached. The half-dozen members of the Facilities Council had debated the question for months—in and out of various forms of council—without being able to reach a conclusion. There were at least four different locations being considered, with strong advocates for each who were quite attached to their personal visions. Finally, we were down to the wire, since the panels were to be delivered in less than a week. Making a decision was becoming urgent. The leader of the Facilities Council decided on a novel approach. He asked the group to do their best to let go all their previous ideas about where to locate the panels and settle into a quiet, open state. Then in a calm voice he took us on a guided meditation.

"Suppose it is five years from now and you are taking a group of visitors on an extensive tour of the Foundation's forty acres, emphasizing our "green" approach to building and providing the power we need . . . The solar panels are a highlight of the tour and you look forward to standing in front of them to extol the virtues of being totally energy independent . . . Where on the land do you stop to make your pitch? "

The six of us "played the game," projected ourselves into the future and went on the tour. It felt very real. When we gathered a few minutes later, we were all surprised to discover that five of us had "seen' the panels in exactly the same place! The sixth member of the group quickly surrendered his slightly different vision and the decision was made.

When group consensus has been chosen as the basis for making a decision, it is often helpful—as in the above example—to have first used various forms of council to explore alternatives. The same is true even when a single person has been given the responsibility for making the decision. The "decider" can benefit greatly by finding out how people feel who will be affected by the decision. Proceeding in this way almost always increases the chances that the final decision will be implemented in a satisfying way.

Council also can be quite helpful when a single individual is facing an important decision, whether a group of supporting individuals is available or not. One begins by creating an "inner council" of the various aspects of oneself that could play a role in making the decision—for example, the heart, mind, body and spirit. Alternatively, the inner circle might include a fearful voice, an optimistic voice, the one who knows the most about the situation and the one who primarily makes decisions intuitively. Other members of the inner council might include a trusted advisor, a parent, a wise grandmother, and/or former teachers and colleagues. Then one sits quietly and moves into a meditative state in which each member of the inner council is invited to join the circle, one by one. After the council is dedicated and the context for making the decision established, each voice is given a chance to speak as the imaginary talking piece goes around the circle. Not only can this process lead to a more productive decision being made, but the person carrying it out ends up learning a lot about how she or he makes decisions in general!

In working with groups exploring ways to make important life decisions, Gigi often uses the inner council process together with the Circle of Law (see Chapter 4). In this approach one goes around the circle three times—using the response council format—speaking to the voices from the various directions that represent the most important influences in one's life as well as archetypal sources of wisdom. The very last voice is that of the "Contrary," which turns our knowing upside down just at the time we think we know what's right. This helps in ways that are often hard to explain but sometimes we have to say "no" in order to finally feel the "yes." As Gigi has expressed:

"Only after the full three rounds do I complete the council, get up and actually see what I end up doing . . . By that time the truth is clear even if that turns out to be "no decision"— and for that I am grateful.

4

DEEPENING
THE PRACTICE

We are an old people, we are a new people
We are the same people, deeper than before
Cauldron of changes, blossom of bone
Arc of eternity, hole in the stone

> —Chant attributed to
> Will Shepardson

I remember a council many years ago, during which the Ojai Foundation staff and board members were struggling with several "us-versus-them" problems familiar to many communities. During stressful periods, each group tended to feel unappreciated, overworked, and not entirely trusting of the other, despite the many close personal ties between board and staff members.

The council unfolded in a distressful way. As hard as we tried, we could not seem to settle our differences and find the harmony we all wanted. We would make a little progress, but then someone would say something inflammatory and we would be back "in the soup." Two hours into the council process, we were as entangled as ever.

Fortunately we had asked three visitors to the Foundation to witness the session. Our instructions to them before the council started had been simple:

> "You are invited to join our circle as witnesses. That means: sit in the circle, listen devoutly, as we all try to do, but remain silent until the very end of the council. At that time we'll ask you for brief comments about what you have observed. We'd like you to focus more on group dynamics than the content of the discussion and tell us what you think might serve us at this time."

The three accepted the invitation and patiently observed our long and arduous journey. We were so strung out by the end of the council that we almost forgot to ask for witness comments! The first witness shared admiration for our perseverance. The second acknowledged that polarization between staff and board in a community was difficult to avoid. She glanced at some notes, added a few words of encouragement, and apologized for not being more helpful.

The third witness completely shifted the energy in the circle. She began by briefly thanking us for the opportunity to witness a group in such a vulnerable state and then, without hesitation or benefit of any notes, described what she had observed. She laid us out bare, clinically describing the factions in our "community culture," the inconsistencies in our positions, and the irony of so much love being lost in the polarization. She spoke without attachment to any of the attitudes expressed in the circle—or to her own observations, for that matter. Her words and images embraced all the positions taken in the circle. Listening to her overview, we remembered our wholeness. Her clarity provided the doorway we had not been able to find.

When she finished, after no more than four or five minutes, there was a long pause. We showered her with expressions of admiration and appreciation: "brilliant," "insightful," "transformative," we chorused. The council leader extolled the exemplary way she had played the role of witness. Of course, we still had our problems to solve, but having been "seen," we felt a renewal of faith in our ability to address them.

The story has an interesting postscript. The day after the council a few of us spoke to our "star witness" in the hope of finding a way for her to stay connected to the Foundation. The conversation leapt from one exciting possibility to another, but nothing "clicked." We found ourselves talking to a bright, entrepreneurial young woman who was going through a major life transition and was not ready to make any commitments. She left the following day amidst promises of continued communication, but we never heard from her again. She had already given us the gift she was meant to give and, hopefully, also received one in return.

THE ROLE OF WITNESS

It is often advantageous to have a council formally witnessed. One approach is to designate a few regular members of the group as witnesses on a rotating basis. Another is to invite an experienced practitioner of council to sit as a witness. Or, as our story revealed, guests can be asked to witness as a way of getting acquainted with the group and contributing to it at the same time. This is often a productive way for a community to honor the presence of a visitor without rearranging the agenda or losing focus. It also honors the spirit of council by keeping the circle open and contributes often to healing feelings of being excluded.

Witnesses sit in the circle, receive and pass the talking piece silently, and at the close of the council are invited to share their reactions, primarily to *the process* itself, including the way the council was led. Witnesses are asked to keep observations about the specific content of the council to a minimum.

Sometimes it is useful to ask for witness comments at the conclusion of a major portion of the agenda or even after a particularly intense round. Witnesses should be identified and introduced to the circle before the council begins and acknowledged at the end, whether or not they actually speak.

Council trains us to be better witnesses. The practice of devout listening involves simultaneously witnessing the speaker and the quality of one's own receptivity. When we speak, we learn to hear ourselves while observing how others are listening. In council we learn to be involved and detached at the same time.

Still, the personal challenge in witnessing can be formidable, particularly when you are also an integral part of the circle. When passions are aroused, it is easy to exceed the threshold of detached witnessing. Decisions may be made that will affect each member personally. If the circle is made up of family, classmates, or co-workers, you naturally care how they feel about you. Their judgment matters. When emotions dominate participation, your internal witness may need some external support. As a witness you are being challenged to transcend your personal perspective and perceive the underlying story as it unfolds in the circle.

Choosing the Witness Perspective

There are many "maps" of human consciousness that can be used as a context for particular witness roles. Witnessing sets the intention to suspend personal perspective and identify with one of these universal points of view. For example, the unifying vision of the four directions, which is integral to many earth-cherishing cultures, offers a variety of witnessing viewpoints. In the Northern Cheyenne tradition, the witness views the circle from the South with the "innocence of a child," the West with the "power of introspection," the North with "logic and wisdom," and the East with the "illumination and the long view of the eagle."[1]

---

[1] See *Seven Arrows*, by Hyemeyohsts Storm, Harper and Row, 1972.

Other witnessing systems associated with the Native American Medicine Wheel include the teachings of the Twelve Sacred Shields, which are intrinsic to the Sun Dance tradition, and the Circle of Law that specifies archetypal aspects of awareness at various positions around the Wheel.[2] The Tarot system can also be used to create a context for witnessing perspectives. One can select any of the cards from the Greater Arcana—such as the Magician (skill and diplomacy), the Empress (fruitfulness and action), the Hierophant (alliance and servitude), the Hermit (prudence), the Hanged Man (wisdom and circumspection), or the Fool (folly and intoxication)—and witness the council from that figure's point of view. Invoking various animal perspectives is another rich source of witnessing contexts. One might choose to observe the council with the unpredictable brilliance and humor of Coyote, the strength and inner wisdom of Bear, the immediacy of Mouse, or Hawk's ability to see at a distance and closely at the same time.

Most people find that keeping in mind a particular perspective or image is a difficult task.

Once many years ago, Jaquelyn, a close friend, and I found ourselves in a place of heightened awareness as a result of a remarkable conversation about the possibility of becoming conscious of our death while still in our bodies. After several hours, I had to leave my co-explorers sitting outside gazing at the stars, since I had promised to cook dinner. They challenged me to sustain our connection by holding the image of the three of us sitting out in the clear night, *en rapport*, while I went inside to cut up the vegetables and put the pasta on to boil.

I couldn't maintain the image for more than thirty seconds at a time. The task of cutting the zucchini would take over my mind and I would forget the starry night and our trio for fully half a minute before I realized what had happened.

---

[2] Ibid, pages 8-10.

Reassuring myself that I would never again forget to remember, I returned to the image of the three of us. But a minute later I had forgotten once more. I persevered for twenty minutes before abandoning the experiment.

Fortunately, sustaining a specified point of view while witnessing a council is not as difficult. Being present in the circle already provides a source of attentiveness through commitment to the basic intentions of council. The challenge for the witness is to focus this attentiveness in a particular way. This can be accomplished with the assistance of imagery (for example, a soaring eagle for the East, a child in wide-eyed wonder for the South) supported by slow, conscious breathing and persistent re-engaging of the desired perspective when one "forgets."

On occasion, a witness may be graced by becoming completely identified with the assumed perspective.

A few years ago, Gigi and I were facilitating a group of prospective council leaders consisting of twenty women and four men (including ourselves). We had decided to use men's and women's fishbowls as part of the training. When it came time for the women to be in the center, we suggested that the men hold the perspectives of the four directions while witnessing. The other three men good-naturedly agreed, chose a direction, and took their places around the circle of women. As I took the seat in the West (the direction they had left unclaimed), the image of a wise and ancient "Grandmother" took form spontaneously in my mind's eye.

The women spoke of their struggle to be empowered in the world. They told story after story of how little they felt supported by the men in their lives, how uninformed their men were about women, and, as a result, how hard it was for them to engage in worldly activities in an effective way. As a talking piece, they used a Northwest Native American knife one of the women had brought to the training; the knife well mirrored the tone of the circle. I battled with feisty and defensive male reactions as I did my best to listen with Grandmother's ears and heart. I imagined a circle of crones sitting around a fire, sharing stories that few men had ever heard. I thought of my wife, Jaquelyn, and other women who had trusted me enough to share some of their pain. I imagined I was healing the bodies of women who had been abused by men. I did a lot of deep breathing.

After the women finished, my three cohorts shared their perspectives admirably, each one holding the knife gingerly in his hands. When it was handed to me, I felt a change take place in my body, starting at my feet and moving upward, as if someone was pulling an invisible rake through me. By the time it reached my arms, "I" was gone. The hand holding the knife gripped it tightly and stabbed the earth several times. At that moment, an ancient, hoarse voice came out of my mouth that startled everyone. Grandmother had taken over. "She" spoke of the power of women, of her disgust at the whining and complaining of the present circle, of the need for women to reveal their power to men and not wait to be recognized. She spoke simply and passionately, all the while stabbing at the earth. Finally she said that the Earth would continue to suffer if women did not *empower themselves* and challenge men to understand the interdependence of all forms of life.

My ordinary consciousness was present enough to know generally what had happened, but afterwards I couldn't re-member exactly what Grandmother had said. Fortunately, one of the women had taken hurried notes. The words looked familiar—and I believed them to be true—but clearly they were not my words. The vocabulary was not mine. I felt tired but elated after the witnessing. Grandmother appeared in my dreams several times during the following month and briefly in another council. I feel a little closer to her wisdom now, thanks to the power of witnessing.

A Place for Humor

Sometimes an ongoing circle finds itself in a solemn mood a good deal of the time. This is neither necessary nor desirable. In fact, a steady diet of solemnity will eventually alienate most people (particularly children). We all know that humor and playfulness are strong allies in group situations; fostering them in a council that has become overly serious can be accomplished by strengthening witness consciousness.

Having access to your playful witness while in council depends on the ability to transcend that portion of your emotional system that tenaciously latches onto a problem. Once the state of witness detachment is attained, an interaction that only a few minutes ago seemed dark and serious can now be pursued and even deepened in a playful way. This is particularly important when a number of couples are exploring their relationships together in council. When one or more members of the circle spontaneously take on a wry, humorous witness role, not only is the solemnity diminished, but serious disagreement is more readily handled and truthful reflection achieved.

My knees ached and I longed for a silent walk along the ridge. Our problems felt heavy and insurmountable. After two days of board meetings, everyone's exhaustion sprawled about the circle. Finances and some difficult staffing decisions still loomed menacingly on the agenda. I knew I needed to shift perspective. Then I caught Gigi's eye, just as she finished a passionate description of how off-center the discussion had become for her. She winked. That was all I needed. Suddenly our seriousness seemed absurd. "We could always open a fast-food stand in town to make up our deficit," I said. A chorus of "creative" ideas followed.

"Pita bread and alfalfa sprouts, of course."

"We could offer fasting programs and cut expenses."

"Or we could video our board meetings and have a smash soap opera series."

"Or a Saturday Night Live special on spiritual centers."

"What a great idea!"

We stayed silly for a few minutes and then got back on track. The final hour of the meeting went smoothly and efficiently.

A spirit of playfulness can be introduced directly and thematically as well. A few suggestions:

- Try some of the games and exercises that have proven helpful in working with groups of children.[3] Many of these are readily adaptable to circles of adults.

- When previous councils have been particularly heavy, consider choosing a playful theme for the opening round of the upcoming session. Themes might include . . .

  Telling a story about a recent "absurd" experience.

  Telling a "the-joke-was-on-me" story.

  Talking about someone who makes you laugh and why they have that effect.

STORYTELLING

Wisdom about the human condition and our relationship to other forms of life was transmitted exclusively by means of the oral tradition for millennia, until the beginning of recorded history a mere three thousand years ago. Since then, both oral and written storytelling has remained a primary way of teaching the young, remembering shared

---

[3] See Council Program Activities Guide: For Use in the Middle School Classroom, compiled by Joan Apter, The Ojai Foundation, 1994, and The Mysteries Sourcebook, available from the Crossroads School, Santa Monica, CA.

beliefs, and relating to the Divine. Traditional stories live in the collective consciousness of a culture and are transmitted through retelling, ceremony and dreams.[4]

How were these traditional stories created in the first place? Did they enter each culture's collective mind as the result of an evolutionary process involving countless individuals over a long period of time? One can only imagine that with telling and retelling, similar personal stories coalesced, were pruned of nonessential details, and, with time, became the lean and powerful traditional myths anthropologists and storytellers know today.

In the past few hundred years, the role of the oral tradition has been progressively supplanted by the written word and, more recently, by the visual media, particularly in Western culture. Yet the power of storytelling to reveal our humanity and the interdependence of all forms of life is still very much alive. We find it reflected in the universal delight of children during story time and the recent resurgence of interest in the oral tradition as a form of education and entertainment.

Story and council are inseparable. The first councils may have arisen spontaneously after a storyteller's tale inspired listeners to respond with associations and stories of their own. Among others, the Northwest Native American story councils still carry on this practice, complete with talking staff and other aspects of the council tradition. And how about old-timers sitting around a potbelly stove spinning yarns, or mothers comparing stories of birth? Or a group of fisherman, athletes, or travelers going on about their adventures? These are all vestigial story councils—not often recognized as such—but story councils nonetheless.

One of the simplest ways to increase the feeling of intimacy in a council circle is to invite stories:

"Tell us a story about
    . . . a grandparent for whom you have strong feelings."

---

[4] *Man and his Symbols*, C.G.Jung, Doubleday, 1964.

. . . a close relative who is hard for you to handle."

. . . the death of an animal you loved."

. . . the way your kitchen smelled when you were little."

. . . the time you were the most afraid for your life."

Or when time is abundant:

"Tell us the very first story you remember hearing as a child."

"Tell us a story that changed your life."

In working with children, particularly a multicultural group, an excellent way to introduce council is for the facilitator to tell a story from a traditional culture and then give each child the opportunity to freely associate the story to his or her own life. The chance to express personal reactions without interruption in a group of attentive listeners further uncovers the story's subtle wisdom. If stories from different cultures are introduced in this way, the children learn to recognize both the differences and similarities among the different traditions. Recognition ultimately leads to greater respect and tolerance. This is one of the basic reasons story councils help ease racial and cultural antagonisms in multicultural schools.

Of course, the power of story councils is not limited to circles of children. If the moment is right, shifting the mood through the gateway of "Once upon a time . . . " can move a group of adults from the logjam of disagreement into greater communion with each other. On a few occasions, when faced with chairing a difficult business, faculty, or community meeting, I have surprised everyone by starting off with a story whose underlying theme related to the difficulties at hand. Then I asked for reactions to the story and offered my own. Approaching a difficult council indirectly through the medium of story often engages people more personally and stimulates insight.

In planning a story council, we suggest the following guidelines.

- Choose a story, whether personal or traditional, that is accessible yet sufficiently out-of-the-ordinary to stir the circle's imagination. If the cultural gap between the story and the group is too large, the story may not be heard. On the other hand, the presence of a new twist, a degree of unfamiliarity, or "touching of the mystery" in the story usually awakens deeper interest. A good story raises more questions than it answers.

- If you find an appropriate story in a book, take the trouble to learn it. Telling is almost always better than reading; it promotes eye contact, greater voice variation, and the opportunity to add a personal touch.

- No two people tell the same story in the same way. Make the story your own. Keep your language simple and lean. Tell the story as if it were unfolding in front of you, right there in the circle. Describing what you see in the moment is more powerful than "remembering" a story. If you have natural gifts or training as a storyteller, great! If not, don't let that stop you. Everybody can aspire to be at least an adequate storyteller—particularly of one's own experiences. When you hear somebody tell a story in a way that awakens your imagination, explore why, and then refine your own storytelling style accordingly.

- When you are leading a story council, don't be surprised if several people choose to pass the talking piece without speaking. Telling a story or associating to someone else's is a challenge for many people at first. It may take a while for a group to come alive as a story circle.

- The fourth basic intention of council ("Don't prepare until you get the talking piece") is a tough one to fulfill in a story council. Stories trigger stories. As associations pile up in your mind, the challenge is to let go, return to attentive listening, and trust that the story appropriate to the moment will come to you when you get the talking piece.

DREAMING

Traditionally, council has always honored and provided a safe place for dreamwork. In fact, sharing dreams that offer guidance to the family or community is one of the oldest functions of council. Even if you are accustomed to working with dreams on your own or with another person, sharing dreams in council and listening to those of others can illuminate the world of dreaming in new ways.[5]

Dreams as Stories

In an ongoing group, the desire to share dreams and visionary experiences is a natural part of the movement towards greater trust and intimacy. Dreams can be offered during a weather report, a brainstorming council, or at any time they seem relevant to the theme. An early morning dream council provides the most practical way to share dreams from the previous night, since most people tend to forget them as the day progresses. The talking piece can be passed around in the usual way or, alternatively, dreams can be spoken spontaneously out of the silence after meditation or drumming.

Analysis and interpretation of individual dreams is usually inconsistent with the spirit of council, since the practice draws invasive attention to one person by juxtaposing analytical and dreaming states of consciousness. In council, we usually listen to dreams as "stories of the night" or "gifts from Dreamtime," with the very different intention of *entering the dreamstate with the dreamer*.[6] This practice, which is similar to that of many traditional cultures, usually generates a nonconfrontational environment that strengthens the sense of interconnectedness in the circle. These reactions can be expressed, or not,

---

[5] See also "The Council Process in Dream and Personal Myth Work," An Interview with Jack Zimmerman, Dream Network Journal, Vol. 10, No. 2-3, Spring/Summer 1991.

[6] For the Aboriginal people of Australia, Dreamtime is not only the historical epoch out of which the earth, animals, and people emerged, but also a contemporary visionary world that is the source of nighttime dreams and visionary experiences.

as the circle prefers, but just the *sharing of dreams* is often sufficient for everyone to feel more connected. This non-analytical approach increases the feeling of safety in the circle and avoids probing deeply into anyone's unconscious material, unless a member specifically invites the group to do so.

The Dreamstar

If an intimate circle wants to interact with each other's dreams and visionary experiences, we recommend a format called "Dreamstar." This powerful way of exploring the dreaming consciousness works best when the circle has developed at least a modest sense of trust and a willingness to take risks.[7]

To create the Dreamstar, an appropriate number of small pillows are arranged in a tightly knit circle beforehand. Then group members are invited to enter the council room silently and lie on their backs with feet extended outward and their heads on the pillows forming the Dreamstar configuration. Soft background music can assist in creating a relaxed mood.

The council leader guides the group through a brief relaxation exercise that releases tension with deep breathing, while focusing on different parts of the body in succession. As relaxation progresses, the leader encourages everyone to bring their night stories and visionary experiences into the present moment by shifting awareness into the dreaming state:

> Now we can enter Dreamtime together, relaxed and ready to connect with our dreams and visions. Tell your story in the first person, as if it were unfolding in front of you right now. Bring us into the dream or vision by sharing the images, sounds, and important feelings as sensually as you can. We'll tell our stories one by one, out of the silence, as we feel called to do so.

---

[7] We are indebted to Maureen Murdock for first introducing us to this practice.

The leader then lies down with the rest of the group. After all the dreams and visionary experiences have been shared, the leader continues:

> Now we are going to weave the dreams together, each as a different reflection of our collective dreamstate. We will search for the common threads in our dreams and perhaps discover how the Dreamweaver is guiding us, not only individually but also as a group. I'll begin the weaving, and then everyone in the circle is invited to continue, one at a time, in any order, as you begin to discover the larger story we are weaving together.

The leader then begins the dreamweaving by noting common elements that arose in the dreams. These might include similar landscapes, common narrative elements (going on a journey, facing fear, death and rebirth, etc.), repeated symbols, animals, bigger-than-life figures, and common emotional qualities. After a few moments, the leader stops and invites others in the circle to continue the exploration. As each person highlights different aspects of the dreaming, a unifying dream story usually emerges. Mythical and personal associations enter the weaving, and sometimes the group reaches a state of collective awareness in which the dreams all seem to have been created by the dreaming mind of a single, multifaceted being. After everyone sits up and forms a circle, the process can be brought to a close by acknowledging the insights gathered during the interweaving and expressing appreciation for the Dreamweaver's gifts.

A group who regularly practices the Dreamstar gradually comes to understand the nature of their interconnectedness in a deeper way. Occasionally group members appear in each other's dreams and, after a while, two or more people may be visited by similar stories of the night. These experiences promote a feeling of intimacy and can become an important part of reinforcing the circle's sense of interdependence.

WITHOUT WORDS

Council is a fertile environment for verbal interaction. Some find their true "voice" in council for the first time. Many expand their ability to express feelings, tell stories, and make clearer statements through their council experience. With patience and perseverance, tending the council garden brings an abundant verbal harvest. But the power of council can be expressed in still moments as well. Pausing between speakers to absorb what has just been said, or holding the talking piece silently while making eye contact with everyone in the circle, can be a profound part of the practice.

Sometimes an entire "silent council" is useful, perhaps during a weekend of intense business or community meetings, when verbal communication appears to be blocked. The shift into silence can diffuse the logjam and eventually lead to a resurgence of speaking from the heart. Even when communication in an ongoing circle is open and flowing, calling for a silent council may help the group integrate previous discussions and make room for deeper listening. At times, experienced council participants can feel wordless as well as full of stories and insights. We have found that, during intensive periods of sitting in council, if time is set aside for a silent circle, it feels like the entire group is taking a long, deep breath before speaking again. This "breath" helps everyone discover what truly needs to be spoken in subsequent councils.

In addition to silent group meditation, nonverbal councils may also utilize some form of movement as their mode of expression. Movement councils are best kept simple and relatively open, thematically. Silent weather reports, expressions of appreciation to the circle, or using movement to describe what the group needs at the moment are typical of such councils. The instructions are given verbally, followed by a period of silence, out of which the movement emerges. Although the talking piece can be passed around as usual, each person placing it in front of him or her before beginning, we often prefer to not use a piece formally and instead each person turns to the next to indicate when they are done.

Silent offerings can be given in a variety of ways:

- *Through mudras:* Each person remains seated and uses only his or her hands, arms, and upper body to communicate a response to the theme.

- *Through movement:* Each person moves about the circle spontaneously, making some form of nonphysical contact with others, if mutually acceptable.

- *Through creating a "statue":* Each person moves until a pose is found that gives his or her response to the theme.

- *Through mirroring:* Each person creates a movement or a pose which is imitated by the rest of the circle.

- *Through passing a movement:* A gesture or movement can be passed around the circle as a "talking stick," changing shape as it is transferred from one person to the next. At the Ojai Foundation, we used to begin our day with one person leading movement for a while and then spontaneously passing leadership on to several others.

People who are more at home with words than with their bodies sometimes find movement councils difficult. For many, such circles require a little courage, mutual trust, the suspension of critical judgment, and a dash of good humor. Those who feel repeatedly challenged by the verbal nature of council may experience silent circles as an opportunity to reveal their passion in a way that is more comfortable for them.

A silent council is best completed with a silent acknowledgment, such as holding hands or joining in a short meditation. Although it is tempting—and sometimes appropriate to do so—discussing a nonverbal council afterwards usually dilutes its power. The challenge is to trust that whatever happened will inform verbal responses when the group meets again.

In recent years Gigi has brought many new forms of sound and movement councils into our trainings. As a consequence —and because they often turn out to be extremely useful in deepening the intentions of council —many leaders now regularly use these forms of wordless councils with students and adults. Here are a few guidelines for introducing sound and movement councils:

- Whoever starts the council begins by creating a repeatable short sequence of sounds, lasting say five to ten seconds —without any movement. After the sound is repeated for a short time, the person turns and passes it to his or her left, and the next in the circle mirrors the sound as closely as possible. When the originator of the sound is clear it has been heard, he or she turns back to face the center of the circle and becomes silent. The new "sounder" —without pausing —transforms the sound gradually into a new sound of his or her choosing. When that sound is being repeated clearly, he or she turns and passes it on. In this way the sounding goes around the circle —without lingering or planning and with "no sound" (silence) always a possibility. When this kind of council is used as part of a training, it is advisable to ask five to seven people to volunteer to do the sounding in a fishbowl with the rest of the circle as witnesses. Working with a smaller number of people in the inner circle usually leads to less performance pressure, particularly if the sound is allowed to go around a few times. Then the leader can ask for witness comments, first from the inner circle and then the outer one. Finally, a second group (and third, if necessary) can go into the center to have its turn.

- It is often good to balance a sound council by following it with some form of movement council—without sound. This gives the circle the opportunity to experience the nature of the connectedness each basic form of such councils can provide—and thus reveal the value in using word-less councils.

- Once sound and movement are introduced separately, they can be used together in a variety of ways. In train-ings, a small new group of volunteers can be the first to try a combined movement and sound council using the fishbowl format.

- One variation that has proved effective is for each person in a sound council to hold on to their sound when they turn back into the whole circle. The attentiveness needed to continue making your own sound while listening to the many sounds of others often helps to deepen listen-ing and increase awareness of the interweaving possible in council.

- We encourage council facilitators to explore these kinds of councils and discover the many teachings they provide. Here are a few comments from participants in a confer-ence, after they met together in a council that Gigi began with sound and movement:

Wow, that was beyond words—a primordial connection!

I was able to get to know and see you all better than talking with you the entire year."

"Yikes, I didn't realize how much I prepare and plan ahead in council. This was my first gateway into true spontaneity."

Copying your sound and movement brought me into a place of deep listening so that now I feel far more present and able to be here."

Once a leader becomes familiar with them, sound and movement councils can be used in a variety of situations: to start the council, shift the field, deepen the listening, or close the circle. Such councils remind us of the many ways we can communicate, be seen, and be heard. Beyond the value of individual insights, sound and movement councils can take us into experiencing a level of interconnection and community in the circle that is sometimes not reached even by "talking hearts," much less "talking heads."

VISIONING COUNCILS

Many of us are familiar with the process of "brainstorming" in which a (usually small) group searches for new directions or solutions to a problem by means of a spontaneous, interactive exchange of ideas. Brainstorming works best when everyone feels free to express themselves and is willing to listen to others attentively; it works less well when a few people dominate the sharing, either through force of personality, skill at articulating, or hierarchical position (CEO, school principal, or community leader, for example).

At its best, the brainstorming circle may generate a synergistic level of insight and creativity that makes it seem as if a "group mind" is at work. Combining brainstorming with council can greatly enhance this synergy. In such "Visioning Councils" the group mind is expressed through what we have come to call "the voice of the circle." This voice can speak through any member of the council and can be recognized by its relatively objective, imaginative, and detached character. Ideally, the visioning process is an intuitive, interactive exploration of the topic that transcends ordinary patterns of rational thinking.

I'm reminded of how Einstein described the way he arrived at the special theory of relativity. The key, he said (to paraphrase), was to contemplate the experimental information with the imagination of a child freed from knowledge of Newtonian physics. Only then could he transcend this traditional mechanistic way of seeing the world. Apparently, genius can achieve this level of freedom alone. Most of us need something more interactive, like a visioning council, to help us free our minds from old patterns.

Sometimes the visionary voice comes through in a surprising way. Gigi remembers a community that tried to convince its founder to attend a visioning council. He refused, probably not wanting to hear his vision distorted by the group, so they decided reluctantly to go ahead without him.

"What happened was amazing," Gigi recalls. "After going around the circle twice, one of the newest members of the community articulated the vision with such clarity it took our breath away. We realized afterwards that the founder's absence had freed the circle from old, deferential patterns. I saw, once again, that discovering a group's vision does not depend on a particular person being present or every member of the circle being well-acquainted with the group. A clear vision can come through anyone who is genuinely open to hearing the voice of the circle."

Being part of a visioning council that works is like participating in dreamsharing, improvising with skilled musicians, or creating a spontaneous dance with a talented group of intimates. Although the process eludes analysis, successful visioning seems to depend on satisfying three basic requirements:

- Setting the intention clearly,

- Heightening group awareness and *esprit,*

- Committing to the practice of open response ("Yes, *and . . .* " rather than "Yes, *but . . .* " or "*No,* because . . . ").

Setting the intention. Focusing a visioning council is often best achieved by posing one or more simple questions, rather than elaborating a number of alternative visions and asking the circle to choose among them. For example, suppose a small private college is facing a financial crisis due to declining enrollment. Taking the more familiar approach, a faculty visioning council might pursue one or more of the following options:

- Survey students to see what courses they would like to take,

- Eliminate courses with less than a specified minimum enrollment,

- Increase teaching loads,

- Hire a professional fund-raiser to increase endowments.

However, a more productive way to start the council might be with the question, "If you had complete freedom to develop a new course, what would it be? Don't be limited by traditional curricula ideas or what we have done in the past." Instead of stimulating a debate on various plans of action, a question of this type might reveal why enrollment is declining (lack of teacher passion, curricula that is out of date, etc.) and eventually lead to a more creative solution as the council unfolds.

Setting the intention for the visioning council requires simplicity and clarity in regard to terminology. For example, a new community searching for a unifying purpose may discover that the word spiritual means something slightly different to each person. In such situations it is helpful to get clear about any ambiguous terms before continuing the process.

Heightening group awareness and esprit. Increasing the esprit of the circle invariably helps break habitual patterns of relating and generates energy for the visioning process. The request for support from the voice of the circle can be empowered through ceremony and group activities before the vision council convenes. The intention of these preparations is to strengthen the group's sense of purpose and create a fertile space for the visioning. Activities might include:

- Joining in a meditation or prayer circle,

- Planning a pilgrimage or "field trip" to a place or project associated with the desired vision,[8]

---

[8] For example, if the intention is to create homeless shelters, then the field trip might be to a nearby ghetto or slum. If the circle's intention is to work with a particular kind of child, then the pilgrimage might be to a school currently dealing with such children.

- Group members spending time alone in the wilderness,

- Working together on a project associated with the group's intentions,[9]

- A backpacking trip, river-rafting expedition, or ropes course adventure (for the strong of heart),[10]

Open response. "No, because" or "Yes, but" responses to new ideas expressed in the circle inhibit the freewheeling creativity that nourishes visioning. A person who reacts in such a manner probably has preconceived ideas of what the vision should be and/or is afraid that the circle will "get off track." These kinds of responses, however well-intended, only limit the rapport and constrict the open flow so important to a successful visioning council.

In a circle that practices "Yes, and" responses, each person's contribution is received openly. If a portion of the contribution is extraneous or off-the-mark, it falls away naturally, as a result of not being reinforced by others, rather than as a result of direct rejection. Open responses are more likely to occur when group members respect each other's visioning capacity and are able to let go of attachment to particular outcomes.

Visioning through open response could be likened to a group of apprentices painting a mural together, guided only by a unifying image. Each apprentice takes his or her turn and then witnesses the work of the others with openness and appreciation. No one knows how the final mural will look, but everyone trusts the integrity of the underlying creative process.

---

[9] For example, building a cabin in the mountains to use as part of a rehabilitation program for teenagers recovering from substance abuse would most likely enhance the group's ability to envision their program in a concrete way.

[10] A ropes course consists of a series of log, rope, and cable obstacles which, at ground level, challenge a group's ability to work together cooperatively, and at elevations of twenty to forty feet, adds the challenge of walking a tight rope or leaping off a platform while securely fastened to "belay" safety ropes.

Towards the end of a relationship workshop Jaquelyn and I facilitated in Santa Barbara some years ago, participants were divided into small groups and given an hour to create brief theatrical pieces about the challenges of intimacy. We video-taped these preparations to see how they would relate to the final presentations. Two groups stood out for opposite reasons when we all watched the tapes after the performances. In the first, group members reacted enthusiastically to each other's ideas with responses such as, "Great!" or "And we could also . . . " This group's subsequent performance was coherent, humorous, and insightful. Most of the reactions in the second group were rejecting: "Oh, no, that would be too hard," "Too corny!" or "We could never pull that off." This group actually ran out of time without coming up with any plan. Their "performance" degenerated into a rehashing of their dismal preparation experience.

For many years the Ojai Foundation included a visioning circle as part of our end-of-the-year celebration with staff and friends. To prepare for co-visioning, we held a council on New Year's Eve focused on the ups and down of the previous twelve months and then shared prayers in a sweatlodge ceremony. After the lodge most of us brought our sleeping bags into the meditation yurt to enjoy a few hours of rest and dreaming time together.

Early the next morning, we began the visioning circle with drumming and a period of silence. The council leaders then set the theme: "You are invited to share your visions and intuitions about the new year. You can focus attention on yourself, your family, the Foundation, or the world—any or all of these. Recent dreams, particularly from last night, are especially invited." Invariably, many of the anxieties, personal challenges, and intuitions expressed about the future were remarkably similar. Sometimes several people would report closely related dreams about the new year. These vision councils helped the Foundation staff serve our extended family more effectively.

COYOTE COUNCIL

As we said in Chapter 1, the talking piece usually travels the circle in the clockwise or "sun" direction. The counterclockwise or "earth" direction is usually reserved for a "coyote council." Virtually every spiritual tradition has a divine trickster: Hanuman, the Monkey God in the Hindu tradition; Hermes, the messenger of the Olympian Gods; and Coyote, the wily creature of Native American *Heyoehkah* folklore. Coyote teaches us primarily by getting into and out of trouble. Traditional coyote stories poke fun at pomposity, solemnity, pride, arrogance, and sensual excess. In our personal lives Coyote sometimes pulls the rug out from under us when we least expect it, by causing us to slip on a "psychic banana peel" that we've inadvertently left in our own path. If we're lucky, from time to time a friend will play Coyote in our lives— although at the moment we may not appreciate our good fortune. For many parents, Coyote's role is assumed by one or more of their children. Although he appears childlike and naive at times, Coyote can be as cunning as fox and as wise as owl. Often he is the butt of his own, and others', jokes . . . and sometimes he has the last laugh.

In an ongoing council the role of coyote is often assumed by an individual who has a low tolerance for taking things too seriously. Such people get restless when the mood turns self-righteous or pretentious, and their natural tendency is to "act-out," coyote-style. These individuals are invaluable in the life of the council, as long as they are confronted if they hide behind their coyote role too much of the time.

When even the presence of a coyote or two is not enough to counteract the heaviness in a circle, a *coyote council* is in order. In this special council, everyone is encouraged to speak in the outrageous, irreverent, and wildly creative voice that is often suppressed. By their very nature, coyote councils rarely stay "on theme."

A coyote council is prescribed when the group suffers from:

• Predictability,

- Lethargy and boredom,

- Adult-itis (loss of contact with its childlike nature),

- Storytime deprivation,

- Symptoms of "there-must-be-more-to-life-than-this,"

- Self-aggrandizement (we are a great group—wise, insight-ful, and aware of our dark places),

- Council-itis (the belief that council is always the solution for every problem).

Gigi and I found ourselves very much involved in a spontane-ous coyote council several years ago when we were facilitating an advanced council training. Two of the participants, who had been asked to set up and lead a role-playing council with Sixth-Graders, designed theirs in a way that brought out the ornery child in the rest of the group. The two of us seized this rare opportunity to play out our rebellious sides, which stirred up a lot of trouble. Not sur-prisingly, our wild coyote behavior became a great challenge for the leaders-in-training, who expressed considerable distress during the witnessing after the session. Gigi and I also learned a lot from the experience, particularly about needing to find ways to express our playful sides during trainings and similar gatherings!

Then there was the time we emerged from a long evening council feeling so uncomfortably incomplete that coyote could not be denied. We rang the meeting bell at midnight, calling everyone who had gone to bed back to the council fire. Initial expressions of disbelief were soon replaced with delight as our outrageous action helped the circle move forward.

When you show up for council and the talking piece is sent around the other way, beware! Don't be surprised if your mind races, your heart pumps a little faster, and you feel more than a little out of control. After all, the council is now in the hands of our four-footed, furry ally!

5
COUNCIL
LEADERSHIP

If we have courage, we shall be healers
Like the sun we shall rise
If we have courage, we shall be healers
Like the sun we shall rise
We are alive as the earth is alive
We have the power to live all our freedom

–Chant attributed to
Starhawk and Rose May Dance

I started out leading councils and council leadership trainings
by myself. Then in 1986, Gigi pointed out to me that a single
leader, although traditional, failed to manifest the vision of
partnership that council inspires. She suggested that a pair of leaders would demonstrate this essential quality as well as bring greater
flexibility and balance to the trainings. She offered to lead the next
gathering of prospective council leaders with me.

The fact that Gigi had been working in council for years, and would be an invaluable partner in training others in the practice, helped me overcome my attachment to the image of the solo leader (a pattern of many males in our culture, which my wife Jaquelyn refers to as the "Lone Ranger" syndrome). Gigi and I formalized our ongoing commitment to the council process at that time through an allyship that has greatly helped us individually and increased our ability to support others in finding the way of council. All of us at the Foundation are now fully committed to a *partnership model* in facilitating most of our educational and retreat programs.

PARTNERSHIP

Co-leadership has many tangible benefits. Having a pair of guides allows each to participate more fully in the circle, knowing that the other is there to "mind the store." Guides can be chosen who have different styles and ways of working with a group. For example, one may have an intuitive gift for "reading" people, while the other is skilled at maintaining an overview and keeping the process on track. Having a man and a woman simultaneously in leadership roles offers additional opportunities for gender balancing within the partnership model.

Co-leadership also resolves the question of when the leader should take his or her turn to speak. One of the leader's options is to initiate the round in order to demonstrate how to deal with the theme. At other times it may be better for the leader to speak last, in order to highlight what took place during the round and bring the session "full circle." When there are two leaders, both of these important functions can be accomplished in a single round.

In an ongoing circle it is not uncommon for some people to become attached to the council leader. This attachment usually incorporates both positive and negative associations to authority figures, as

well as other familiar consequences of *transference*.[1] Working in partnership diffuses the power and focus of these projections, particularly
if the leaders are honest and open about their differences in front of
the group.

Of course, dual leadership is not always possible. Having two
teachers available for councils in a school program is a rare luxury.
However, in community, business, and large family settings, the opportunity to break the solo leadership pattern often does exist and is
well worth pursuing.

Many ongoing groups organize their councils around a rotating
pattern of leadership. Rotation is particularly appropriate when the
circle is comprised of peers (or, as ceremonialist and teacher Elizabeth
Cogburn used to say, "cohearts"). In this case anyone in the group
is capable of leading the council, either individually or in partnership. Obviously, rotation of leadership distributes the transference
throughout the group.

When council is conducted in settings characterized by traditional hierarchies (such as most large corporations, government agen-
cies, and schools), rotating leadership can help to counteract the in-
hibiting effects of the organizational structure by empowering those
further down the administrative ladder. The benefits of rotation in
these situations include uncovering new talent, breaking patterns of
intimidation, and creating greater organizational intimacy. Having
someone other than the administrative leader guide the council often
stimulates the group in a playful and productive way. The intrinsic
partnership nature of council is strong enough to significantly affect
even the most well-established organizational hierarchies.

Rotating leadership among students can be effective in a school
council program as well, once the children have become familiar with
the mechanics of council and a substantial level of trust has been
established. Young people usually rise to the challenge of leading a

---

[1] We use the term transference in the classical sense to describe the process through which
a person expresses emotions and patterns of behavior that relate to repressed experiences
from the past. The process is stimulated by an authority figure, who becomes the object of
the person's repressed impulses.

council and particularly enjoy choosing themes. The teacher or another adult can participate as a member of the circle with the option (agreed on in advance) of intervening, should the group move onto shaky ground.

Family councils also benefit from a rotating leadership. Letting each family member in turn choose the theme and lead the council empowers the children and helps the parents remember what it is like to follow someone else's script.

During our annual "Gathering for Carriers of Council" at the Ojai Foundation, Gigi and I always turned over leadership to pairs of participants for many of the councils. Each pair was asked to decide what the next group focus was to be and what form of council should be used in order to keep the process moving in a productive way. We participated fully in the councils and then offered witness comments, along with everyone else, after each session was complete. At the 2007 Gathering, we stepped back further and turned over the leadership of the Gatherings to the whole circle. Two experienced trainers were chosen to lead the Gathering in 2008 (which I attended as an Elder-participant).

When a group is comprised of both experienced and less experienced members, an effective plan is to choose pairs of leaders, one from each subgroup. The more experienced person acts as a mentor to the other, particularly in preparing for the council and talking about the session afterwards. During the council the pair does its best to share the functions of leadership in a balanced way. Gigi has made it a practice, when first introducing council to communities and organizations, to partner with one of the members or staff. This heightens the training for the chosen individual and eventually facilitates transferring full leadership to the organization.

Other factors that are important in creating balanced partnerships to lead council include gender, age, individual backgrounds and race. Whenever possible, partnerships that reflect both the wholeness and diversity of the group are very much in the spirit of council.

The Challenges of Leadership

A council leader becomes fully empowered when he or she is able to meet three interrelated challenges:

- Fulfill the basic intentions of council in an exemplary way and build council discipline on this foundation of discipleship.

- Develop a heightened perception of the council's "Interactive Field."

- Become a steward of council by integrating authentic participation with a well-developed capacity for witnessing.

The purpose of this and the following chapter is to explore these three challenges, particularly elaborating on what we mean by *heightened perception*, *Interactive Field*, and *stewarding a council*. At the outset, we want to acknowledge that the title of *council leader* is not entirely satisfactory, since for many people the concept of leader automatically implies a hierarchical structure, which is not a predominant characteristic of the council process. Other leadership titles we use include:

- *Caller of Council:* This title emphasizes the invitational attitude inherent in effective leadership. In many ways the leader serves as the host or hostess of the council.

- *Council Chief or Road Chief:* These are both traditional terms, whose use is also limited by hierarchical (as well as masculine) associations with the word *chief*. On the plus side, *road chief* (the term used for council leaders in the Native American Church) is unpretentious—down-to-earth—and rightly depicts council as an extended journey of communication.

- *Guide:* This term emphasizes that every council has a life of its own that can be guided, but not controlled, by the leader.

- *Carrier of Council:* The word *carrier* suggests that, once initiated, the leader serves the practice of council as a sacred commitment.[2]

As we shall see, becoming a steward of council involves full commitment to serving the circle and to the path of council as a spiritual practice. In this respect, the title *carrier of council* is the most appropriate of all, and we often refer to someone who has substantially met the three challenges of leadership as a carrier of council. For variety, we will use all of these terms interchangeably with *leader* in the course of our discussion.

THE FIRST CHALLENGE

Being a Disciple of Council

Whatever the leader's other capabilities, he or she must be an accomplished practitioner of the basic intentions of council: speaking from the heart, devout listening, leanness of expression, and spontaneity. By *exemplary* we mean passionate and authentic. Ideally, carriers of council fulfill these intentions with a fervor that extends beyond functional adherence into the domain of discipleship. When leaders "walk their talk," everyone in the circle is challenged to do the same. Then council discipline evolves organically from the leader's modeling and does not need to be imposed in an authoritarian manner.

To help leaders walk their talk, we suggest that they should first look inward when difficulties arise in leading a group. The basic

---

[2] In the Native American tradition, the medicine person who takes care of the ceremonial pipe is often called the "pipe carrier."

question to ask is, "Have I been practicing the four intentions devoutly in the way I relate to the circle?" If a robust yes is not forthcoming, the leader should recommit to the intentions without wasting energy on self-judgment. The stronger this commitment, the more members of the circle will be inspired to improve their own council presence in a similar way. On more than a few occasions I have found myself growing irritated with someone in a way that goes beyond the content of any issues we might be debating at the moment. When I witness my reactivity, invariably I find that I have not been listening to that person attentively. Then my biggest challenge is to shift into devout listening without beating myself up for being less than an exemplary leader. When I am able to accomplish this, a softening takes place which usually releases the tension between us. Meeting such a demanding challenge requires perseverance. Living the four intentions consistently is usually difficult for a new leader. Doubt and self-judgment about one's capabilities are not uncommon at first, but the experienced leader grows accustomed to discovering which skills need improving without having a crisis of faith. To reiterate: *The challenge is to note the need for change and make adjustments without falling into debilitating self-judgment.*

Building Council Discipline

Every ceremonial journey has its risks and challenges. The increased sensitivity and heightened awareness that ceremony offers require a strong "container" in order for participants to feel safe enough to engage fully. In some traditional ceremonies, one or more people are assigned to be "soul watchers," to patrol the ceremonial ground and help build a physical and spiritual container for the other participants. Soul watchers maintain the boundaries of the ceremony and provide whatever personal support is needed to protect participants during the experience.

The ceremony of council also requires soul watchers to help create a safe container. Although everyone in the circle shares responsibility for making the council a safe place to communicate authentically, the leader is obliged to pay particular attention to dangers along the ceremonial journey. This is especially true when the circle is comprised of young people or adults inexperienced in council. We refer to this challenge of leadership as being a good road chief. The *road chief* is usually the council's main soul watcher.

Like a guide on a challenging backpacking trip, the road chief has explored the trail before and is familiar with the terrain. When the going gets rough, the road chief makes sure the group is focused and attentive to each other's safety. In council, this assignment involves being able to readily handle the more common breaches of council discipline. These include:

- Arriving late, taking unscheduled breaks, or leaving before the council has been completed.

- Making brief but regular comments out of turn or disregarding other council guidelines, such as those that might be associated with a specific spiral or response council format, agreed upon in advance.

- Assuming a body position that indicates lack of attention or respect (lying down, facing away from the circle, appearing to be asleep).

- Purposely treating the talking piece with disrespect (in a moment of anger or rebellion).

- Poking, leaning against, or otherwise physically distracting a nearby member of the circle.

Although anyone in the circle is free to comment on council discipline or its absence when holding the talking piece, it is primarily the leader's responsibility to maintain the integrity of council if a breach occurs. Several ways to intervene are possible; their suitability depends on the particular behavior, the time available, size of the circle, degree of familiarity with council, and the leader's self-confidence:

- Make eye contact with the individual(s) involved while silently reaffirming basic council decorum. When the leader is experienced (and a disciple of council), the impact of his or her presence and attention is often sufficient to handle all but the more extreme breaches of discipline.

- Wait until the talking piece comes around and address the issue as a member of the council.

- Wait until the current speaker is finished and verbally reaffirm council practice or the guidelines agreed upon.

- Interrupt the proceedings and reaffirm appropriate council behavior and/or address the individual(s) involved directly.

Repeated breaches may require more vigorous responses, including talking to the individual(s) after council. When the group is just starting up, it may be necessary to frequently reaffirm and explain the ground rules. In the long run, this time is well-spent. Letting a circle establish poor council behavior, even if limited to minor breaches, such as making brief comments out of turn, is harder to correct the longer it is tolerated.

When members of the circle regularly disturb the flow of council and do not respond to direct personal reflection, the leader has two options. The first is to "turn into the skid," for example, by asking each member of the council to answer the question, "How do you see this behavior affecting the circle and what do you think we should do about it?" When other approaches fail, the second option is to ask those responsible for the breaches of discipline to leave the circle, until they are ready to participate appropriately. The following provides an example of this situation.

Stephen had been struggling with his group of sixth-graders for several weeks. One or two of the students had extremely short attention spans. Others had never had the experience of being listened to by their classmates. Attentive listening seemed to be foreign to the entire group. Stephen had tried a variety of focusing exercises, to no avail. Most of his energy was going into keeping the kids from interrupting each other. Finally, after four weeks of teetering on the edge of chaos, he decided to express his frustration on a personal level.

"We can't go on like this," he said, holding the smooth stone the group had been using as a talking piece. "I sound more and more like an angry, nagging parent. Frankly, I don't look forward to coming to this class any more. As much as I love council, this circle doesn't seem to be going anywhere. What shall we do? I've run out of ideas. I need to hear from you."

Directly acknowledging what was happening broke the pattern. The students began to talk about their own frustrations and boredom with the councils. That discussion led to another about building trust, when they met the following week. Slowly the group came into focus. Stephen and the school counselor decided to ask the student with the shortest attention span to use the council time as a study period, until he was willing to follow the basic intentions of council. By taking the risk to give responsibility for the council's success back to the students, Stephen had established a level of authenticity that focused the group and brought the council to life. Once group members began to listen to each other, they had no difficulty in reintegrating the exiled student a few weeks later.

Even when council attendance is not optional (in a school program or important community meeting, for example), it is helpful if the leader reminds participants that they can "play the game of council" according to the basic intentions and still find room for a lot of creative expression, a little wildness, and even a touch of rebellion. Naturally, the extent to which this is possible depends on the group's and the leader's ability to maintain a strong yet flexible container.

If personal health concerns, an urgent phone call, or other emergency leads to someone's sudden departure from the circle, the leader can simply acknowledge the absence, provide whatever help the individual needs, and then reconnect with the council process. As we said earlier, each circle needs to have an agreement at the outset about taking designated intermissions or, for long or open-ended councils, allowing individuals to slip out unobtrusively during the session for brief breaks.

THE SECOND CHALLENGE

Heightened Perception of the Interactive Field

Earlier we noted how finding the council's true purpose is analogous to the feeling of being led by an unseen conductor who knows the music the council is meant to play. We call this underlying music the "Interactive Field" of the council: *The Interactive Field is the dynamic interweaving of all the people in the circle, together with an ineffable presence that seems to guide the circle towards meaningful interaction.* The council leader's basic challenge is to perceive and support this Interactive Field, which is accomplished by entering a state of expanded awareness we call *heightened perception.*

In the state of heightened perception, the experienced council leader intuitively senses (sees) the web of connections among members of the circle. This intuitive *seeing* provides a spontaneous and direct way of knowing that differs radically from rational observation. Intuition is an important part of our sixth sense—a direct way of observing reality that is unlike normal sensory perception. Intuitive awareness can astound us at times, because we are not used to acquiring knowledge—to *knowing* something—without first going through concrete processes of sensory perception and mental evaluation. Council can stimulate a state of heightened perception in which intuitive capabilities are expanded into the realm of "psychic" or direct insight.

Heightened perception can be activated in many ways. Sometimes I become aware of a new movement in the circle's Interactive Field through another person's tone of voice or through making prolonged eye contact. In our family councils, I often experience the door to heightened perception opening as a result of one of my children's startling insights or forceful confrontations. For example, when my son challenges me to acknowledge that I have been less than frank in some interaction with him—and he is right—my defenses are penetrated, I am disarmed, my parental role falls away, and briefly, until my patterns reassert themselves, I see myself and our relationship with heightened clarity.

For those familiar with the process of "scanning" the body's energy field,[3] the Interactive Field of the council can be thought of as the constantly changing energy field of the entire circle. This dynamic field arises from the complex interweaving of the "subtle bodies" of the circle's members. Entering the state of heightened perception means having the capacity to use one's "subtle senses" to see the energy field of the full circle. Each person in the circle has the potential to discern the field using these subtle, energy-sensitive versions of our ordinary senses. Part of a leader's job is to scan the circle, like a revolving antenna, "embracing" each person with heightened perception and listening devoutly. When the council leader perceives the Interactive Field in this more refined way, others in the circle are more likely to enter a state of heightened perception through the power of "intuitive resonance." Then, as more people see the Interactive Field, the energy of recognition further illuminates the field, making it yet easier to *see*.

This mutually enhancing relationship between the state of heightened perception and the Interactive Field is an example of the profound inseparability of self-awareness and awareness of other. Recent psychical research suggests that we become conscious principally through becoming aware of others.[4] To quote from Fred Alan Wolf's summary of this recent work:

---

[3] *See Joy's Way*, by W. Brugh Joy, J. P. Tarcher, Los Angeles, 1978.

[4] See *The Dreaming Universe*, Fred Alan Wolf, Simon and Schuster, 1994. Also see Montegue Ulman, "Dreams, Species-Connectedness and the Paranormal," Journal of the American Society for Psychical Research 84, no. 2, April 1990

> . . . consciousness is not just our personal recollection or reflection. It is not a property of a brain in isolation, but of a brain in communication with other brains. Thus we are conscious because we are in communication with other human beings . . . one's being is centered not in one's self but in the relation between one's brain and others. (p. 189)

This radical view of consciousness implies that the experience of seeing all the relationships flowing into the Interactive Field in council leads to council members becoming more conscious and more perceptive *individually*. As a result, each member of the circle is then able to see the Interactive Field more clearly. Thus, contemporary psychical research (as well as the traditional shamanic perspective) supports our observation that a council's collective state of heightened perception and its Interactive Field are mutually enhancing.

The first and second basic challenges of council leadership also enhance each other. Being a disciple of the four intentions of council requires a commitment of *ordinary attentiveness* which, at the outset, primarily involves the ordinary senses. However, as we listen more devoutly and speak more from the heart, the subtle or intuitive senses become activated and the gateway is opened to the *non-ordinary attentiveness* that is the foundation of heightened perception. With the birth of heightened perception,[5] our ability to fulfill the four intentions of council is greatly strengthened, because the subtle senses have now been added to our ordinary capacities for listening and perceiving. Thus meeting the first challenge of council leadership paves the way to fulfilling the second, and vice versa.

Being in the state of heightened perception also enhances the way we speak. The term *streaming* has been used to describe this experience. The words appear to be coming through you without benefit of processing by your ordinary conscious mind. Some of the images, and even the point of view expressed, may feel refreshingly different.

---

[5] Parapsychologist Charles Tart uses the term "lucid waking." See Waking Up: Overcoming the Obstacles to Human Potential, Charles Tart, New Science Library, 1986.

"Who was that?" you wonder after streaming. The source of streaming is not entirely unfamiliar, however. You have heard that voice before; the experience is one of *deja vu*. Perhaps it was in a dream, or a time in nature when you merged with the surroundings, or a joyous moment in relationship. I remember a time when an entire group shifted awareness because a few individuals moved into streaming consciousness:

> When we began the council, our circle was still bathed in the late afternoon sunlight that flooded in through the large windows. The entire faculty was present, only a few of whom had been in council before. "What are the most important challenges the school is facing right now?" was our theme. The initial speakers—the Headmaster, Dean of Students, and a few of the older teachers—spoke directly to the topic, outlining the school's staffing and curricular goals for the new year. Then, halfway around the circle, a young English teacher, who had begun in the same rational vein, drifted into a story about his father. The strong feelings embedded in his tale of estrangement and reconciliation moved us out of our heads and into our hearts. As the listening deepened, the door to heightened awareness opened for many in the circle.
>
> A few moments later, the school custodian described his conversations with students as they worked together in the vegetable garden. As he spoke in his slow Western drawl, the awareness of the circle quickened further. Lonely children and the need for closer connections between students and teachers had clearly become our theme, but no one needed to speak it directly. Instead, many described their own loneliness and inability to connect with adults when they were children, in voices that were soft, slowed down, and without a trace of self-consciousness. A few described the school's inability to reach many of the children, but without placing blame or making judgments. No one was defensive. By the time the talking piece returned to me, we had entered a state of communion,

sitting now in the shadows created by the single candle in the center of the circle.

The insights shared while streaming do not feel like those arising from the familiar process of conscious thinking. When someone asks about the source of such insights, one might say, "I'm simply report-ing what's coming through." You take responsibility for what you are saying, but not full credit. (There are even occasions when the stream-ing goes so deep that it is hard to remember the content afterwards!) This transpersonal quality of streaming helps to avoid inflation, on the one hand, and undue self-judgment on the other—both of which limit the extent of heightened awareness.

Just as the words "Once upon a time . . . " entice a child into a deeper state of listening, streaming stimulates greater attention. In-deed, becoming aware that you are streaming may be your own first indication that you have entered a state of heightened perception. Streaming is contagious. When an entire circle streams, council mem-bers become uncommonly aware of the group's Interactive Field. The illusion of being separate from others in the circle dissipates and the wholeness of the circle becomes a palpable reality—"Such is the King-dom of Heaven," to quote the last line of an Aldous Huxley novel.

Greater access to the state of heightened perception is one of the principal benefits of being a practitioner of council. To use Charles Tart's terminology, council is a pathway to "lucid waking." As seeing develops and becomes available outside of the council context, the ability to communicate with others is greatly enhanced. For example, many council practitioners develop the ability to *see* in advance if what they have to say will truly be heard. Such perceptions are invalu-able in helping them decide how and when they choose to speak.

Keeping Thematic Councils on Track

Watching for abrupt shifts. When it is important for a council to maintain a thematic focus, the leader can track what is happening by watching the Interactive Field. As the talking piece goes around the circle, the leader carefully watches this continuously changing "energy movie." As long as there are no jarring breaks in the unfolding story, the leader continues listening and witnessing silently.

If the Interactive Field should shift abruptly, the council leader tracks the excursion to see if the basic agenda is changing. However clear the original focus, a change is *always* a possibility. The leader then has several options:

- Recognize the change as appropriate and support the new focus.

- Continue to track the Interactive Field until the situation clarifies.

- Comment on the shifting energy pattern when the talking piece comes around. Ask for others in the circle to give their reflections and put the talking piece in the center. Suggest that the whole group decide what to do.

- Consider changing the council form (into a fishbowl, for example, if a few individuals need more time or attention, or an issue needs to be clarified).

- Intervene when the change in the Interactive Field is clearly inappropriate and there is no need to involve the whole circle in refocusing the council.

A few situations are straightforward. For example, say the first person to speak obviously has misunderstood the theme. Except for what was transmitted in initiating the council, the Interactive Field is still undeveloped. The road chief quickly assesses whether the theme or focus needs changing (perhaps the situation was misread) and if not, interrupts and refocuses the council.

As the Interactive Field develops, the leader may face a variety of more complex judgment calls. General guidelines are difficult to formulate. Some leaders rarely, if ever, intervene. Others, particularly those who work with young people, find themselves in many situations where intervention is appropriate. It would be more instructive to give examples of the kinds of shifts that can occur in a council's Interactive Field and, in each case, describe how the leader might track the process. In citing these examples, we are stressing the witness role in council leadership. Bear in mind that the leader integrates this capacity with authentic participation in the circle, and normally would not be as strongly focused on tracking the Interactive Field as conveyed by these anecdotes.

Going on too long. This is one of the most common problems in council. Generally, when one or more people go on too long, the energy in the Interactive Field slowly dissipates and the focus of the circle begins to fade. The loss of attention is cumulative; soon even an inexperienced council leader will see what is happening. Imagine that you are the council leader in the following example.

> About thirty people are gathering in a large, high-beamed living room for the opening council of their reunion weekend. Many in the group had worked together intimately for more than five years and a few had kept in touch with each other since that time. But the group has not met together for fifteen years and most people have no idea what to expect. The basic intention of this first council, which was set by the committee planning the weekend, is to honor the past and clear up any lingering unfinished business. As the leader, you address this intention after the candle has been lit:
>
> "Looking back with the wisdom of the present, what role did the group play in your life twenty years ago? How did it help you; what were your problems with it? Do you have any unfinished business from those days that needs expressing now?" You look at one of the co-planners of the weekend to see if she wants to add anything. She smiles. You review the rules of council, introduce the talking piece, and send it on its way.
>
> Several people speak briefly and positively about their past experiences: The group had been important to them; they have missed being part of an intimate community; they were glad to

see everyone again. So far the sharing is predictable and rather superficial; the Field is of low-intensity and waiting for direction. No one takes a significant risk until Esther gets the rattle. She rests it in her lap, debating whether to plunge in or not. You send her a supportive silent message ("Go for it!"). She begins: "I have some unfinished business . . . "

Esther speaks about the lack of acknowledgment and hurt she felt twenty years ago. She says she was not alone in feeling that way. Then she offers an awkward apology for having shifted the mood. In fact, she has activated the council. You suspect she is holding onto more than she shared. You *see* that part of Esther's personal story is that she carries hurt a long time. The next few people speak from a slightly deeper place, but the Field is more or less suspended where Esther left it.

Then Mitchell takes up the stick with a sweep of the hand that says he's been waiting impatiently to speak. He begins in "narrative consciousness," describing events of twenty years ago. You hope he will leave his narrative soon and move more directly towards the intention of the council. He doesn't. His narrative continues, year by year. You recognize Mitchell's agenda: "I have an opportunity to tell my life story to a congenial group. I may not get the chance again for a long time." You silently remind him of the council's size and purpose. Then you notice that several people are quite engaged, probably those who hear in Mitchell's story portions of their own. You take that in. However, a few others, including members of the planning committee, are growing restless. You *see* that the Interactive Field, set by the original intention and activated by Esther, has now been split into two distinct parts.

Split fields create a dilemma. You wonder if anyone down-circle from Mitchell might be able to refocus the council on the original theme. It is hard to tell, but most of these people are new to the practice and probably not up to refocusing. You scan the experienced members of the group, one by one; they have all spoken already. A few communicate through eye contact: "I hope this guy stops soon, he's driving me crazy. This is not what we're supposed to be doing." But they leave it up to you.

You take a deep breath. Mitchell is up to 1983, only half way through his twenty-year history. You shift your position on the pillow and your mind wanders. Then you realize that you are not listening devoutly to Mitchell. You feel chagrined and immediately give him your full attention. Now your perception shifts; you hear an "Everyman" quality in Mitchell's narrative. The underlying story is clear: I've been starved for community for fifteen years. You see that others in the circle feel the same way. But the restless ones do not agree. They are afraid others will follow Mitchell's example and the council will go on forever. You *see* that it won't, although Mitchell sounds like he might. You know you would gently interrupt anyone else who went on as long as Mitchell. One Everyman Story is sufficient.

Mentally, you step back and look at the council from a greater distance. Suddenly you see that the two Fields you thought were separate are part of one larger Field. Telling a life story is part of bringing the circle into the present. Mitchell's saga gathers in the threads of the twenty years that have elapsed since the group shared personal stories on a regular basis. Mitchell was part of that practice. Had the community continued, his narrative would have been part of the collective history. You reach inside somewhere for more patience. You silently communicate what you have seen to the restless ones.

You wait Mitchell out, taking the opportunity to practice devout listening. He takes eight more excruciating minutes to get to the present. Several people after him thank him effusively for revealing so much and helping the circle come alive. You are relieved to hear the confirming remarks. However, after the council, three members of the planning committee ask you why you failed to stop the long monologue. They feel you indulged Mitchell and rationalized your nonintervention in the name of patience. You remind them that the leader intervenes only as a last resort. Besides, you go on to say, what serves some in council to hear and say does not necessarily serve others.

But councils like the one just described are opportunities to practice a willingness to make room for all points of view. So you also honor the planning committee's position and remind yourself to take a closer look from that perspective the next time a similar situation arises.

Collective/personal shifts. The circle has been focusing on a group issue when someone abruptly shifts into personal business. Example:

A group that has worked and sat in council together for a long time is exploring the question: "How can our group do its work in the world more effectively?" After several people have spoken directly to the issue and a strong Interactive Field has been established, someone starts talking about a personal health problem that has limited her council attendance. You note the shift in the Field and send a silent message to the next person to get the circle back on track. You soon discover, however, that he is not seeing the Field the way you are. Inspired by the previous speaker, he launches into a detailed description of marital problems that have consumed much of his energy over the past few months. Instead of briefly acknowledging that he has been unavailable to do the group's work in the world because of personal problems and then turning his attention to the group as a whole, he is going on and on about his personal situation!

You consider the possibility that the personal focus is actually what the group needs. Perhaps there has been too much emphasis on group activities and insufficient time for dealing with individual journeys. However, as the minutes drag by, your agitation increases. You see the Field losing energy and shifting in an unproductive way. Your seeing is confirmed by your growing disinterest in what the speaker is saying and a definite restlessness in your body. You check around the circle and see that others are also losing their focus. After listening for another few minutes, during which you continue sending him strong silent messages to get back on track, you decide to intervene:

"Peter," you begin. "I'm sorry to interrupt, but I believe we're losing focus. I hear you saying that your personal life has made it difficult for you to participate in the work right now, but you are providing a level of explanation that is taking us away from looking at the challenge of working together more effectively as a group. Besides acknowledging your personal un-availability, do you have something to say about that topic?"

Peter is a strong council player and so he responds by say-ing: "The bottom line is that I'm distracted by what's going on with Marjorie and me. I guess that means I've become an obstacle to the work of our group. I see that in going on about my relationship just now I'm continuing the pattern. So I'll stop and try to reconnect to the group. I can talk about my personal stuff later on, maybe at another council."

A different Peter might have felt put down by the interrup-tion and become angry or withdrawn. Either of these two re-sponses might require the group's further attention, but that still might be more productive for the council than listening to Peter drag out his story a while longer.

Personal/collective shifts. A shift away from the personal can also significantly change the Interactive Field. Example:

Community members are feeling the stress of working nonstop on common projects and need to get current with each other personally. An in-depth weather report council is planned to clear the air and help everyone reconnect.

As the talking piece goes around, many revealing stories are told, some joyous, others troubling. Inspired by the storytelling, an Interactive Field emerges that weaves together several themes: working hard and feeling unappreciated, not enough time for personal renewal, and trying to maintain a private life while fulfilling community responsibilities. People take bigger risks in revealing their struggles as the themes emerge and the Field becomes stronger. Even though many of these challenges remain unresolved, the circle is moving towards a nourishing level of intimacy.

Then Bella, the newest member of the circle, gets the talking piece. She looks a little pale as she begins to describe a book she is reading about the disastrous state of affairs in schools across the country. Bella is a former teacher and the issue obviously means a lot to her personally, but she focuses almost entirely on the content of the book. You see the Field begin to shift. Bella is not giving a personal weather report or responding to someone else's. In heightened perception you see her discomfort with the level of intimacy in the circle. You hear that Bella's real story is her fear about revealing herself in the group. Perhaps it doesn't feel safe yet, perhaps she has never felt safe in any group, perhaps her feeling of isolation is too frightening to reveal to anyone. She is telling this deeper story between the lines of her continuing book report.

You send Bella a silent message: "Take the risk to tell us you're not ready to share deeply. It's okay not to feel safe. And as far as the book is concerned, perhaps you can tell us how the plight of the schools affects your life personally." The focus of the circle begins to diffuse. You see that others are feeling Bella's avoidance. Harry sends you a "what-shall-we-do" look. You make eye contact with him and tell him silently that the circle needs to learn how to take care of itself and not rely on you too much.

As Bella goes on, you decide to watch the Interactive Field a little longer. Though there is a loss of energy, the Field is still intact. You notice who is next to speak and see that she has the ability to reconnect with the main intention of the council. You relax. That immediately brings the insight that Bella is carrying the voice of shyness and fear for the whole circle. No one else has spoken that voice as yet. You check that perception . . . and see it confirmed. Now you are clear that Bella should finish without intervention. Her avoidance is important for everyone to hear. You set the intention to help the circle acknowledge her voice at the end of the council without putting her on the spot . . . Perhaps you'll check in with her after the council as well.

Being with pain. Some people have a strong urge to relieve another's emotional pain as soon as it is expressed. The Interactive Field in council can be about relieving pain, but timing is important. A shift in the Field may occur when someone interrupts council in an attempt to comfort or "heal" another's pain prematurely.

Notice I said *may.* The shift is usually minimal or nonexistent, if the reaction is authentic and not self-serving or when the person in distress asks for support directly. Asking for physical comfort in council rarely disturbs the Field in an unproductive way unless the request is a result of an ongoing manipulative pattern.

The council has been focused on the theme for a while when Marilyn describes a painful personal situation in a way that evokes verbal empathy from many who follow her in the circle. You see that the previously established Field has shifted to a primary focus on Marilyn. The feeling in the circle is growing heavy. You are alert to the situation, but no action is required. When Jesse gets the talking piece, he begins using his turn by putting the piece down in front of him and then springing to his feet: "I just want to give you a hug," he says to Marilyn. "More words from me won't help right now." You *see* the contraction in the Field relax, as the emotional charge hanging over the circle is relieved. You wait quietly with the rest of the circle as Jesse and Marilyn hug. The feeling is loving and genuine. Jesse returns to his seat, picks up the talking piece and goes on. The Field begins to expand again. You send Jesse a silent message of gratitude for his sensitivity to both Marilyn and the circle.

Alternatively, suppose the stick has been placed in the center after the first round of the council and Marilyn realizes she is feeling incomplete about her story. She decides to say something to the circle: "I need to ask for support before we stop. I feel vulnerable having shared so much with you all today. I'm not sure what to do . . . Maybe a hug would help." Michael, one of the group's premier huggers, accommodates.

An abrupt change in the Field may occur if a person attempts to discharge someone else's discomfort to avoid exploring the issues that underlie it. For example, suppose Marilyn is one of the first people to speak. She tells her story in a way that does not elicit immediate expressions of support. You *see* she is capable of working on the problem herself or asking for help when she needs it. The Field "hangs over her" for a moment, but is still fluid. "Bernice," who obviously reads the situation differently, springs to her feet from across the circle and envelops the startled Marilyn in her arms. "Words can't do it," Bernice says hugging her vigorously.

You feel jarred. The scene has a slightly distasteful quality. You *see* that people are unmoved by the embrace; you see that the hug mostly served Bernice's needs. Since she spoke out of turn, you decide to say something as she sits down again, before the person after Marilyn picks up the talking piece.

"I need to make a witness comment before we go on. Bernice, I appreciate your desire to comfort Marilyn, but you broke council in doing so. I have come to trust this process enough to question your timing. As the talking piece goes around, we all have the opportunity to react to her situation, including hugs if we like. The circle is here for her when and if she asks for our direct support."

Bernice looks a little crestfallen. Others speak to the issues raised by Marilyn's story. When the talking piece gets to her,

Bernice holds it silently for a while. You feel a subtle shift in the Field and then notice the tears in her eyes. She cries quietly for a moment before speaking. "Marilyn's words brought up a dark period of my life when . . . " Bernice tells a moving story that engages the whole circle. By the time she is through, the Field has expanded, a theme has emerged which encompasses both Marilyn and Bernice's stories, and the council is off and running.

Embracing someone in council can be done silently and nonphysically. In fact, devout listening and *seeing* are, in part, exactly that. If you feel the urge to nourish a person after he has spoken, it is a good idea to check out your own needs first. Perhaps his story touched a desire in you to be comforted. If so, you have the choice to acknowledge that, perhaps even out loud when you get the talking piece. If the hug you wish to give is authentic, you can try offering it silently from a place of heightened awareness—and also physically after the council.

Challenges to the leader. A number of challenging situations can arise that directly involve the leader. Examples:

Part way around the circle, someone changes the theme deliberately after speaking critically of the one you suggested to start the council. Why is the well-established Field being challenged? Is the theme appropriate? Have you been too controlling in setting up or leading the council? Is questioning the theme an indirect way of challenging your leadership?

If you react to the challenge as a personal affront, you will probably lose track of the Field and get swept up in the turbulence of the confrontation. Then the council may run into trouble. If the council is ongoing, you might suggest that someone else lead the next circle and so diffuse a possible power struggle. Or you can simply wait it out and speak to the issue when you have the talking piece. If the challenge continues, you might suggest a small fishbowl as in the following situation.

It is the end of a stormy council with a community in which you play a central role. As soon as you put the talking stick in the center, Mark snatches it up quickly. "I've been sitting here getting angrier by the minute," he blurts out, glaring at you. "I don't like the way you've been leading these councils. You say you want everyone in the community to take more leadership responsibility, but I don't believe you. You're willing to talk about self-governance, but you still act like you know what's best for us—and you always get in the last word."

You wait a moment before picking up the stick to recover from the force of the confrontation. You see that you are being asked to look at your need to control and how you play out the role of leader. However, at the moment you are still the road chief. You see that the Field has been irrevocably altered, but the new direction is unclear. You pick up the stick slowly: "It won't surprise you to hear that I feel differently about the situation. Mark, you're not happy with my way of leadership, or anyone else's, as far as I can tell. However, now that you've brought up the issue in council, why don't you and I step into the center and let Betsy take over as council leader—that is, if the circle is willing. In a fishbowl we can all take a deeper look at what's going on." You look around the circle for a response and hear a chorus of "Ho's."

"I've wanted to do this for a long time," Mark says as he picks up his pillow. Your leadership has been challenged directly. The confrontation may have been difficult for you to see as part of the Interactive Field, but playing it out in a fishbowl could be just what the circle needs. By acting in this way you have honored the spirit and form of council, despite the direct personal challenge. Your leadership abilities and need to control, as well as Mark's problems with authority, will now be explored. And by witnessing you and Mark in the fishbowl, others in the circle will have a chance to deal with their own issues about authority and control.

6

BECOMING
A CARRIER
OF COUNCIL

My words are tied in one with the great mountain
With the great rocks and the great trees
In one with my body and my heart
Will you all help me
With supernatural power
And you day and you night
All of you see me
One with this world

> —Yokuts chant, collected by
> A.L. Kroeber, circa 1920

B eing a disciple of the four intentions of council and learning to read the Interactive Field fulfills the first two challenges of leadership. To become a carrier of council, the leader also has to meet the third challenge of becoming a steward of council. This path begins by exploring models of stewardship and undergoing trainings and apprenticeships. Becoming a steward, however, ultimately requires *surrender to the wisdom of council* as the primary teacher. In many ways the situation is similar to becoming a musician, actor, or any professional, for that matter. The initial stages of learning involve attending school, finding mentors, and becoming an apprentice. Finally, all of that is incorporated *and surrendered* along the path of direct experience.

THE THIRD CHALLENGE
STEWARDSHIP

Being able to *participate* and *witness* at the same time provides the foundation for council stewardship. *The critical skill in this respect is to be able to see oneself as part of the Interactive Field.* To understand how to meet this challenge, we need to explore further the art of *seeing*. Although we continue to focus on the experience of leadership in this chapter, it is important to remember that everyone in the circle faces similar challenges and harvests comparable benefits from the practice of council.

Balancing and the Art of Streaming

We have described how witnessing the Interactive Field of council in a state of heightened perception is supported by the intention of devout listening. The remaining three intentions involve self-expression: speaking from the heart, conciseness, and non-anticipation. How do these become part of the leader's ability to *see*? In other words, how does the aspiring carrier develop the art of streaming?

Because the leader is also a participant in the council, learning to balance participation and witnessing during self-expression can be approached by a leadership apprentice in the same way as anyone else in the circle. For example, the leader can ask the three questions suggested in Chapter 2:

1. "Will what I say serve me?"

2. "Will what I say serve the circle?"

3. "Will what I say serve the whole?

However, the leader also has the responsibility of serving the circle by being particularly aware of the Interactive Field and his or her relationship to it. By speaking and witnessing simultaneously from a state of heightened perception, the leader inspires others in the circle to do the same. The following guidelines can be helpful in accomplishing this objective (and are appropriate for others in the circle as well).

- Practice non-anticipation diligently. Wait until you have the talking piece to *look* as deeply as you can at the Interactive Field.

- When the Interactive Field is well-defined and expanding, enter more lightly and express yourself in a way that illuminates the Field for others in the circle.

- When the Interactive Field is undefined or dim, enter more vigorously to give the circle additional energy with which to work.

- Take the risk of speaking more personally and passionately when others in the circle lack inspiration to speak from the heart.

- Pay attention to the connection between the Interactive Field and how much you reveal yourself personally, particularly with new circles and in groups of children. Before doing a piece of personal work, consider whether doing so will strongly redirect an already well-defined Field. Make your decision on the basis of what will serve both yourself and the circle. Generally, exposing intimate details of your life tends to reduce others' transference to you as the authoritative presence in the council. If the circle is looking to you to "make the council happen," being more personal may help break this dependent pattern and establish a stronger Interactive Field.[1] One way to recognize excessive reliance on the leader is to watch where people look when they are speaking. If most people shift their gaze around the circle, that is usually an indication the leader is not dominating the council. If people tend to look primarily at the leader while speaking, that should be noted and ways of diffusing the transference considered.

This may seem like a lot to think about all at once, but *seeing* is the central process in heightened perception, not thinking. With practice, considering all these alternatives before and during sharing becomes second nature.

Being in Service

Being able to *see* the Interactive Field while one is speaking is a capability that must be used wisely to avoid manipulating or controlling the council. As always, the key to using personal power in an enlightened way requires that the individual surrender to "the greater good." To the extent the council leader effectively serves the circle and communicates authentically, the capability of speaking while

---

[1] However, this is not the case in councils of children. It is rarely appropriate to ask a circle of young children to involve themselves in your current personal issues, although commenting on them or on problems you struggled with as a youngster, may be of great service to this type of circle.

in a state of heightened perception will be used wisely. Surrendering to this level of service is an essential part of becoming a steward of council.

As we have said, it is ultimately the council process itself that teaches a leader how to be a steward. To empower this level of teaching, the leader makes a commitment to practice council as a path of personal awakening. This means acknowledging that *the ultimate authority of council resides in the whole circle.*

Fortunately, council has many built-in checks-and-balances that serve to prevent the leader from exerting too much personal authority. Since council empowers individuals, the circle is inherently self-balancing, even when the leader is perceptive and more experienced than others in the circle. When the four intentions are practiced diligently, the Interactive Field is perceived realistically and the leader surrenders to serving the circle. Stewardship is thus empowered as a path of awakening. This is the Way of Council.

Stewardship is built on a foundation of service, not control. The steward of land seeks more than the satisfaction of personal needs from the piece of land he oversees. By "listening" and relating to the land directly, the steward learns what is possible to grow and build. What happens on the land finally emerges out of the steward's visionary and physical relationship to it.

Similarly, the council steward's gift lies in serving and empowering the circle, not controlling it. When a council is well-stewarded, people leave saying, "That was a strong council," rather than, "So-and-so is a great council leader." Self-assurance, humility, and the absence of both inflation and false modesty are the aspirations of the council steward.

Parallels With Shamanic Training

As a path of personal awakening, learning to steward council has much in common with traditional forms of shamanic training. The basic intention of the carrier of council is to enter a state of heightened perception for the purpose of serving others. Several researchers of the shamanic tradition have emphasized that utilizing heightened perception to improve conditions in the ordinary world is the challenge of the contemporary shaman.[2] The paths of council stewardship and shamanic training resemble each other in the following ways.

Being at home in both worlds. The shaman is experienced at journeying "between the worlds"—that is, he or she knows how to enter a state of awareness in the spirit domain and then safely return to ordinary reality. The council leader's ability to participate fully in the council, while simultaneously monitoring the Interactive Field, is an analogous capability. The shaman's heightened state of perception is evoked through a trance induction that usually involves some combination of drumming, dancing, meditation, and the ingesting of sacred plants.[3] The carrier of council evokes the state of heightened perception through preparatory rituals—sitting in silence, praying, connecting with place, setting the circle, and initiating the council—and subsequently by practicing the four intentions.

Recognition of energy patterns. The shaman learns to identify energy patterns in the spirit world and relate them to physical reality. The accomplished carrier of council is able to make similar connections. By utilizing the subtle senses, the carrier *sees* the energy patterns that comprise the Interactive Field and, through experience, learns what is happening in ordinary reality to create those patterns. The Interactive Field provides an overview of the energetic complexities of "concrete" reality that is virtually impossible to perceive using the five senses and rational thinking. In time, a leader's perceptual skill increases if he or she works closely with other leaders. Two experienced carriers will *see* the same Field, although they may use somewhat different language in describing it.

---

[2] *The Way of the Shaman: A Guide to Power and Healing*, Michael Harner, Harper and Row, 1980, and *The Spirit of Shamanism*, Roger N. Walsh, J.P. Tarcher, 1990.

[3] See *The Spirit of Shamanism*, Roger N. Walsh, J.P. Tarcher, 1990, and *Food of the Gods: The Search for the Original Tree of Knowledge, A Radical History of Plants, Drugs, and Human Evolution*, Terence McKenna, Bantam, 1992.

Non-attachment to outcome. In making the journey to the spirit world to heal illness or improve the well-being of the community, the shaman petitions Spirit to reveal the cause of the difficulty and guide the process of healing. The shaman sets a strong intention before making the journey but is not attached to the outcome. Indeed, the guidance received may be that healing is not possible at that time.

Similarly, the challenge for the council leader on the stewardship path is to support the intentions of the council without attachment to what actually happens in the circle. A particular council may not resolve the issues being discussed. The truth of council—that is, the meaning of the Interactive Field—may be that resolution is not possible within the expected time frame. *Seeing* that, the carrier of council helps the circle avoid forcing a resolution by encouraging patience.

Non-attachment also includes letting go of any notions one holds about what it means to have a "good" council—a difficult challenge for many council leaders, particularly those who guide circles of children. The desired council scenario usually includes deep sharing, attentiveness without the need for imposed discipline, humor, perhaps a few tears, and, above all, enthusiasm for the sanctuary of council itself. Needless to say, while all these outcomes may be desirable, they do not always occur. Holding on to a desire for an ideal council usually limits risk-taking and authentic experience.

When councils that do not meet most people's expectations are viewed as failures by the leader, an environment is created in which participants either may try to please the council chief by behaving like "good" members of the circle, or rebel against this tendency by undercutting council discipline. In both cases, the basic intentions of council are compromised and the Interactive Field is "flattened" or disrupted accordingly. In contrast, the carrier of council who avoids pushing the council towards a particular outcome supports authenticity in the circle, which in turn allows the Interactive Field to flower.

Accessing wisdom. The shaman's knowledge and healing capabilities are inseparable from the traditional ceremonies and beliefs of the tribe. Similarly, carriers of council can become teachers and healers when the circle and the moment empower those capabilities. The wisdom articulated by the carrier (and others in the circle as well) is inspired by what happens during the council; it is not planned as part of the formal predetermined teachings.

Taking risks. In our culture priests, teachers, physicians, and therapists often establish a psychological boundary in relation to their parishioners, students, patients, or clients, which protects these helping professionals from the vulnerability of personal exposure. In contrast, council carriers, as in the shamanic tradition, open themselves to a level of vulnerability at least as high as other members of the circle. This risk-taking can inspire intimacy, diminish the distinction in authority, and lead to a significant strengthening of the Interactive Field.

"Don't you think that council was a disaster?" Sabrina asked, as we discussed one of the longest councils I have ever led. My highly esteemed colleague had been introduced to the process just a few days before.

"Not exactly," I replied. "But it was certainly long and difficult. Mathew must have gone on for at least fifteen minutes."

"Which set the tone for the others," Sabrina added pointedly. "Mellie went on even longer. I couldn't believe you didn't stop them. I thought I'd have to leave the circle."

"I'm glad you didn't, I answered. "I debated whether to interrupt or not, but I didn't have a clear picture of what was happening, so I let them go on."

"I would have stopped Mathew after five minutes. Going on longer was an indulgence. I think we lost a lot of people during the council. I hope we get them back tomorrow."

Sabrina and I finished our discussion and decided to begin the following day's council with a weather report.

During the lighting of the candle the next morning, Sabrina's comments echoed in my mind. I looked around the circle and *saw* that I had to start. I held the stone for at least a minute in silence, unsure, waiting. When I finally spoke, my voice sounded throaty.

"The weather in here [*pointing to my chest*] is heavy...sad mostly, and a little anxious. I think I blew it yesterday. [*Several people sat up straighter on their pillows.*] Our council went on too long, but I wasn't clear enough to see how to focus it. I think my uncertainty had to do with co-leading a weekend with Sabrina for the first time. My admiration for her is intimidating. This is her first experience with council and I wanted everything to go well. That's not a good state of mind for a council leader..."

I paused, but no more words came so I passed the stone. Several people thanked me for what I had said and shared their own feelings about the long council. When it was her turn, Sabrina looked at me admiringly from her place across the circle. "Speaking the way you did, and seeing how others responded, brought council to life for me. Now I see how real the process can be. Your trust in yourself and the circle allowed you to step out of the leader role. Thank you for taking that risk."

I thought Sabrina had been generous in her reaction and worried that my "authority" would be compromised by what had happened. However, by suppertime my fears had completely dissipated. Sabrina and I guided the evening program in a strong way. I *saw* more clearly in the council the next morning than I had in a long time.

Character Attributes

Carriers of council develop certain leadership qualities that support the state of heightened perception. The following four are fundamental.

Patience. The leader on the path of stewardship is in touch with the broad movements of nature and the human condition. There is deep understanding that *everything unfolds in its own time*. The Interactive Field of the council is like the proverbial river that cannot be pushed. One can set intentions and interact with the Field, but what will be, will be. If council is governed by impatience, the Interactive Field "stiffens" and contracts.

When first experiencing council, you may have to subdue a restless body and overactive mind in order to listen from the heart. As your commitment to devout listening grows stronger, however, patience becomes an ally, and even long councils can be joyous. Patience is the skill that permits the carrier of council to *see* clearly and function effectively without distortion caused by restlessness.

Perseverance. Often vision and insight alone are not enough to transform negative thoughts, uproot entrenched emotional patterns, or heal the body. But even strong resistance and a stubborn mind can be won over by perseverance. Although not as glamorous or charismatic as many other character traits, perseverance is essential on the path of council stewardship. Perseverance helps you overcome frustration when the truth of council is "no resolution is possible now," and brings you to the next session with renewed openness and commitment. Equally important, perseverance helps build the trust that even your greatest personal barriers to effective leadership will eventually be overcome. The situation described in the following story is not unusual.

Sheila had been working with a particularly resistive group of sixth-graders twice a week for several months. The dominant girls in the class decided at the outset that council was "nerdy" and did their best to sabotage all of Sheila's creative activities and council themes. All but one or two of the boys had miniscule attention spans; many spent the council time fidgeting or poking their neighbors. Sheila struggled to maintain council decorum with little success. Chaos reigned on more than a few occasions. There were days that she drove home from school in tears, wondering why she was subjecting herself to such torture.

But, with support from some of the other council facilitators, Sheila persevered. She had the students "picture" their feelings with marking pens; she tried to teach them songs and chants; she dug up new activities particularly appropriate for eleven-year-olds. A few attentive moments here and there were all the group could muster.

Then three weeks before the end of the semester Sheila confessed her frustration to the group. She had done that before, but finally her diligence paid off. First one and then another from the "in" clique of girls spoke authentically in the circle. One admired Sheila's willingness to keep on trying; another apologized for being so "bitchy"; a third confessed she was really beginning to look forward to council. Spurred on by the girls' shift in attitude, the boys' behavior improved rapidly. By the end of the semester, Sheila was enjoying well-focused, strong councils.

Compassion. Functioning compassionately inspires the Way of Council. The compassionate council carrier practices the four intentions of council fervently and in so doing invites council members to bring the full range of their feelings to the circle. Compassion fuels our ability to *see* and makes it possible to include ourselves when viewing the Interactive Field without self-judgment.

The carrier of council knows not to confuse compassion with sentimentality. Being compassionate is not the same as being "lovey-dovey" (as the kids at Heartlight used to say). Buddhists talk about "dark compassion"; experts in parenting speak of "tough love." Compassion is based on the truth of what is happening, not on a fantasy of reality. Sometimes only a little extra attentiveness opens the door to compassion, as the following story exemplifies.

Lola knew a little of Russell's history before he sat in the circle with us for the first time. After introducing the council theme and intention, I welcomed him briefly, as I always do new members of the circle. But Lola *saw* that my comments would not be enough to help Russell feel at home. She stopped me as I was passing the stone to the person on my left. "I'm sorry to interrupt, but I want to welcome Russell too," she said. "He's just come from Salt Lake City, where his father is in the hospital. Besides applying for one of our staff positions, he's here to visit his oldest son who he hasn't seen for almost a year..." She went on for a minute or two, touching on her reactions to the abundance of darkness in his life. When he was passed the stone, Russell spoke of his family's current difficulties in an intimate way that would not have been possible without Lola's intervention. As I closed the council, I thanked her enthusiastically for being so responsive to Russell's discomfort.

Capacity for knowing. The carrier of council develops a capacity for knowing be being able to read the Interactive Field. This capacity makes it possible to communicate with the "Imaginal World" or, in more traditional language, the Realm of Spirit.[4] In Biblical times, for example, people were said to *know* God when their life was shaped by spiritual devotion. Similarly, a man and woman were said to *know* each other through the mystery of their erotic intimacy.

In our culture, this vision of knowledge has largely given way to the more superficial desire to "have information about." Knowing *about* comes from the *outside* in. The carrier learns to acquire knowledge from the *inside out.* The capacity for knowing acquired along the path of council is developed through a process of experiential learning that is literally the council leader's "way of power." The following is one of many stories I could tell.

When the question about dealing with rebellious children arose from a teacher in the council training, Gigi said she

---

[4] See *Creative Imagination and the Sufism of Ibn Arabi*, Henry Corbin, Princeton University Press, 1969.

wanted to give a response rather than letting me answer the questions about circles of children, as I usually did. She began a little haltingly, but soon gathered momentum and, within a minute or two, was speaking with a full head of steam. Her insights impressed me. I heard wisdom from a source that seemed to come from beyond her direct experience in councils of children, perhaps from the many circles of teachers she had led, or from her own childhood, perhaps from the "voice of the circle" that blesses us on occasion. When she was through, I commented on how much I had learned from her response— and how innovative it sounded. She confessed that the ideas she had presented sounded fresh in her own ears as well. That precipitated a fascinating discussion about how the circle can bring out the hidden innovative teacher in all of us.

SACRED LEADER
SHADOW LEADER

At this juncture, we would like to have an imaginary dialogue with any readers who feel a little overwhelmed by our exploration of council leadership. Perhaps some of you thought that leading a council meant learning a few rules, getting a talking stick, and sitting in a circle with a few well-intentioned people. Council format is deceptively simple, but the path of council stewardship can be mysterious and difficult. In this respect council and meditation are very much alike. Both forms are simple and easy to teach, but when one commits to the practice, there is much to discover. For example, all this time we have been talking primarily about the "sacred leader" of council.

Come again?

We've been talking about leaders who are not only perceptive and devoted, but also well-intentioned and self-aware. No one quite fits that description.

I'm glad to hear that. I've been feeling a little inadequate.

We're not talking about limitations of skill and experience. We're talking about that part of each of us that can compromise our best intentions *without our being aware of it*. We're talking about the "shadow leader."

Sounds ominous.

Failing to realize the shadow leader exists *can* lead to a host of difficulties. When we take for granted that our actions and perceptions are based only on our conscious intentions, we're asking for trouble. Being attentive to the possibility of *our own* unconscious motivations and hidden personal agendas is essential to being a carrier of council.[5] Every leader has a sacred side and a shadow side. The sacred side governs as a "steward of the realm," devoted to the well-being and empowerment of the entire community. The sacred leader is willing to face any personal obstacle in fulfilling that intention.

Sounds like the carrier of council.

Exactly. On the other hand, the shadow leader is interested in personal power. We may think we're devoted to empowering others, but the shadow-leader-part-of-us is out to strengthen its authority and bask in the glow of admiration. Sometimes our shadow leader is clever at calling attention to itself even when professing service to the circle.

Gigi remembers a time when she listened attentively to the problems and concerns of a circle of colleagues for several days, at the end of which she was asked to lead a council. When the talking piece came to her, the shadow leader emerged in the form of the "overcritical witness." She went around the circle pointing out ways each person could improve or "tune" his or her way of functioning in the group. The *content* of her observations was accurate—even brilliant—but there was a forcefulness and insensitivity of *timing* and

---

[5] The sacred and shadow leaders are particular forms of the archetypes of the sacred and shadow king or queen that appear in folk tales and traditional mythologies. For example, see *King, Warrior, Magician, Lover*, Robert Moore and Douglas Gillette, Harper, 1990.

manner in her witnessing that left the circle feeling a little judged and raw. Looking back on the experience, Gigi realized she had reacted strongly to the intense listening of the previous several days. She wanted to "fix" everybody in the group in order to avoid having to listen to so many distressing stories in the future. That unleashed the shadow leader and prevented her from being fully responsive to the needs of the circle.

In leading the councils, our shadow side can subtly use the circle for self-enhancement rather than the development of the Interactive Field. Believing we have entered a state of heightened perception, this side of us fails to see how self-involvement has seriously distorted our *seeing*. Sometimes the shadow leader slips in so smoothly that we are in its grip before we know it. Even when a carrier of council has been on the stewardship path for a long time, the danger always exists.

I recognize the pattern. The diabolical part of it is that I usually don't know when my shadow side is running the show.

That's exactly what "shadow" means.

So what can be done to keep the shadow leader from doing too much damage?

By the very nature of the beast, there is no guarantee you can keep the shadow leader from affecting the circle. But there are a number of precautions you can take to limit the dangers of unconscious leadership.

- Before council begins, always remind yourself that you have a shadow leader part and recommit to the practice of self-witnessing.

- Whenever possible, lead council with a partner. It is not likely that two shadow leaders will take over at the same time. If you see the shadow side of your partner, do something about it. A simple signal or a whispered comment is often sufficient, although direct intervention, either with or without the talking piece, may be necessary on rare occasions. If you are suspicious but unclear about what is going on, talk to your partner after council.

- Let the circle know that you want to hear their comments when any aspect of your leadership disturbs them. If the council meets regularly, ask to be evaluated periodically.

- Some leaders begin to feel vaguely uneasy or tense when they slip into a shadow leader pattern. Track your own shadowy reactions and feelings during the council—and afterwards (with your co-leader or someone else from the circle). Look for patterns. In particular, pay close attention when someone in the circle says something or behaves in a way that irritates you, particularly if your reaction is stronger than their behavior warrants. The individual may be reflecting an aspect of your shadow side in the form of a disowned and disparaged quality. This is one of the main ways council acts as a circle of mirrors. Being alert to shadow reflections is a productive practice for every member of the circle. Experienced council participants often give special attention to the individual sitting directly across from then in the circle. The person holding that seat seams to provide shadow reflections a disproportionate amount of the time. We often use the description, "He or she sits across the circle from you," in talking to people about individuals who "push their buttons."

- If you lead councils frequently, make it a point now and then to join a circle in which you have no leadership responsibilities. Being "just a participant" can lead to insight about your shadow leader, particularly those aspects related to power and control.

- Last and most important, remember that *the power of council resides in the circle*. Commit to the stewardship path. Practice the four intentions and the art of *seeing*, doing the utmost to include yourself in the field of view. The more completely you enter a true state of heightened perception, the more likely the presence of the shadow leader will be detected. At the same time, turn to the council regularly for leadership—in your heart and mind as well as in your actions, when appropriate. At these moments, let go of your need to guide, intervene, or do anything but *trust in the circle to take care of itself.*

For example, imagine that you are co-leading a council that has been going on for a long time but still has a lot of business to accomplish. You feel yourself getting a little tense, but remain in heightened perception (you think!), doing your best to keep the Interactive Field fluid and strong. The talking piece has been in the center for a while. You take it, and after passionately exhorting the circle to get on with the issue at hand, your co-leader picks it up.

"I know we still have a lot to do," she begins, "but I need to interrupt the discussion for a moment." She looks at you intensely. "I feel you're pushing the circle."

You take a deep breath and listen. She continues: "You're on a roll, which may be distracting you from what's really happening. I'm not sure the circle can reach a resolution right now and I feel you're not entirely open to that possibility. I don't know whether it's because you're in a hurry to finish or because you have a personal stake in the outcome of our deliberations. I may be off, but that's what I see."

You feel as if you have been caught with your hand in the cookie jar. You *see* that you have been *seen*. Part of you is angry and defensive. You remember the times when your partner was on an even bigger roll! A self-righteous rebuttal is just about to pass your lips. Fortunately, the part of you that knows you've been *seen* is directing verbal traffic.

"Okay, I'll back off a while," you say in a shaky voice. "You carry on alone while I refocus."

STEPPINGSTONES

Typically, the path to becoming a carrier of council includes some of the following steppingstones.

- You hear about council or join one and get interested. Then you may forget about council for a while.

- A friend tells you about a great council he attended. You remember your experience and decide to find out more.

- You call someone who has been involved with council for a while and she tells you about her experience with a women's wilderness group...or he tells you about a men's group...or a writing circle...or a school project...or a program at the Ojai Foundation.

- You sign up for a program that involves council or participate in one with some regularity.

- After a while, you gather your courage and try leading a council in your classroom, community, business, or family. It works okay, but you realize how much there is to learn. You hear about a council training and sign up.

- The training knocks your socks off. You see that council is much more than a form for respectful group communication. You get a taste of what is possible when people practice speaking and listening from the heart. It feels like you've just discovered ice cream!

- You decide to get serious and commit to an internship at a local public school—perhaps through the Los Angeles Unified School District's "Council Practitioners Center," or you decide to seek a council mentor, or you decide you want further training qt the Animas Valley Institute or PeerSpirit. Perhaps you explore the roots of council in indigenous cultures, in your own ancestral tradition or in the natural world.

- You lead a few councils in your family, your community or your workplace—with varying success. Some days you feel council is the only solution to the world's problems. At other times you wonder why you are sitting in a circle trying to involve so many disinterested and uncooperative people.

- You persevere and begin using council more regularly in your work, your community, your family, and/or your intimate relationships.

- You find council entering your way of thinking whenever the need for authentic communication arises. Occasionally you hear yourself sounding like a council missionary. One day, when somebody asks what you've been doing, you include "leading councils" in your response.

- You want to refine your skills by counciling with other leaders, so you attend a gathering in a community or at an institution that has embraced council as the basis of its group practice (the annual "Gathering of Carriers of Council" at the Ojai Foundation, for example).

- At the gathering you realize the honeymoon is over. You are surprised to feel disconnected from everybody and even bored. You question all the fuss about council. You are turned off by the group's rituals and tired of feeling like a Kindergarten student. After the gathering you begin to question the focus on spirit, sacred space and ceremony. Most of all, you are tired of sitting, listening, talking, and "being empowered." You want to get things done on your own in the world.

- Mysteriously, after living with these feelings for a while, you find yourself moving ahead again, more aware than ever that it is time to risk making council yours, to find your own way of leading, and to surrender to the stewardship path.

- You are fast becoming a carrier of council!

A SUMMARY OF TASKS

We conclude this chapter with a review of the various steps a leader can take in conducting a council. To emphasize our commitment to partnership, we will assume that two leaders are available to guide the circle.

1. *Preparing for council.* This includes reflecting on what has happened in previous councils if the group is ongoing, selecting themes, and choosing the form(s) to be used at the upcoming meeting.

2. *Preparing for leadership.* Some leaders prepare for council in a ceremonial way by:

   Connecting with place through prayer, "walking the land," or making an offering.

   Centering oneself through meditation.

   Reflecting on each person in the circle.

   Praying for guidance and support.

   Carrying out one or more of these rituals together provides an additional attunement for co-leaders.

3. *Preparing the setting.* Getting ready for the council includes cleaning and beautifying the meeting place, arranging the pillows and chairs, creating the "center" of the circle (candle, flowers, etc.), choosing the talking piece, and collecting whatever musical instruments are to be used.

4. *Transition.* When it is appropriate, some leaders like to drum before the council starts. Drumming offers a way for people to center, "sets the field," and is an excellent transition into council work. Some leaders like to play recorded music suited to the moment as people arrive. Instead of drumming or music, some leaders use singing, chanting or silence to set the field. A sensitive council leader can tell a lot from listening carefully during the transition period; the cohesion and attentiveness of the group are self-evident from the sounds of music making or the field created by silence. This in turn can influence the way the leaders start the council. For example, an angry or fragmented circle becomes apparent in the quality of the group's silence, particularly when the circle regularly sits together and comparisons can be made.

5. *Welcoming and opening the council.* A quiet moment or the silence after drumming provides the final transition to the opening of council. The few moments following this quiet period are important in setting the tone of the session. Some circles join hands, sing, chant, and/or smudge each person with sage or cedar to open council. Then the leaders honor place, acknowledge the council hosts, take note of any significant absences from the circle, discuss guidelines for confidentiality and taking breaks, and thank the group for the opportunity to serve the circle as leaders. Some of these duties can be assigned to others in the circle.

   If the council leaders are being hosted by a community, conference conveners or other individuals, it is important to acknowledge that, honor the hosts, and give them an opportunity to speak before the council begins. In some situations asking the elders of a community for permission to convene the council is traditional protocol

   Then the leaders ask that someone light the candle and offer a dedication. When appropriate, the person who contributed the talking piece is asked to relate its story or how it may be connected to the group, the physical location and/or the current agenda. Then the leaders set the theme, review the basic intentions of council (if necessary) and begin. Generally the leaders sit next to each other, so that one will start, and the other complete, the circle. The solo leader decides at this moment whether to set the tone of the council by speaking first or waiting until the end of the round to weave the threads of the council together.

6. *Transmitting the spirit of council.* Throughout the transition, welcoming, and opening ceremony, leaders have the opportunity to transmit the spirit of council by shifting into a state of heightened awareness. By witnessing the circle as it gathers and listening carefully to the drumming, chanting, or the silence during the transition period, experienced leaders instinctively choose a voice quality and rhythm that suite the moment. If the group energy is low, the leaders' tone and pace might intensify accordingly. If several group members seem agitated or stressed, the leaders might speak quietly with a calming tone. However, when the agitation is about the issue at hand, the leaders are well-advised not to dispel the charge before council begins and so lose energy for the session. Whatever the mood of the circle, the leaders' primary responsibility is to open the door to heightened perception and transmit their devotion to the four intentions of council.

7. *Maintaining the state of heightened perception.* During the council the leaders help each other *see* what is going on in the circle. Regular silent affirmation of this intention and eye contact are useful nonverbal practices in this regard. More explicit mutual support can be given verbally as part of the normal council format.

8. *Spontaneously shifting the form.* The leaders may *see* that a different form of council is necessary after the talking piece has gone around the circle (possibly even before that). For example, If the group Is too large for a full round but It Is still important to hear every voice, a simple request to give ones name and affiliation or place of residence can be enough to evoke the 'remembering of council' that can be so powerful. A song and/or a holding of hands can also bring the gift of council to a large group even if there is not enough time for everyone to speak. Perhaps putting the piece in the center, starting a second round with the same or different theme, or shifting into a fishbowl format to sharpen the focus or emphasize witnessing would serve the circle. The two leaders check with each other about these alternatives by making eye contact or having a brief conversation, possibly in full voice so the rest of the circle can join the dialogue. Alternatively, the leaders can agree before the council begins which one of them will make such decisions.

9. *Summarizing the council.* Although it is not always necessary, before closing, the leaders can review the council's highlights (describe what they *saw*), identify items for individual action, suggest the appropriate theme and process for the next meeting, mention who will be leading that council, and so on. These remarks can be made by the council chief who speaks last in the circle or shared by both. Alternatively, putting the piece in the center and asking for a few members of the circle to "pop corn" one sentence highlights of the council can help everyone to remember the story of what took place. If the council is part of a leadership training, this is the time to reflect on the process and share teachings about the path of stewardship.

10. *Calling the witness comments.* After the summary and before closing, comments from the witnesses are invited. The talking piece is passed to each witness, after which his or her contributions are acknowledged by the leaders and others in the circle.

11. *Closing ceremony.* It is important to mark the closing of council (if only briefly) with a song, an expression of appreciation, a circle of hands in silence, an offering or "dedication of merit" (as in Buddhist practice), or some other brief ceremony. When people drift away from the circle without closure, the power of the gathering can be dissipated. Marking the closing of the circle also helps set the field for the next council. If the group will not be reconvening, it may be good to acknowledge this and suggest other ways in which the purpose and themes of the council might be continued.

12. *Postmortems.* While the experience is fresh and the leaders (hopefully) still in a state of heightened perception, they can briefly reflect with each other about the just-completed council. (A single leader would do well to talk to another member of the circle, or even better, someone outside the circle who knows council.) Their reflections might include a discussion of any miscommunication that occurred between them, their effectiveness as leaders, and the appropriateness of thematic material and forms that were used. If one or both of the leaders are new to the work, a more extensive evaluation might be undertaken, with the caution that lengthy discussion and analysis can drain the energy and dissipate the magic of the council experience.

7
COUNCILS
OF CHILDREN

Humble yourself inside your children
You got to bend down low
Humble yourself inside your children
You got to know what they know
And we will lift each other up
Higher and higher
And we will lift each other up

—Chant of unknown origin

Since schooling began, there have always been teachers who sit with children in the spirit of council. For many years, groups of elementary school students gathered together in "sharing" or "magic" circles have become a familiar occurrence in both public and independent schools. Self-esteem and community building programs, which stress open communication with students, are finding greater acceptance in the public domain during the past twenty-five years. Many of these activities are directed towards the amelioration of specific problems—drugs and violence, for example—and utilize methods of group communication that have intentions similar to council.[1]

As I have described earlier, the leap into formal councils with children began for me with the inception of the Heartlight School in 1980. We started each day with a weather report or thematic council with all the children, ages five through eighteen. We also used the council process as part of Heartlight's "Mysteries Class," which involved middle and high-school students, and met three times a week throughout the year. We chose this name because the topics for council exploration, reading, artistic expression, and personal writing that made up the "curriculum" of this class, were based on what the children identified as the mysteries—the compelling questions—in their lives they wanted to explore more deeply.

In 1983, the Heartlight experience inspired Paul Cummins, then the Headmaster of Crossroads School in Santa Monica, California, to invite me, along with Maureen Murdock, Ruthann Saphier, and other educators, to initiate a *Mysteries Program* at his school. Crossroads is a college preparatory elementary and secondary school with a substantial tuition deferment program that allows many talented Asian, African-American, and Caucasian students to join the student body.

The Crossroads Mysteries Program grew rapidly, eventually including all middle and high school students, and is now a well-established part of the school's core curriculum. [2] Since 1983, many other college preparatory independent schools in Southern California have initiated council programs, most of which are still active. These include: Polytechnic (middle) School in Pasadena, Happy Valley (high) School in Ojai, Chadwick (middle and high) School in Palos Verdes, New Roads (high)

---

[1] "For example, see *School-Based Impact Program: Impact 1 and 2*, Los Angeles Unified School District: Office of Instruction, Training Manuals X-134, revised 1990 and X-135, 1988. The Non-Violent Communication Network has also sponsored many educational programs based on their methodology.

[2] This program is described in *The Mysteries Sourcebook*, available from Crossroads, 1714 21st Street, Santa Monica. CA 90404. See also Appendix I.

School in Santa Monica, Highland Hall Waldorf School in Northridge, Oak Grove and Ojai Valley Montessori Schools in Ojai, and Archer Secondary School, Pressman Academy and Odyssey Schools—all in Los Angeles. Over the years other council-based independent school programs have started in Colorado, the San Francisco Bay area, and the Pacific Northwest.

As early as 1980, many of us started dreaming of bringing council into the public schools. However, apart from individual teachers who were willing to use council in their classrooms, the first "official" public school council programs (that we are aware of) did not start until more than ten years later. These include the New York City Alternative School Program begun by our colleague, Rachael Kessler (now leading the Passageways Institute in Colorado), and the Palms Middle School Program in Los Angeles, initiated by my colleague Tom Nolan and myself in 1992.

During the period 1992 - 2005, the Palms Program provided weekly councils for as many as two thousand middle school students from Latino, African-American, Caucasian, Asian and other racial/cultural groups that make up the Palms Student Body. Palms also incorporates a gifted Magnet School as part of its academic program.

By 1995 the Palms Program had become a model for council programs in other public schools in the Los Angeles Unified School District (LAUSD), as well as other districts in Southern California and several schools through the country. In the years that followed, programs were started by trainers and facilitators from The Ojai Foundation's Center for Council Training (CCT) in several LAUSD middle schools (Daniel Webster, Marina Del Rey, Walter Reed, Horace Mann, Mulholland), and a few elementary schools (Open Magnet Charter, Wonderland). High school programs were started in Malibu High and Ojai's Nordoff High School. Some of these programs flourished for several years but were not absorbed into the educational mainstream of the school. Others continue to this day (Open Magnet, Daniel Webster, and Malibu, for example).

Although the Palms Program was successful for many years, the bulk of the councils were still being led by trained CCT facilitators from outside the school. Only a handful of teachers were active as council leaders, even after ten years. The use of outside facilitators required a considerable fund-raising effort each year and an ongoing need to acquaint new teachers and administrators with the value of having such a program. By 2004 it had become clear that:

1. For council to be well established in a school—both educationally and financially—a significant portion of the faculty (and administration) had to be trained in the practice and enthusiastically support the program. Furthermore, a critical element in sustaining a school program is in the establishment of a "School Council Leadership Committee," that gathers to consider the needs of all stakeholders in the school community and uses council to fulfill its mission.

2. A unified council program office in LAUSD was needed to provide the necessary leadership and coordination for both initiating and sustaining council programs.

In 2005, The Ojai Foundation was awarded a substantial three-year grant by the Herb Alpert Foundation in Santa Monica to start a "Council Practitioners Center" (CPC) in LAUSD with exactly this mission and several members of the Palms Council Program Leadership Team at that time (Joe Provisor, Monica Chinlund and Natalie White) are now playing key roles in the CPC. We will have more to say in Appendix I about the CPC, the logistics of starting council programs in schools and "the mentor model" for involving teachers and administrators as council leaders from the beginning of the program. In this chapter, however, we want to describe our more personal experiences sitting in council with young people, particularly in connection with the Crossroads and Palms Programs as they developed in the Eighties and Nineties.

I had asked Tom Nolan to co-lead the first councils at Palms with me for a variety of reasons. Besides being an educator (now Dean of Students at Crossroads), he was an actor and a successful musician—talents that had made him invaluable in the council work he had been doing at Crossroads for many years. In order to gather material for this chapter originally, Tom and I talked for several hours at Crossroads a number of years ago. It occurred to me then that "listening in" on an edited version of our dialogue would be a good way to hear what we have to say about making council available to both public and independent school students as a regular part of their curriculum. Our dialog (with a few further edits) still feels useful to me now, many years later.

STORIES FROM THE FRONTIER

Tom Nolan: Encouraging children to speak from the heart is a strong message. It helps educate them about their emotions by asking how they feel and then giving them the opportunity to wrestle with expressing an answer. Speaking from the heart empowers children by giving them the opportunity to say to a group, "This is what I think, this is what I feel." When an institution invites honest expression, and then responds respectfully, students are willing to become more involved and responsible in their own education. Council becomes a channel for self-expression, which deepens as it is acknowledged and cherished. For a school to give children a place to speak in this way may seem revolutionary to some educators.

Jack Zimmerman: It is revolutionary—as long as what the children say is received with full respect, no matter how strange, disagreeable, or even violent it may sound. Everything in council is sacred: anger and despair as well as love. How many teachers and administrators in schools really want to hear what the children have to say—uncensored, unadorned, unadulterated? The willingness of people in a school community to truly listen to each other is what makes council revolutionary in schools.

Tom: So many children, even the so-called advantaged ones, have surprisingly few opportunities to speak their voice and know they will be heard. It's sad. What we're doing with the children's council project is so important, particularly now that we have brought the practice into public schools. There are many stories to tell.

Prejudice

Tom: The invitation to start the Council Program at Palms grew out of concern about the cultural factionalism at the school. Our program began on the heels of the violent civil disturbances in Los Angeles that occurred in 1991 as a result of the much disputed verdict in the Rodney King trial. It was a time when the Palms school administration felt particularly concerned about the lack of understanding and potential for violence among the many racial groups on campus.

I remember doing a council with a group of sixth-graders who were mostly of Hispanic origin. There were Guatemalans, El Salvadorans, Nicaraguans, Mexicans, and Colombians. There were also several Asian, Caucasian, and African-American kids. The topic of the council was *prejudice*. I asked them to tell a story about "someone you were prejudiced against or a time when you were persecuted by others."

Every kid had a story, either about themselves personally or about deep-seated prejudice in their families. There were stories about El Salvadorans who didn't like Guatemalans, Mexicans who didn't like El Salvadorans, Nicaraguans who didn't like Mexicans, and Koreans who didn't like the Japanese. Some stories were more familiar to me: African-Americans who didn't like Caucasians, Caucasians who didn't like African-Americans, Japanese kids who didn't like Chinese kids.

Listening to the stories showed the kids that prejudice is universal. But as council continued through the semester, I heard more and more statements, such as:

"You're somebody I never would have talked to if it weren't for council."

"I never would have had lunch with you or hung out with you."

"I feel like I know you now—and you're not so bad!"

"I might even have been afraid of you, but I can speak in front of you now. I'm not afraid anymore."

Once the kids identified their prejudices, we took the discussion to the next level. We saw how, on an individual level, prejudice is generated as a by-product of our need to label people and then maintain that system of identification. By the end of the year, through direct experience, these kids had let go of a lot of prejudice, because council gave them the opportunity to share stories and hear one another in a new way.

The Toothpaste Incident

Jack: Council can also be helpful in dealing with problems that arise spontaneously in a group of kids. On the first Palms Student Retreat at The Ojai Foundation in 1995, three high-spirited sixth-grade girls did an incredibly good job of smearing two of the boys sleeping bags with toothpaste one night. The girls had identified Ojai as a "camp," and at camp that's one of the mischievous things you do.

I sat with the two boys in their tent. One was brokenhearted and wept. He took it personally, even though we assured him that the girls had no way of knowing whose bags they were smearing with toothpaste. He was so upset, he couldn't go to sleep. The other boy didn't take it so hard. The girls' thoughtless actions, although not unusual, left me with a feeling of betrayal, since we had spoken passionately at the opening council of being at Ojai to build bridges between us all.

Before the next morning's council started, the other facilitators[3] and I decided to abandon our previous plans and deal
with the toothpaste incident. I couldn't let go of my displea-
sure with the girls. The old aphorism that "kids will be kids"
wasn't helping me very much. I didn't ask who had done it
or reprimand the group. I just told them I was upset and why.
The council took off almost immediately. The three girls identified themselves and described how bad they felt. "We didn't
think," they said. "It was just something to do." Indeed, they
hadn't known whose bags they were smearing. The less affected boy spoke eloquently about how it felt to crawl into his
bag and feel the mess. The other boy didn't say much, because
he didn't want to cry in front of the group.

That circle brought the whole group together in a way no
prepared theme could have accomplished. An ordinary incident became a strong teaching in the context of council.
Some of the kids recognized the episode as a metaphor for
more serious thoughtless actions and behavior.

We say we want students to learn how to take responsibility for
their own actions, but the deeply embedded authority structures that
dominate many schools work against this goal by creating an "us-and-
them" dynamic. The result is that kids either go into denial about
their responsibility or use most of their energy resisting authority.
This familiar polarization eliminates the possibility of real "authority
partnership" with children. Young people need ways to enhance their
sense of inner authority through opportunities to develop it naturally
and through modeling authentic adults.

Council encourages authenticity and shared responsibility; both
qualities help students become more self-authoritative. The heart of
the leader's job is to maintain the integrity of the process of council
without taking an authoritative position about the content. Admit-

---

[3] Educators who lead councils often refer to themselves as facilitators, so we will add that
term to our list of titles for council leaders.

tedly, this is a "fine line" to draw. If the leader fails to support the forms and intentions of council strongly enough (particularly when a group is just starting up), the process won't work. But if the leader's behavior or attitude becomes too authoritative, polarization takes place and students are likely to withdraw emotionally.

One reason this fine line is a challenge for many leaders is that, as lovers of council, they tend to project a desired outcome onto the group. When council is just starting up, the kids watch to see what the game is—as they always do in school. They "sniff out" what the facilitator wants. If council is dominated by the leader's hidden agendas, students soon pick this up and play the game the way the facilitator wants it played. Or they rebel. Either way, the councils lose energy. Facilitators have to know themselves well enough to identify their personal agendas, so that they do not unconsciously shape the councils they lead.

Tom: Your toothpaste story shows how a minor, spontaneous incident can bring kids together more effectively than a big political issue. I remember a council group at Palms that had many factions, including a few really shy kids who were not used to speaking in front of anyone and would "pass" all the time. Then one day we just stumbled into a council about "your dog or a dog that you knew." Every kid had a dog story—an emotional dog story—and the group came together for the first time. That led to a council about rain the next time we met. Every kid had a story about some experience in the rain. The simple universal experiences are often what bring the kids together.

Jack: Stories about animals or nature give children a chance to reveal themselves indirectly. Dogs are easier to talk about than one's friends or oneself. Themes like these help kids approach important material "through the back door."

Khalil's Dream

Jack: I recall another story that demonstrates council's remarkable ability to support students' self-esteem.

During the first year of the Palms program, when we both co-facilitated part of the school's leadership class, my half of the group included a very shy seventh-grade Iranian boy. By spring, however, "Khalil" had become trusting enough to share that he was struggling with an invitation to become part of a gang. Joining would give him status and personal power, which he lacked, but several of his friends were advising him not to succumb and he had a lot of his own reservations. The leadership circle gave him strong support for not joining the gang. The group's regular teacher and I talked about our personal experiences with gangs and cliques when we were students.

Then one day Khalil mustered the courage to tell us one of his dreams. A few of the kids had shared dreams before, which we listened to as "stories of the night," without offering interpretations. Sometimes the kids would react to the speaker's dream with comments like, "Oh, I had a dream like that." Khalil's dream had a distinctly mythical quality to it. The complex story took place in an earlier time in Iran and involved two opposing factions, one darker-skinned than the other. The darker-skinned faction, which included both young and old people, was led by his grandfather, who was a traditional peace-loving Muslim. The lighter-skinned militant faction was represented by a group of young people, who were relentlessly trying to get Khalil to join their "culture." After a long struggle, just as he was about to succumb to the gang, a white horse with a long flowing mane appeared. He grabbed the horse's mane, mounted, and escaped.

Several students commented on the obvious connection between the dream and Khalil's current struggle. I acknowledged his courage in sharing the dream and talked about how important dreams can be in helping us understand who we are. Then a week later, Khalil took me aside before council started. On the previous day, while he had been standing in line in the cafeteria waiting to get his lunch, he suddenly found himself transported into his dream. Once again, he was in Iran, in earlier times, surrounded by all the light- and dark-skinned dream people. At the same time, he knew he was in the cafeteria listening to students laughing and talking while they ate.

By telling me his story, I felt Khalil was inviting the whole circle to get involved. I asked him whether he would be willing to describe what had happened in the cafeteria and then tell his dream again. He agreed. (I also let the school counselor know what had happened, so he could keep in touch with the situation on a daily basis.)

The cafeteria story and the second telling of the dream riveted everybody's attention. I broke the silence after he finished: "Khalil's dream was so important for him that it returned a second time while he was in school and awake. Because he chose to tell us what happened in the cafeteria, I thought we could honor the dream's importance by sharing whatever reactions we have as we listened to him tell it again. We're doing this to help Khalil hear his own dream more deeply." Then we passed the talking piece around.

Since we had been listening to each other's stories all year, the kids had no difficulty in relating to the dream as "Khalil's story." They made associations to their own dreams and personal experiences and suggested why Khalil's dream was so important for him. Many of them commented on what we had come to call "the story under the story" (in this case, the conflict in all of us between our "good" and "bad" parts). They showed compassion for the struggle he was going through and came up with some imaginative associations to the horse with the long mane. I didn't need to say a word. When it was my turn, I simply affirmed the circle by acknowledging the compassion and insight that had been offered to Khalil.

Khalil blossomed in front of our eyes. By the end of the council he was sitting straighter and even looked bigger. Telling the dream again and receiving all the feedback had been a strongly affirming experience for him. A few days later he told us that he had decided not to join the gang—at least for the time being.

Hearing Khalil's important dream was healing for all of us. We identified with his conflict. It is a shame that some of us still relegate dreams to another world, which we deal with primarily through therapy and analysis, if we deal with them at all. In fact, dreams and personal stories are cut from the same cloth. Council offers a safe place between the worlds to share them both.

Tom: Dreams and stories are doors into one's interior life. Children have a limited number of ways to identify with each other's interior lives. Dreams are a universal way. Some of my most difficult council groups have been united through the sharing of dreams. A kid will tell a grizzly dream about falling or being chased by monsters and then another one will say, "Oh, I had a dream like that!" and we're off and running. Soon we're all feeling very united. Naturally, sharing shadowy dreams can be self-revealing, but the kids feel pretty safe because the revelations are hidden in the story of the dream.

Jack: For me, telling shadowy dreams or stories is like sharing difficult feelings. Hearing that others have had similar feelings dispels my sense of isolation. I discover that I'm not the only person in the world who feels that way or has scary dreams. Council provides an opportunity for everyone to make that discovery.

A variety of challenges arise when dreams are welcomed into circles of children. My advice to facilitators is . . .

- Ask yourself if you feel the circle is a safe place for dreams to be shared. Would you tell a dream of your own if you thought it appropriate for the children to hear?

- Let the children do most of the responding to each other's dreams.

- Enter in primarily to affirm the circle and keep the process from getting too heavy or out of balance. Most children enjoy exploring their dreams. However, facilitators should watch for indications that a child's curiosity about his or her dream has been replaced by defensiveness arising from feeling evaluated or judged. As soon as the dream-sharer shows any discomfort of this kind, the facilitator should step in and relieve the pressure. This might involve reframing the discussion by making some general comments about dreams or moving the circle away from focusing on the individual child.

• Most important, avoid taking an authoritative position with a statement like, "This is what the dream means . . ." When a leader plays that role, the circle loses its power.

Tom: I believe dreams can breathe life into a council because they give us a glimmer of our spirit. Dreams are a window to spirit. They involve altered states that are mysterious and inexplicable. When kids enter that realm with each other regularly through the intimacy of sharing dreams and stories, an honoring takes place in the group. Maybe that's why councils about animals can be so potent as well. Most kids feel animals—particularly wild animals—are closer to spirit than humans. That's why they identify with animals more than most adults do. Kids are less arrogant about their humanness.

Jack: In a way, not only dreams but all stories are doorways to spirit. Just hearing the words, "Once upon a time . . . " can initiate a shift in consciousness . . . which brings us to the next topic, since I know you like to initiate children's councils with stories!

WORKING WITH STUDENTS IN COUNCIL

Starting Out

Tom: When I introduce council, I often begin by saying that every one of us is living a story with a beginning, a middle, and an end.

As we go through our lives, many people contribute to the telling of our story: ancestors, grandparents, parents, friends, and, of course, ourselves. During the early part of our lives, others take a primary role in helping us tell our story. As we grow up, the pen lands more frequently in our own hands. Hopefully, by the time we leave high school, we are writing our own stories most of the time.

After that, I might describe how the wisdom of our species has been passed down through the art of storytelling since the beginning of time—which is how the "good stuff" is transmitted from family to family, tribe to tribe, and generation to generation. I tell the kids that everyone is invited to tell their dreams and personal stories in council, and then, as others share their reactions and associations—that is, as the circle mirrors the storyteller—we all learn more about our humanness and how to get on with daily life.

I usually start in a simple way. Before I even mention council, I'll often pair kids up and tell them to interview each other, as an introduction to telling stories in a circle and learning to listen. Questions might include: Who do you live with? Where do you live? What's your favorite food? What kind of music do you listen to? What's the best book you ever read? Non-threatening questions work the best, because kids are often shy at first. When they return to the circle, everybody introduces their partners by using the information they learned from the interviews. This simple first step begins to set clear guidelines about *listening* and *speaking* in council. It works because it makes a game out of listening. The kids have to try and remember what their partners tell them; they are not allowed to write anything down. Hopefully, their partners congratulate them on how good a listener they were.

Jack: Each child also gets to see himself or herself in a new way, through the eyes of the interviewer.

Tom: And through the responses to the questions, the kids immediately begin to notice similarities with others in the circle they didn't know before. One that comes up often—sadly, from my point of view—is, "I don't have a favorite book." Other common statements with which the kids identify include, "I live far away from school," or "My father doesn't live with us anymore."

To help the kids get comfortable telling their own stories, I might begin a council by selecting a favorite story of mine and then invite them to connect my story with their own lives. Generally I use short, traditional stories from various cultures to enhance our multicultural intentions and to model the brevity, clarity, and art of good storytelling. Then all I have to do is frame the story a little—that is, comment on its theme and what it might be saying about the nature of the human condition or the culture from which it came—and be a good listener. Of course, it is always a boon to the council to have a few kids who are natural storytellers, just as some kids are natural athletes or singers.

Because of the importance and power of story, I believe the more comfortable facilitators can be with all kinds of stories, the better. Kids can tell horrifying stories, but that's part of the process. The facilitator has to know how to contain a strong story in the circle and work with the wildness that may come out of it.

Jack: I remember a third-grade boy who, in a deadpan voice, described a time when he pulled the legs off a bug, one by one, until the insect stopped moving. The story produced a strong set of reactions, even though it wasn't that unusual, I think because the boy seemed completely without remorse. I didn't react but I asked a lot of questions when my turn came: "Have any of you ever done something like that? What is it in us that does that? Do adults do things like that? Does Marty's story have anything to do with violence?" We ended up having a riveting council about thoughtless brutality.

And not too long ago, a girl in one of my middle school councils described watching her father, in a drunken rage, hit her mother after a shouting argument about money. Some of the other girls in the council got mad and started crying, after which we all drifted into a depressed silence. Finally, I suggested we put the talking stick in the center and let people say how they were feeling, when and if they felt ready. It took us more than a half-hour to wade through the emotions enough to identify some of the underlying issues: alcoholism, men's rage and impotence arising from losing a job, women's fear and anger of men's violence, the stress of poverty, children's terror when their parents fight, and so on. The discussion continued for several more councils, during which many of the kids demonstrated amazing insights and passionately insisted they would never be part of a scene like the girl had described when they became parents.

But back to initiating council...One of my most compelling first council sessions came about spontaneously.

I had arrived at Palms a little early, all prepared to introduce council to the leadership group. As the students gathered, their teacher (my co-facilitator) introduced them one by one. Their names intrigued me. Many were native to the student's language and culture. There were Israeli, Iranian, Latino, African-American, Asian as well as Anglo names. On the spot I decided to let go of what I had planned and hold a council on names. I asked the students to say their names, tell what their names meant in their own language, for whom they were named, who named them, other reasons why they were given their particular names, how they felt about their names, whether they had any nicknames, and if they had ever wanted to change their names. I was amazed how much we all learned about the cultures represented in the circle, not to mention the kids!

In some cultures people are given new names as part of certain rites-of-passage ceremonies. In our society, our names don't usually change, except for the dropping of diminutives and nicknames as we mature. That's why we made the "Naming Council" part of the rite-of-passage retreat for Crossroads seniors at The Ojai Foundation. You remember how this playful ritual goes.

When the talking piece comes to—say, Mary—she rises and walks slowly around the inside of the circle three times. While she does this, everyone focuses on her, allowing images, phrases, or names to enter their mind spontaneously. When Mary returns to her seat, the person to her left takes the talking piece and shares the names or images that came up for him or her (if any) while Mary was walking the circle. The naming continues around the circle. When the piece gets back to Mary, she comments on any or all of the new names she just received, thanks everyone, and passes the piece on to the next person to be named. The naming ceremony usually deepens the intimacy of the circle and also generates a lot of good-natured humor.

Tom: Speaking of humor, humorous stories are an excellent way to start off a new circle. Let's face it, traditional schooling is not very funny. At school, I laugh the hardest in councils with children. When the kids feel safe with each other, the facilitator can introduce themes that naturally elicit humor, such as, "Tell a story about an embarrassing moment you experienced." The facilitator's basic challenge is to create a safe container in council for kids to laugh. Creating this container usually requires a discussion of the difference between laughing *with*, and laughing *at*, people. Making that distinction gives the facilitator an opportunity to step in if the laughter becomes disrespectful.

Introducing Students to Ceremony

Tom: I downplay ceremony at first when introducing council to students, particularly high-school students. I begin with councils that talk about personal and cultural rituals and then invite the students to create simple rituals that are intrinsic to the class. We might spread out a small blanket for the center piece, turn down the lights, choose a different person each time to dedicate the council, sing a song, or honor a student's birthday with a council in which each person has the opportunity of offering a verbal gift. The ceremonial quality of council usually emerges gradually as time goes on.

Jack: I gather you are using the words *ceremony* and ritual in a different way.

Tom: Yes. For me, ceremony is a state of being; it means sharing a heightened sense of presence in the circle, whereas ritual has to do with personal and cultural patterns of habitual behavior—such as singing the National Anthem before athletic events, watching the eleven o'clock news every night, and always putting a five-dollar bill in the collection basket on Sunday. Some of my ongoing councils never become ceremonial in nature. I let the natural desire for the sacred grow slowly and organically within the circle, rather than trying to impose it on the students. You can impose the use of rituals; you cannot impose reverence for the circle.

At Crossroads we may start a council by sitting in chairs and using something as mundane as a pencil to identify who has the floor. Then a talking piece of greater meaning can be introduced, such as the crystal used by last year's seniors, or an old penny-whistle that a member of the circle can play remarkably well. Finally the kids may make one for themselves—a rattle one group created out of an ornamental gourd purchased at the local supermarket comes to mind. We let them warm up slowly and work together to create ceremony.

In introducing ceremony to groups, I always try to remember that every situation is unique. For example, people in a church group might have a more relaxed attitude about ceremony than a group of high-school students. But the reverse might also be true. Sometimes, teenage kids are so hungry to acknowledge their "ceremonial selves" that they devour the opportunity as soon as it becomes available.

Jack: I agree that ceremony has to emerge organically, but there is another reality that has to be honored as well. If we avoid ceremony starting out with a new circle, we may succeed in not offending anyone, but we may also miss the opportunity to invite a numinous quality into the council early on. There are times when my instinct tells me to "go for it" (more often with adults, but sometimes with children too). For example, I might tell a story in a more dramatic voice, accompanying myself on a drum, rather than in an ordinary narrative way. Or I might even take a greater risk and suggest a few moments of silence, during which each person is invited to imagine a person in the circle they hardly know becoming a new friend. After all, ceremony is one of the ways we invite the mythical into a group. Sometimes people need to experience that at the outset to appreciate that council can be more than a secular process.

Generally, I find that children, particularly young children, are more open to ceremony than adults. Their games can be quite ceremonial in nature. Children's games often involve serious purposes, setting complex rules, and the assignment of special powers. Sometimes the games involve imitating adults in much the same way that people from traditional cultures perform ceremonies in which they take the roles of the gods in mythological dramas and dances. Since most adults in our culture have lost the capacity to create ceremony, it is particularly important to support children's natural ceremonial proclivities.

Tom: The challenge is to let ceremony emerge in a way that doesn't run smack into people's belief systems. For example, I now talk about the creation of sacred space as the lining up of heart and mind with the environment in a conscious way.[4] Although we have a long way to go, people are beginning to awaken to this possibility. The leader, just by creating that space internally, can help others attune to it too. The kids feel it almost immediately.

Jack: That touches on one of the central challenges of council leadership. On the one hand, leading a council appears to be "no big deal." You call the circle, choose a theme, find a talking piece, and maintain a certain level of order and integrity. But there is much more to leadership than that. To use your words, the leader is also asked to be aligned, heart and mind, with the circle and the environment in a way that fosters the spirit of council. Some facilitators have a hard time achieving this internal alignment. They carry out the council procedures, but they are insufficiently *aligned* internally to evoke a similar quality in others.

Tom: The ability to maintain this inner alignment grows out of seeing yourself as a steward of the circle, rather than using council to put on your own show. Alignment also means being awake, fully awake. My image of the great council leaders—you call them carriers of council—is that they embrace the entire circle, seeing it and serving it at the same time. Surrendering to being in service is quite a challenge for facilitators, which is why we say to prospective leaders: "If you are going to facilitate council, know that you will be continually involved in working on yourself, because all your own issues are bound to come up."

---

[4] I am grateful to our colleague, Zachary Terry, for this insightful metaphor.

Embracing the Rebel and the Saboteur

Tom: The rebel and the saboteur are often the strongest voices in the circle. In most schools, the notion that students have an empowered voice is already a rebellious idea. The rebel is often the one trying to turn that idea into a reality. So if the rebel's voice is given expression and brought into the circle, he or she can become the leader of the group. Allowing the rebel's voice to be heard proves to the rest of the circle that the council facilitator really meant, "You can speak from the heart here." If the rebel is silenced, the kids will know that the council isn't "for real." Instead they learn that they can say what they want—as long as they agree with the facilitator.

Jack: Suppose the rebel is sabotaging the council process itself by purposely talking out of turn, mimicking other people, or interrupting.

Tom: There is a spectrum of behavior to consider here. Some kids should not sit in council at a certain time in their development—innate restlessness may be as much the issue as sabotage. And then there are kids who can be so intent on sabotaging the council that you need to ask them to leave. Usually the risk of self-revelation is so threatening to these students, they need to attack the integrity of council in order to prevent that possibility from happening. Fortunately, much more often, the saboteur is the kid who is searching for the boundaries and so can be useful in creating them. I often sit the saboteur right next to me for ready access in constructively shaping the council!

Jack: I remember a charismatic fourteen-year-old by the name of "Skipper," who joined one of our early Heartlight wilderness trips.

Generally our group held together well, but this young stranger had a gift for inciting the unexpressed rebel in the other kids. Despite his age, Skipper fancied himself a fully empowered visionary and it wasn't long before he became the lightning rod for a major rebellion. At one point Skipper started leading half the group out of camp, because he thought the site we had chosen was filled with "dark spirits." (I think Skipper's spiritual insight may have been related to the abundance of mosquitoes at the site!) After an hour of loud confrontation, I told the Heartlight kids that breaking the integrity of the group by leaving meant they were no longer in the school. That stopped the exodus, but the rebellion was diffused only after I invited Skipper to sit in a place of honor in our subsequent council and personally welcome every member of the group back into the circle. He agreed. During the council, we discussed the rebellion and Skipper explained his reservations about the place we had chosen to camp. Slowly the group re-created a new, although slightly shaky, sense of wholeness, noticeably expanded by Skipper's unpredictable presence.

Tom: Facilitators always have to remember that the shape of children's councils are created and destroyed and then created and destroyed again. That's part of the teaching. For example, with my sixth-graders, I often have an incredible council—in which everybody listened to each other, and was heartfelt and self-revealing—followed the next week by one in which the kids treat each other like dirt. Intimacy is frightening, so they have to back off for a while. When that happens, the facilitator can always make fear of intimacy one of the themes for the next council.

BRINGING COUNCIL INTO THE MAINSTREAM

Jack: Introducing council into the educational mainstream is happening more and more as educators, students and parents discover the rich harvest that a school council program provides. There are many challenges, of course, including dealing with racially, culturally and economically diverse circles of children; finding a common language with which the circle can communicate; dealing with many different religious beliefs; and repeatedly convincing reluctant teachers and administrators that council is worth all the effort it takes. Fortunately, the opportunities are as enormous as the challenges: increased capacity for student expression, nonviolent means of resolving conflicts, greater racial and cultural understanding, the possibility of building a stronger school community and even improved academic performance—to name but a few.[5]

Multicultural Challenges and Opportunities

Tom: Generally, if you have a culturally diverse group of kids, there is no need to stimulate multicultural issues; they arise naturally through the telling of personal stories, since most kids have a strong cultural identification by the time they are seven. If the facilitator models the behavior of honoring others' traditions, the kids will usually learn to appreciate the common threads that connect their diverse cultures and to respect the differences.

In a school with a diverse student body such as Palms, the opportunities to explore multicultural issues are unlimited. All you have to do is choose a simple theme, such as "Tell us what your family does around the December holiday time" or "How does your family let you know that you are growing up?"

Jack: This indirect approach is ideal, because kids tend to resist "politically correct" multicultural themes when they are introduced directly. At Palms, we end up dealing head on with racial and cultural issues less often than expected, because so much of the work is done indirectly.

---

[5] In 2000-2001, WestEd, a major education evaluation organization conducted a school-wide council program at Palms. Along with the expected social-emotional findings (that students feel more connected to their classmates, their teachers, and the school, safer on the campus, and more confident about speaking authentically and listening more openly), the WestEd study noted an actual increase in GPA for students exposed regularly to the council process. An evaluation of 207 social-emotional programs such as council, recently published by "CASEL" (the Collaborative for Academic, Social, and Emotional Learning) reaches a similar conclusion.

Tom: The best work in council is always done indirectly by giving full voice to the kids. The results we hope for usually come in through the back door.

Jack: When the school's student body is more or less culturally and racially homogeneous, the facilitator has two basic options: Choose council themes that directly deal with prejudice and lack of understanding or proceed more indirectly through stories and analogies of academic, athletic, or economic prejudices. Direct themes are familiar to teachers who use "moral dilemmas" to explore values with their students. For example, a facilitator might pose the following scenario to the kids, "Suppose you were invited to a party at which all but one of the kids had the same racial and cultural background as yourself. Suppose several of your friends began picking on the minority kid. What would you do?"

Examples of indirect themes are:

- Tell a story about a time when you felt everybody in your class was smarter than you or when you were impatient with someone at school who was slow to understand what was going on in class.

- Tell a story about a time you were chosen last, or near to last, when two captains were picking people for their athletic teams.

- Have you ever been poorer than most people in your group? How did that feel?

- Have you ever been richer than most of your friends? How did you feel about that situation?

Tom: When strong cultural animosities flare up in the circle, the leader has to steadfastly maintain the form and intentions of council. If students can meet the challenge of sharing their fear, anger, distrust, and differing viewpoints within the framework of council, then the process can continue. At the very least, the kids will agree to disagree about the issues at hand.

When the intentions of council continue to be broken, the leader may have to interrupt the process and ask the students whether they are ready to participate respectfully with each other. If the intentions continue to be broken after that, the leader should probably end the council. The point to stress is, "If people are not listening to each other and their hearts are closed, there is no council anyway."

Jack: I've had to shut down councils for this reason only a few times over the years. In all but one instance, it felt like the group was testing my boundaries and devotion to the process—and in each of those situations, council discipline improved in the sessions after the shutdown. In the exceptional instance, I had been invited by a group of acrimonious adults to help them settle their internal battles with the help of council. I had the (false) impression that the group members knew a little about the council process before they invited me. It turned out they really wanted a "parent" or, better, King Solomon, to settle their disputes. The idea that they would actually listen to each other attentively and search for "the truth of the circle" terrified them. Their level of anger didn't permit them the opportunity of really trying. I hung in for half an hour before deciding that "discretion was the better part of valor" and abandoning the effort. I never heard from the group again.

Finding the Right Language

Tom: The language used to describe council and introduce themes should be as secular as possible, particularly when working in public schools. Spirited experiences occur regardless of language, of course, but many people can get hung up on words and trappings.

Jack: I remember when we started at Palms, we had to reword a Halloween council theme we had used for years. We used to say, "Since Halloween is a time when we honor the dead, let's tell stories about how the spirits of our ancestors are still present in our lives." Several teachers at the school were concerned that this theme implied the existence of ghosts, which was inappropriate from the traditional

Christian point of view. It was easy to remedy the situation by substituting the word *memories* for *spirits*. We were a lot more sensitive about language after that, which I think helped strengthen the program and make it accessible to a greater variety of people.

It is entirely possible to conduct council programs for children (as well as adults) without using any spiritual language.[6] The question that arises, however, is whether a linguistic secularizing of council promotes a false impression, which will end up offending more people in the long run. A more honest approach, when talking to educators considering the use of council, might be to acknowledge that spiritual issues do arise in council and, more to the point, that some people do have experiences of spirit in the circle.

In dealing with the challenges of language, it is always helpful to check in with your own honest feelings about sensitive words. For example, "spiritual," "sacred," and "ceremony" can have widely different meanings and conjure up a variety of images depending on the person to whom you are talking. In a heterogeneous group, having a council just to discover the range of associations to such words can be quite enlightening. As a general guideline, we suggest using words in a way that is generally appropriate for the circle, while still having the courage to sometimes use a word that will produce a charge in order to give it new life and perhaps even a new definition. An experienced council leader is willing occasionally to rock the boat, while at the same time being sensitive to using language that meets the circle where it is. Ultimately, handling the delicate issue of language is an ongoing judgment call for each council leader—and each school.

Dealing With Religious Beliefs and Practices

Jack: Although our practice of council with children has evolved in a way that has little to do directly with traditional Native-American

---

[6] Rachael Kessler, Peggy O'Brien, Bonnie Tamblyn, Adam Behrman and the other authors of the *Mysteries Program Source Book* at Crossroads have done an excellent job in this respect.

ceremonies, we occasionally still hear the question, "Are we practicing another culture's religion?"

I don't believe we are. Whenever I dig underneath the cultural and historical influences associated with an unfamiliar spiritual tradition, I invariably discover a core of teachings that seem remarkably familiar. I feel "at home" with the deepest roots of many traditions. At its core, council has Buddhist, Greek, and Quaker roots—as well as Native American. Our practice of council arises from this core level.

Gigi often reminds me that women in many cultures have been sitting and working in circles for centuries. Indigenous peoples all over the world honor their interconnectedness with nature and their surroundings in circle ceremonies, which reflect a way of life all but forgotten by the modern industrialized world. In the archetypal levels of the psyche, however, these universal circle practices are still part of all of us. But beyond all that, the vast majority of Americans are a mixed breed—*Metis*—and it seems natural to use a form of group communication that welcomes all opinions and cultures.

Inviting kids to talk about their own traditions and practices leads—almost without exception—to honoring the differences that make us unique and discovering common threads that bring us together.

Tom: Yet the religious issue remains a thorn for a few teachers and parents, usually those of a fundamentalist background.

Jack: I remember a Crossroads student who came to me in an agitated state after a few weeks of council. "I'm beginning to feel in the circle like I feel in church," she said. "But we don't talk about Jesus and the Scriptures in council, which makes me feel like I'm doing something wrong." I listened to her for a while and invited her to talk about her love for Jesus in the circle, but she felt that would be even more inappropriate. Finally (with her permission) I decided to call her parents. After a long conversation with her mother, we agreed it would be best to excuse her daughter from the council. Fortunately this situation has arisen only a few times in working with thousands of children.

Tom: In fact, we have the opposite experience most of the time. I've had many religious kids who are very comfortable in council and actually end up understanding more about their own path. In a way, practicing council is like meditation. Anyone can meditate, regardless of spiritual affiliation, and as a result, deepen his or her relationship to that tradition. Council works the same way.

Should Council Leaders Be Specialists or Regular Teachers?

Tom: My answer is simple: They should be special, regular teachers! Facilitating council has made me a better classroom teacher and administrator; I am better able to understand kids and work with them.

Jack: Ho! The question is particularly important when launching a new program. At one independent school that introduced council to their high-school freshmen, all the grade-level teachers went through a brief council training before the program started—too brief, as it turned out. Some of the teachers did well as facilitators, but those who were less inclined towards council struggled and the program eventually floundered. When we began the council work at Crossroads, we wanted to set the new program on a strong foundation, so we used facilitators who had been through intensive training and had apprenticed with an experienced council leader. For several years this group of specialists worked successfully, but separately, from the regular faculty. As a consequence, the lack of knowledge about the program created doubts in some teachers' minds. So neither extreme is ideal.

A practical solution is to have a few carriers of council available to train academic teachers at the outset of the program. The carriers spend their time co-leading circles with the teachers and mentoring them. Hopefully, by the second or certainly the third year of the program, the teachers will be ready to carry council leadership on their own. (For a more detailed description of this "mentor model" see Appendix I.)

In the best of all worlds, the entire school faculty and administration would be familiar with council before launching the children's program. But it is only recently that some charter schools and small independent schools have explored this possibility.

Tom: Crossroads has come a long way in that respect. Council has been introduced systematically to the entire faculty and every new teacher participates in a council internship as part of his or her introduction to the school. Besides helping them understand the council program, this gives teachers a general frame of reference for how we talk to children in the school.

All our facilitators meet together in council frequently—it is built into their schedules. Having a support group for the teachers who are facilitators continues their training and gives them a place to deal with the personal challenges of leading council.

Councils of Teachers, Administrators, and Parents

Jack: Teachers and administrators can also use council in faculty meetings, although the traditional leadership roles most administrators assume in running these meetings may not be consistent with the spirit of council. One way of diminishing the debilitating effects of conflicts about authority is to invite an outside facilitator periodically to lead a faculty council, so that every administrator has the experience of becoming an integral part of the circle.

Tom: I know that problem well! When the hierarchical context dominates council, something significant is lost.

Jack: What can you say about parents' reactions to council?

Tom: Usually fear about council stems from ignorance, which can lead to a lot of individual parent conferences if council has not been explained to them or they have not experienced it themselves. An occasional parent who tries council might say, "This scares me to death, I can't deal with it." But for the most part, once parents sample the program and realize that it is nonsectarian and does not violate—in fact, supports—their basic ethical code, they relax. That's what happened at Palms. I think we did a smart thing when we began that program. We introduced council to all the parents in a letter and invited those who were interested or had concerns to come in and "have a taste" of the process.

The closing council with the parents that first year at Palms was valuable too. One thing I noticed was that the majority of parents who attended said, in essence, that their kids were introverts who had been helped to find their own voices through council. Many parents reported that their children talked about school and shared their feelings more at home. Telling us that was a way of saying, "Thank you."

Jack: When they see how council has helped their children, some parents want to start their own circles. We've started ongoing parent councils, but they don't seem to last very long.

Tom: In my experience, many of our parents don't feel they have the time, and, besides, they are unfamiliar with the notion of parents creating an ongoing support group for each other. Our parents are very involved at the level of supporting school activities, but they do not view the school as a place in which to focus on their personal needs and concerns. Fortunately, that's beginning to shift through our parent education program, where we often use council.

Jack: Using council in a parent education program is an excellent way to stimulate the formation of ongoing parent council groups. When that's ready to happen, the school can provide facilitators until the parent councils become self-sufficient. It takes time for parents to view their children's school as a community that can nourish their own interior lives.

THE POWER OF COUNCIL

Jack: In the early years of the Mysteries Program at Crossroads, one of our biggest challenges was to avoid having the program become just another successful school activity, isolated from the mainstream of the faculty and regular courses. We emphasized, again and again, that council had the potential to strengthen teaching methods and improve the effectiveness of academic studies, environmental education, and the entire human development curriculum of which Mysteries was a part. Most of all, council facilitators kept reiterating that using council to deal with important school-wide issues and crises would strengthen the sense of community in the school. Most of the students saw the potential of council from the beginning, but it took some of the administrators, teachers and parents many years to really get the message.

Improving Methods of Teaching

Tom: Once teachers become familiar with council, it can be used to deepen class discussions. One of our ethics teachers uses council with his seniors to help students listen to each other's opinions on "hot topics." He feels council is indispensable to a classroom teacher. However, our teachers are more likely to drop into council when dealing with class dynamics than with class content. They see council primarily as a problem-solving device in their academic classes.

For example, in a recent self-defense training class, the teacher ran into some cynicism and resistance. After five minutes he could see the kids were not willing to participate in any appropriate way. So he moved into council and asked them to describe a time when they had committed themselves fully to learning something. That reframed the whole situation for the students and the impasse was overcome. As always, the gift of the good facilitator is to *turn into the skid*.

Jack: Beyond giving them a tool to deal with classroom dynamics, I've seen council change the way teachers teach. At Palms, several of the regular teachers report that council has helped them work more effectively with students, now that they have heard so many more of their stories about the pressures of family life and homework.

Tom: Council improves a teacher's ability to hear children on a deeper level—to hear the story beneath the story. It also provides a concrete experience of co-teaching with students. In council everyone is both student and teacher. In the classroom a good teacher is perpetually in a state of learning, particularly from the students. We learn about the material we are presenting and also about our methods of teaching. Obviously students give us our most useful feedback—and not only from test scores and grades. If we ask for a council devoted to evaluating the class—and if we listen—we can hear quite clearly how we are doing. As council has become an integral part of the school program, more teachers are asking for evaluations. When teachers model the respect that council creates by listening to the kids, the respect is returned in kind.

Jack: I dream about a school in which classroom teachers hold a council with their students every few months to explore the theme, "How do you feel about what you're learning and how I'm teaching?" It goes against the grain for many teachers to put themselves in the line of fire that way. But the alternative is highly inefficient. Complaints about teachers or classes normally take a tedious route: from student to parent to administrator, and finally, back to the teacher. This indirect route is based on mutual fear and distrust. It makes much more sense to deal with the problem directly between teacher and student.

Tom: Council is also a constant reminder that kids are quite capable of teaching one another. They solidify their own learning when they help other students.

Expanding the Academic Curriculum

Jack: Council can spark new curriculum ideas. At Palms, an English teacher is integrating council with her eighth-grade class by having the kids write and illustrate a handbook, possibly in the form of a children's story, containing practical advice for incoming sixth-graders. The idea is to create an "easy-to-use, no-nonsense guide to middle school," prepared by their "elders." The books will be presented ceremonially before the end of the year to the elementary schools in the neighborhood. This project fits in beautifully with the overall theme of the eighth-grade council program, which is the rite of passage from middle school into high-school.

Tom: I think there is still a lot of relatively unexplored curricular territory in which council could be of great assistance. For example, at Palms an Eighth-Grade teacher has begun to use council to deepen her classes' investigation of the art of storytelling. I love it when the kids understand that each of their lives is a story—an inherently dramatic story—that is full of teachings for themselves and others. Looking at their own stories in the context of traditional storytelling would add to their understanding of both. Then they could develop the art of storytelling in new ways, both orally and in writing. Stories also help us align ourselves with the environment and face the challenges of the human condition. In all spiritual traditions, telling certain stories is one of the main ways of creating sacred space. Stories can be keys that open the doors to universal truths.

Jack: That reminds me of the "Saga of the Army" at Heartlight.

One year we didn't have any girls in the middle group when we started school in September. The nine boys, ages eight through eleven, often used our morning councils to keep the rest of the school abreast of their imaginative recess-time games. Soon we were all familiar with their ongoing narrative of an intergalactic war between primal forces of good and evil. The story was played out during free times, using the small G.I. Joe toy figures that were the rage then. The boys wore camouflage clothes to school, and so identified with their story that they became known in the school as the "Army." When we finally found a girl brave enough to join our middle group, she had to identify herself as a "camp follower" to feel a part of the middle group. Eventually, two of the boys developed strong crushes on Rachel, and that even more powerful "triangle story" broke up the Army!

Supporting Environmental Education

Tom: Council is an excellent form for group building when working outdoors with kids, because it is nature-based. Both nature and council are "circular events," so council fits beautifully into an environmental education program. When working in nature under challenging physical circumstances—on a ropes course, wilderness fast, or backpacking trip, for example—it is necessary to get continuous and honest feedback from the kids to know exactly how each one of them is handling the experience. Council is an effective and efficient way to do that. And, as always, council provides the opportunity for kids to teach and support one another, which is particularly valuable in physically challenging situations. (For a more in-depth discussion of rites of passage and council in natural settings, see Chapter 13)

Strengthening the Human Development Program

Jack: When council was first introduced at Crossroads in 1983, there was no Human Development Department at the school. That came into being a few years later. Now the department includes environmental education and community service, as well as the Mysteries Program, and is a strong presence in the school. Administering these three programs in the same department has helped to bring council into the other two. Deciding a few years ago to make the human development chairperson a dean reflects how important this part of the curriculum has become in the school community.

Tom: How do other schools administer their council programs?

Jack: In independent schools they are often administered by the human development department, which allows council to be integrated with health education programs. Normally, public schools sponsor human development activities through their counseling office—when they are fortunate enough to have one! We discovered at Palms that having one or more school counselors intimately involved in facilitator training and administration of the council program is essential.

Dealing With School Crises

Tom: After the "riots," the big fire in 1993, and the 1994 earthquake, we used council throughout the school to give students and teachers a chance to talk about their fears and experiences. In large part because of council, the school felt even more like a huge family during those difficult days. We felt fortunate that there was a familiar context in which the kids could discharge a lot of their anxiety.

I also think of the "mourning circles" we've had at Crossroads. Council has been extremely useful on the rare occasions when a student has died. A long time ago a seventh-grade boy was hit by an automobile near the school and died a week later. During the week of anguish and the period of mourning, groups of seventh grade and other students met in council throughout the school to express their feelings.

Jack: I remember how student reactions varied tremendously. Those who knew the boy well were shocked and grief-stricken; for many, it was their first encounter with death. Some, who didn't know him well, didn't share the deep emotions and felt a little guilty and excluded. Then there were a few kids who had unfinished business with the boy—an argument the day before the accident or a feeling that they had teased him too much. Those kids had a hard time with his death and needed an opportunity to express their feelings of incompleteness. As you might imagine, the councils were strong. Afterwards, many teachers, students, and parents expressed gratitude that the kids had been given an appropriate place to deal with the torrent of emotion that swept through the seventh grade during those few weeks.

I can still remember the agony Paul Cummins went through then. (He was the headmaster at the time.)

> That week happened to be the final session of an early council training that included Paul and several other school administrators. He came to the group distraught and down on himself. Naturally, I abandoned what I had planned and we became a support council for Paul.

"What right do I have to be headmaster of a school, if I can't make sure the kids stay alive," he began. Obviously, he needed a place to let down and grieve, since he had been holding so much together at school and with the boy's family.

The group readily identified with how he felt; several in the circle had been through similar trials. After Paul spoke for a while, we all responded with stories of our own. There were expressions of sympathy and reassurance, of course. A few of us offered the opinion that ultimately one can't take total responsibility for others. One headmaster suggested it was hubris to believe anyone had the power to guarantee those in his care would not be harmed. "Only God can do that," someone else agreed. I remember how these words awakened Paul from despair and brought him into the circle in a way that the earlier offerings of sympathy had failed to do.

Tom: We also held mourning circles more than fifteen years ago when a much loved student died in the spring of her senior year after a long struggle with leukemia. She had been vitally engaged in the school since seventh grade and the entire community went into mourning. We held several councils the day after she died that gave everyone an opportunity to voice their feelings.

LIMITATIONS AND POSSIBILITIES

Jack: What comes to mind when you think about the limitations of council?

Tom: My first thought is the choice of inappropriate council themes. "Tell a story about a teacher you really hate," is an example. That kind of theme usually calls forth a negativity that is rarely productive.

Jack: Right. But as we've said before, when a class or teacher becomes a cause for concern, there are productive ways to explore the situation in council, assuming the teacher is willing to hold one. An appropriate question to ask students might be, "What does, and does not, work for you in this class?"

Tom: That's what I would call "positive reframing of a shadow issue." To do that, the teacher has to be really available.

Jack: Council is definitely not a place for "ragging" on teachers or students who are not present. When someone has something to say to a person in the circle, there are productive and safe ways to handle that in council.

Another limitation in doing council in schools is the tyranny of the bell system. It taxes a facilitator's ingenuity to anticipate reaching some kind of closure in exactly fifty-four minutes.

Tom: Fortunately, after a while, facilitators get to know the rhythm of their groups and are able to bring closure pretty quickly.

Jack: Still, it is hard to stop when the council has come alive just in the last five minutes. If that happens, I usually summarize the issues the group has uncovered as part of the closing. This builds a bridge to the next session and gives the circle the option of picking up where it left off.

Tom: We both know that there are more fundamental limitations in doing council with a group of students than bad themes and tight scheduling. As the circle feels safer and safer to the kids, they begin to voice their deeper problems, some of which can be devastating. The extreme is when a kid "drops the bomb"—that is, talks about suicidal intentions or experiences of abuse, both of which have to be reported. Working with intense personal despair in front of a bunch of kids is not safe. School councils are inappropriate when raw material comes up that requires a lot of deep work with one student.

Jack: I agree. Fortunately, "the bomb" is less likely to be dropped if facilitators have been clear about their obligation to report such information. In that case, the child carrying the story usually speaks to the council leader first, outside of council, which makes it possible to bring in the parents and a school counselor in an appropriate way.

If an abuse or suicide story bursts through in the moment, I suggest that facilitators interrupt the council, reiterate their obligation to report the information, and then help students gain some measure of resolution. What works the best for me is to explain why it is inappropriate for the group to focus strongly on the storyteller. It is important, however, that everyone in the circle have the opportunity to say something about the story they just heard.

I might say, "It is not appropriate for the whole circle to go deeply into what Cassie just told us. This is a highly charged situation that requires the special skills of a trained counselor—and a lot of attention. Other members of her family need to be involved. I will talk to her after council and make sure she gets the help she needs. What I'd like to suggest is that we take some time now to listen to each other's thoughts and feelings about the general problem that Cassie's story exposes . . . And if you have any questions about this way of responding to Cassie, please bring them up in the council as well."

Reframing the discussion after "the bomb" in this manner usually allows students to release some of their emotional tension in the discussion that follows. At this juncture, I usually restate the confidentiality agreement we made originally and ask council members to decide whether it needs revision. Council themes and activities should be chosen carefully in the weeks that follow. Dealing with the spontaneous revelation of abuse or suicidal intentions challenges even the most experienced council leader.

Tom: Ho! All this leads me to the questions we get from parents sometimes about the differences between council and therapy. Without sitting in council themselves, it's hard for parents to understand.

Jack: This might be the moment to retell the story of Mrs. Simmonds from Palms.

You were there, so you remember how she sat in the back of the room looking decidedly unhappy as I was telling the roomful of parents about the council program. As soon as I paused, she said: "I'm Julie Simmonds' mother. You make it all sound so wonderful, but I have a serious problem with the program." Several people turned around to see who was talking. "Suppose a child gets into some deep feelings. Are all the council leaders trained to deal with that? Council sounds like a therapy group. I don't think that's why we send our kids to this school. If I want my daughter to have therapy, I'll arrange private counseling."

The challenge was familiar. "Your question is a good one," I began, trying to sort out my thoughts. "Sometimes council does help children get in touch with feelings they've been holding inside for a while. Clearly council leaders need to be skilled in dealing with emotional material. But council is not group therapy. Good council leaders and good therapists function differently."

I wondered how much more to say. Mrs. Simmonds leaned forward, crossed her legs, and rested her chin in her hand. Her body language said, "You have to say a lot more than that to satisfy me." I got the message and went on.

"First of all, I don't deny that council can be therapeutic—by which I mean healing. Some of the aims of therapy and council are similar. They both set out to expand self-awareness and self-acceptance. They both can improve the way an individual relates to others and functions in the world.

"But council and traditional therapy go about achieving these ends in a different way. In one-to-one therapy the focus is entirely on the client, who feels (rightly) that the therapist— who combines parent, priest, doctor, and teacher—is there to serve the client's process. Even in group therapy, each person's *primary objective is to work on him- or herself.* Therapy is vital and effective when the client's emotional bonding to the therapist— the transference—is strong.

"In a school council (as in any council) the focus is simultaneously on the individual and the whole circle. *Healing is supported by the student's relationships to other students and adults in the group—and to the circle as a whole.* The council leaders act as guides and hold firmly to the practice and spirit of council, but (and this is where traditional group therapy and council differ markedly) they also share appropriate personal ma-

terial in the circle like everyone else. This reduces the transference to the council leaders significantly. Indeed, there is
usually less transference to the council leaders than there is to
the whole circle.

"Council and therapy are quite different on the functional
level too. Therapy is, at different times, analytical and confron-
tational, nourishing and supportive. In therapy, unconscious
patterns are identified primarily through direct intervention
by the therapist. Council, however, is far more focused on syn-
thesis than analysis. Students gain insight about themselves
largely through sharing their stories, dreams and feelings—or
listening and identifying with those of others in the circle.
When we attempt to tell our stories to others fully and clearly,
we end up listening to them in a new way. The telling itself
within the context of the circle brings about a critical re-ex-
amination that leads to increased self-understanding. *In short,
students end up digesting and integrating their experience of council
acting primarily as their own therapists.*

I noticed a few eyes were glazing over, so I stopped. Mrs.
Simmonds hadn't moved at all. "The best thing would be for
you to join a council, I said, looking at her directly. "It's difficult to talk about these issues in the abstract."

Tom: At that point, I remember suggesting we do a council with the theme, "Concerns and questions about council."
We arranged the chairs in a circle and began. Many of the
parents expressed enthusiasm for the program. One mother
said, "I wish I had been able to join a council when I was
in school. Then I might have been able to talk honestly to
my mother, and my whole life would have been different." A
father said he thought the school was courageous to initiate
the program. When it was her turn, Mrs. Simmonds held the
stone talking piece gingerly. After a long pause, she said she
still had misgivings, but would wait and see how her daughter
felt after a few weeks of the program. When the stone came to
me, I acknowledged her for taking that risk.

Jack: Ironically, council's biggest limitation may be its magic. Sometimes people believe the form itself is so powerful that, just by doing council in a school, the whole community will come together. This belief confuses the form and spirit of council and also begs two important questions: Does the school community share a common vision? Has the school integrated council sufficiently into its hierarchical structure?

Tom: Starting a council program usually creates what I think of as *pockets of enlightened communication.* But, unless there is wide support for the educational vision of the school, and the administration is comfortable using council to help make decisions, a stronger community may not materialize. These two goals could be achieved as part of an expanded council program that includes teachers, administrators, and parents, along with students.

Jack: Once there is alignment of vision and the use of council in the daily life of the school, the possibilities are unlimited. Many of us have dreamt of a time when the way of council becomes more accepted as an integral part of the education of children. The great potential of council is its power to *draw out* the wisdom each person brings to the circle—and that, after all, is what education is all about.

Tom: *Ho!*

8

FAMILY
COUNCILS

C ouncil sometimes gets started in a family because of some crisis, large or small. Here is my friend Perry's story.

We used to meet occasionally to discuss important family issues, but it became clear last August that stronger measures were needed. The kids were home all summer, playing and doing their best to avoid chores. "We're on vacation," they kept telling us. Naturally, Anna and I disagreed, but we got tired of badgering them all the time and finally, in desperation, decided to start regular family councils.

By the second session, the kids realized that passive resistance wouldn't work any longer, so they shifted strategies.
Bridget's approach involved reminding us that she was doing
more than her brother, a dubious argument since his efforts
were virtually nonexistent. Tommy saw I was about to blow
my stack, so he tried a more subtle approach: "I wish you'd
be tougher with me," he said, giving me his sincere look and
shaking the twisted piece of driftwood we used as a talking
stick for emphasis. "You should just assign the job, tell me
what happens if I don't finish on time—and then be tough!"
Trying to shift the blame, I thought. Clever! But I had time to
calm down while he went on about something else. If just the
two of us had been talking outside of council, we would have
gotten into a battle for sure.

"Fine," I said when I got the talking stick, "I agree that I've
been too soft on both of you. From now on I'll really crack the
whip—deadlines, consequences, and all!" Bridget rolled her
eyes and gave Tommy a drop dead look.

Hoping to go beyond such mundane interactions, Anna
began the third council by asking the children to share their
feelings about the family. After a round of innocuous gener-
alizations, Bridget somehow found the courage to speak from
her heart:

"It feels like I come after your work and social life," she
said to Anna in an unsteady voice. "You never want to talk
about my friends or what I'm into. You don't seem really interested in what goes on in my life. You're always busy. You say
you care, but . . . "

Anna sat frozen on her pillow, while Bridget went on passionately for several minutes. Her eloquence surprised us.
"There's no one in the world I love more deeply than you!"
Anna said when it was her turn to speak. "It hurts me to hear
you say I don't care. Nothing could be further from the truth
. . . But I do have to admit your crushes and intrigues don't
grab me like they grab Dad. His involvement in your social life

is more than enough for both of us. But I never stop caring about you."

Bridget picked up the talking piece as soon as Anna had finished. "I don't get it! How can you love me and still not want to know about my friends? That's what's important to me . . . You could at least be a little interested."

I told Anna her snide comment made me feel funny about all the time I spend discussing Bridget's latest crush. Tommy said he thought crushes were "stupid," which elicited a small explosion from his sister.

"I didn't mean to be judgmental," Anna assured me when the piece of driftwood got to her again. "To be honest, I'm jealous of your relationship with Bridget. We used to be really close . . . " For a moment, she looked directly at Bridget without speaking. "I miss you," she said finally. "You're either with friends all the time or talking on the phone . . . or with Dad. We hardly spend any time together." She put the stick down slowly in the center of our circle, close to Bridget.

"I didn't know you *wanted* to be with me," Bridget began, her voice slightly breaking. "Mellie's mom is always wanting to know about her friends and all, but you and I hardly ever talk . . . " She went on for a while, trying to get comfortable with the shift in feeling.

"You have to *ask* Mom to talk," Tommy observed when it was his turn. "She doesn't just come into your room to hang out, like Dad does." He paused for half a minute while we all waited. "Maybe she's shy like me," he said finally in a quiet voice.

I was touched by what Tommy said about Anna. So was Anna. We both said so when it was our turn in the council.

"You shouldn't have to invite your mom to talk," Bridget began stubbornly, picking up the stick from the center. Then she softened suddenly. "But I'm glad you don't just bust into my room like Mellie's mom does when I'm over at their house. And there are things I can't talk to Dad about . . . "

"I think it's time for Dad to spend more time with me and Mom with you," Tommy announced. "I've got important stuff to talk about," he added looking at me.

"I'll bet," Bridget interjected, dismissing him with a toss of her head. Tommy put the stick down without saying anything more. I reminded Bridget not to interrupt and told Tommy I'd be glad to talk to him about whatever was on his mind.

Since I knew his kids pretty well, Perry asked for my reflections after he told me this story some time ago (Bridget and Tommy were thirteen and ten at the time). Perry's eyes had been opened by that council in many ways, so there was little for me to add. I did point out that Bridget seemed devoted to putting Tommy down. "He's intimidated by her because she makes friends so easily," I told him. "Everyone is drawn to her. Tommy seems to have one good friend or plays by himself." Perry knew all that, of course, but not in the way it hit him after that council. He began paying more attention to the kids' relationship. Several months later, he told me Tommy and he had deepened their connection, and Anna and Bridget were spending more time together too.

WHY BOTHER?

When people first hear about family council, many question the importance of formalizing communication among a few people who talk to each other all the time. The answer is simple: Talking and communicating *can be strikingly different in the dynamics of family life.*

Take leisurely dinner table discussions, for example. Even when a family regularly enjoys this vanishing pleasure, mealtime conversations can be dominated by underlying family patterns. Parents often set the tone and agenda and naturally take on the responsibility of maintaining order. Often, the more articulate members of the family dominate the discussion. Authentic dialogue is rare.

Family council can help transcend this and other patterns—such as those that arise in families that are so busy they hardly ever share a meal together . . . Even parents who feel they enjoy open communication with their children are amazed to discover new levels of honesty and intimacy when the family commits to a regular practice. Hidden agendas become overt, children and parents feel empowered in new ways, and the family begins to function more as a community of allies than a collection of disparate individuals. For some families the improvement may not be dramatic but is welcome nevertheless. For others, the new sense of openness is in marked contrast to the dysfunctional patterns they had come to accept as an inevitable part of family life.

Council can make a big difference in a family's quality of life for two basic reasons:

- The communication process itself is given far more attention in council than during ordinary family get-togethers.

- Honest interaction is hindered when family members are caught up in the habitual roles that so often dominate family life. Council provides a safe container in which to risk breaking out of deeply ingrained family patterns.

In some cases these risks are formidable, which is one reason many families procrastinate before committing to regular council. Often they "have been meaning to do it" for months before the first session finally takes place. Busy schedules, one or more disinterested family members, and the familiar line, "We just don't seem to get around to setting up a council," are the reasons often given. Sometimes there is considerable fear lurking behind these "reasons." Regular council can uncover painful feelings and destructive relational patterns that have lain hidden for years. Understandably, some families don't want to rock the boat.

A child who knows council from school may be the missionary who converts the family. But not every student who enjoys council in school wants to bring the process home. It is one thing to sit in circle with one's classmates, and another to speak from the heart with Mom, Dad, brother and/or sister. More often one of the parents is the council initiator, trying to convince a resistive spouse and one or more disinterested children. Consequently, perseverance is essential in getting family council started.

It's worth it. A regular practice helps family members support each other through difficult times, encourages even the shyest child to expand self-expression, and stimulates open communication outside of council. A family that councils becomes more conscious of their destructive patterns and how to transform them. A family that councils together keeps on growing together.

FINDING THE RIGHT SETTING AND SCHEDULE

The first steps in creating family councils involve scheduling, commitment, and establishing the setting.

Scheduling. Agree on a regular schedule, such as every Sunday afternoon or an evening when no one has classes, jobs, or meetings. Trying to schedule council week-by-week usually doesn't work. Choose the optimal time and conduct the council with whoever can attend. If Mom is out of town, the family can council with Dad. If Sabrina is rehearsing a school play for two weeks at the regular council hour and a better time can't be found, go ahead without her. The more regular the meetings, the more family members will schedule their lives around council. Holding council once a week works well for most families. However, it is better to strongly commit to regular council twice a month than imposing a weekly schedule on a busy family. Agree that special councils can be called (by anyone) when an issue arises that cannot wait until the next regular meeting. The rest of the family then does their best to accommodate the "caller," at least for a brief session. Following the regularly scheduled council with a family meal extends the intimacy in a celebratory way.

Commitment. "After three months of hassling, I finally got my family to try council last Sunday," Nancy began. Telling me the story brought back all her frustration. "It was a complete disaster. The kids wouldn't talk—unless someone else was holding the talking stick, of course. Billy couldn't sit still for a moment and Seth rolled his eyes or giggled every time anyone said anything serious. I spent half the time reminding them of the rules. John was patient with the kids —actually, *long-suffering* is a better word. But his expression said, ` I told you this was a crazy idea.' It was our first and, I'm afraid, our last council."

"I hope not," I told her. "Some families take to council right away, but some don't, particularly when the children are young. You have to commit to regular sessions for at least a month or two, before you can tell whether it's going to work. Council can come together unexpectedly the moment something authentic happens that engages the children. They usually get past the resistance when they see that council can serve their own interests, not just yours. Be creative in choosing the themes, ask John to actively support you—and keep trying. They're testing your devotion to the idea of open communication in the family."

Establishing the setting. Maintain the integrity of council by avoiding interruptions. Turn off the telephone and ask those in the household not in attendance (somebody watching the baby, for example) to interrupt only in case of emergency. Consistency in this regard is important. When a family allows their councils to be easily interrupted, the focus diffuses and fewer risks are taken in speaking authentically.

Small children. It is hard to predict how young children will adjust to council. Some three- and four-year-olds do fine; some six- and seven-year-olds don't. Generally, five seems to be a good age at which to initiate council with children—with appropriately chosen themes, of course. Parents with infants-in-arms are usually fine, if the parents can stay focused and agree to leave the circle should their babies become a major distraction. In some families young children (say, three to five years old) are told they can leave the circle before council is over if they get restless.

Meeting with part of the family. Holding councils with portions of the family from time to time can be very productive. For example: father and the boys, mother and the girls, the parents and one child, or the teenagers alone (or with one parent). These sessions offer the opportunity to deal with such topics as sexuality, drugs, and dating behavior in a way that might not be possible in the full family setting.

On the other hand, some of the most gratifying moments in family council come from watching younger children learn from their older brothers or sisters. For example, if a ten-year-old girl feels safe in the circle, she can ask questions about adolescent issues and be given appropriate explanations by her older siblings as well as her parents. In the long run, each family needs to find their own way to expose younger children to sensitive topics without overwhelming them.

NURTURING THE PRACTICE

Creating a cohesive family life is increasingly difficult in our culture. The pressures of economic adversity, cultural assimilation, single parenthood, and relentless stimulation from the mass media all combine to assault and challenge each member in one way or another. Many of us feel we lack the time, patience, and ability to create family practices that serve intentions similar to those of council. For example, how many parents think in terms of rites of passage for their children? Some Jewish families celebrate the bar- or bat-mitzvah when the children turn thirteen, and in the Catholic tradition the passage to adulthood is marked around twelve with a Confirmation ceremony. But many of us have grown up without celebrating this major transition— or any other, for that matter. In fact, important life passages occur at five when children first start regular school, at the onset of physiological puberty, when they start to date or learn to drive, and more subtle developmental milestones such as becoming more aware of the power of the "Imaginal World," which occurs with remarkable generality around seven. There are also passages in a child's moral development, about which many educators, whether they have read Kohlberg or not,

are very much aware.[1] These are no less life-altering than the more obvious milestones, since they mark the movement of largely self-involved
behavior to that which includes a greater sense of responsibility to
other people, embracing of moral values and awareness of society as a
whole. Families who establish a regular council practice are more likely
to help children celebrate these rites of passage. * (For more about this,
see Cahpter 13.)

Discovering the Family Story

Council can improve the quality of family life by illuminating the
story of how the family functions as a whole. This underlying *family
story* weaves together the individual stories of each family member and
shapes the ongoing dramas, conflicts, and joys of family life.

The principal forces that play a role in determining family stories
include:

- The parents' values and the sometimes radically different
  values of the children as they grow older.

- The (mostly unconscious) erotic patterns that strongly
  influence family relationships.

- What the children learn about marriage and intimate
  relationship by living with their parents.

- The way in which the children live out the denied or
  unconscious aspects of their parents' personalities.

- The ongoing negotiation for power and authority.

- The way family members experience their bodies.

---

[1] "Promoting Moral Growth: From Piaget to Kohlberg," Richard H. Hersh, Diana Pritchard
Paolitto, and Joseph Reimer, Longman, Inc. 1979. See also *Natural Learning Rhythms*, Josette
and Sambhava Luvmour, Celestial Arts, Berkeley, California.

- How family members "push each other's buttons" (the family's "emotional wiring").

- The different and possibly conflicting ways that family members create meaning out of experience. This could be called the "epistemological confusion" in the family.

Although this list may appear daunting, exploring the family story doesn't have to be a solemn and onerous task. Discoveries in council arise more from seeing the story directly in a state of heightened perception than from labored analysis of family dynamics. The process can have its playful moments too. However challenging, the journey is worth taking. The more we know about our family story, the more consciously we can reshape it to avoid the unproductive patterns of family life.

If a family perseveres in the practice of council, its story will eventually unfold before everyone's eyes. Typically, parents and children take up familiar roles during the first few councils. The family skeptic, the tease, the bored one, the shy one, the parent or child who wants more cooperation from others—all these "characters" automatically play their accustomed parts. During this phase, frequently occurring topics include clarifying family agreements, calls for less fighting among the children, and more joint family activities.

As useful as these early councils are, they have a predictable quality that is less than inspiring. Moments of spontaneity are rare. Being locked into our roles in the family story makes speaking from the heart and attentive listening more difficult. As long as everyone is immersed in the story, there is no one available to call the family's attention to habitual patterns. Without this witness, no one sees what is going on and there is little opportunity for change (since family members are the trees, it is hard for them to see the forest).

Council comes alive when someone takes the risk of stepping outside normal family roles and patterns. Sometimes the breakthrough requires the catalyst of a family crisis. Or a family member may be blessed with a spontaneous moment of courage, as in the story that opened this chapter. Supported by the intentions of council and her parents' per-severance, Bridget let go of enough fear to speak her truth. In that moment Bridget's feelings were strong enough to overcome the non-confrontational pattern in her relationship with her mother.

Once such breakthroughs of authenticity occur, the family's appe-tite is awakened and moments of heart-to-heart communication occur with greater frequency. Soon family council is off and running.

More than ten years ago I was counseling a high-powered, professional couple with two children: a thirteen-year-old boy, Terry, and a nine year-old-girl, Emilie. Maria and Dennis were both strong-willed and creative individuals, who loved each other deeply, communicated regularly—and still went through volatile periods when their marriage seemed to be coming apart. I used to hear from them primarily during these un-stable intervals, when our work together included family ses-sions and an occasional family council.

Terry and his mother were extremely close. At that time, he still saw Maria as perfect, which I remember feeling was unusual for a boy his age. Emilie was sharp as a whip, a little closer to her father than her mother, and definitely somewhat of a "loner." The family bonds were strong enough, but some-times the kids got lost in the powerful dynamics of their par-ents' relationship.

The family had been doing weekly councils for quite a while, when Dennis reached out for support. A week earlier, on Maria's return from a "visit with friends" in the Northwest, she confessed to Dennis that she had had a brief affair, while away from home, with someone they had both known for sev-eral years. The affair was over and, from Maria's point of view, did not threaten their relationship, but, as might be expected, Dennis didn't see the situation in the same way. Maria's trip had occurred after a difficult period in their relationship, dur-ing which some strong differences in values and child-raising philosophy had created a feeling of distance between them.

After several long nights of concentrated dialogue, after the kids had gone to sleep, Maria and Dennis had cleared some, but not all, of his painful feelings of betrayal. The atmosphere around the house had been tense and grim for days.

Dennis told me that he and Maria felt able to work it through on their own, but he was worried about the kids. His concern had developed after their most recent family council a few days earlier. He told me the story of the council in exquisitely painful detail. I can still remember the anguish in his voice many years later.

The family gathered in their screened-in porch in the late afternoon, sitting on the old green pillows as they had done so many times before. For a while, they watched the sunset in silence. The feeling of anticipation they usually enjoyed before family council was distinctly absent. It was Emilie's turn to lead the council—that is, open it and set a theme, if she could think of one that would serve the family. All of their previous councils had focused on improving the feeling of cooperation in the family, arriving at agreements about chores, settling the typical older-brother/younger-sister difficulties between Terry and Emilie, and deciding where to go camping during next summer's vacation.

Emilie unwrapped the blue cotton cloth and took out the old Mexican rattle their family used as a talking piece. She held it in front of her for a moment, took a deep breath, and began. "It's been miserable around here since Mom got back—and it wasn't so great before that either. I thought you were both mad at me or something. I actually wanted to go to school yesterday morning just to get out of the house. I couldn't figure it out for a while, but I've decided that something is going on with the two of you that doesn't have to do with Terry or me. So I want a status report on your relationship. I want to know what's going on." Then, she abruptly handed the rattle to Maria.

Caught completely off-guard, Maria stared at the rattle for a few moments, waiting for inspiration. Later she told Dennis she felt like a drowning person seeing her life pass before her. She was flooded with images of Terry and Emilie as babies, their first day in Kindergarten, and so on up to the present. She debated about how to respond to Emilie's challenge. How honest could she be? What was appropriate for Emilie and Terry to hear? Dennis told me that, despite being stunned by Emilie's challenge, he knew that her leap out of their usual council pattern signaled the end of an era. He looked at Maria with as much compassion as he could muster and silently communicated that it was okay with him if she wanted to speak openly.

"Dad and I have been struggling lately," Maria began. "We've hit some rocky places in our relationship, especially since I got back . . . I spent some time with Samuel, an old friend of ours, while I was gone . . . That has been difficult for Dad and me . . . " Emilie looked confused. Terry stared at Maria as if he had never seen her before. He couldn't restrain his frustration.

"What are you talking about!" he blurted out, completely forgetting council protocol. Dennis gave him a quick look and then let go. If ever there was a time to feel supported by the family circle, this was it. He hoped that they had sat in council often enough to honor the spirit of the practice, if not all the details of the form. Maria was looking at Terry with such terror that Dennis couldn't resist bailing her out. He reached for the rattle, which she surrendered with relief.

"What Mom—Maria—is trying to say (Dennis told me that it seemed very important not to refer to her as 'Mom' in that moment) is that she spent some intimate time with Samuel while she was gone last week." Dennis paused for breath. "And that has caused me a lot of pain, even though—"

"What do you mean by *intimate time?*" Terry would not be denied. "Stop beating around the bush!"

"I mean that they were intimate with each other, they—" Dennis started to answer, but Maria interrupted him by taking back the rattle.

"It's not right for you to be answering for me," she said to Dennis, finally meeting Terry eye-to-eye. Resignation joined fear in the expression on her face. She answered her son's question in a voice that was raspy, but a lot calmer than before. "I was sexual with Samuel on two occasions while I was gone. We didn't plan it; it just happened . . . and it won't happen again. Samuel and I both know that. What I did doesn't change how I feel about Dennis."

"How can you say that?" Terry shot back. Emilie put her finger to her lips and held out her hand for the rattle. Maria gave it to her reluctantly. Dennis told me he couldn't fathom what was going through Emilie's mind at that moment.

"How could you be with anyone but Dad?" was all she said before putting the gourd down in the center of their small circle. Instantaneously, Maria's eyes filled with tears. Emilie's innocence was like a sword. Dennis told me that the anguish in Maria's face completely melted his own anger and pain. Terry grabbed the gourd.

"How can having sex with Samuel not change how you feel about Dad—and how he feels about you?" Terry shouted, looking at Dennis for the first time. Dennis told me he felt something stir between them, an ancient identification that he had never felt on such a deep emotional level before.

"Because I had sex with Samuel and I make love with Dad—Dennis," Maria answered, reaching out and touching the gourd still in Terry's hand. "I'm fond of Samuel, but being intimate with him is not what our relationship is about. We both saw that clearly. What I did was wrong. It has caused Dennis and our relationship a lot of pain—and now I see that it has caused both of you pain too. I'm truly sorry, more sorry than I can express right now . . . Sometimes people have to learn the hard way by making mistakes."

Terry continued looking at Maria, still in a state of shock, but his disbelief was mixed now with a new kind of recognition. Maria told Dennis later that, at that moment, she could feel the deep bonding between them stretch and snap in a few places. Then, suddenly, Terry shifted his attention to Dennis. "Have you ever had sex with another woman since you and Mom—Maria—got married?" Terry asked. Dennis' heart sank. Too much was happening all at once. He wanted to be there for Terry, to catch him as he fell away from the closeness with Maria. But, by that time, Dennis knew he had to answer truthfully.

"Once, more than ten years ago, when we had been together only a year or two, I went away for a weekend with another woman. It was a time when Maria and I were unclear about our commitment to monogamy. After a few days I knew I was on the wrong track. I knew that I only wanted to be with Maria. We went through a lot after that, but it ultimately strengthened both of us—and our relationship. That's the only time I've been with another women sexually; I feel both of us are through acting out in that way."

Dennis told me he saw Maria literally wince at the words "acting out." Terry started shaking his head and groaning to himself quietly. His eyes were glistening with tears, but he held them back. Emilie reached for the gourd. "If you two separate, who would we live with?" she asked, looking at the gourd.

"First of all, there's not going to be any separation," Dennis responded immediately, upset that Emilie even had to ask such a question. "Maria and I are working this through and we're going to be all right. I'm sure of that now, although there were moments during this past week that shook my trust. We're okay. There won't be any separation."

"But what if there was?" Emilie insisted.

"Once, I had the thought that, if Maria and I ever separated, Terry might like to live with Maria and you with me," Dennis said. Dennis' words produced an immediate reaction that surprised both Maria and him. Terry stopped shaking his head and came back to life. Emilie picked up the gourd, sat up straight on her pillow, and spoke in a strong voice.

"I want to be with Terry always, whatever happens to the two of you. Terry and I don't separate—ever. If you two stop being together, we would both live with one or the other of you. Either way would be okay with me, as long as you don't split us up!" She put the gourd down in front of Terry and waited for confirmation from him. He nodded, cleared his throat, and picked up the gourd.

"Emilie is right. We have to stay together and take care of each other, no matter what happens." Maria told Dennis later that, at that moment, she felt a mixture of guilt, grief, and joy unlike any feeling she had ever experienced before. Dennis was blown away by Emilie's strength. Terry was blown away too. He smiled at Emilie in a way none of them had ever seen before.

Dennis said they were still integrating the council days later, which is why he wanted some guidance from me. He was concerned about Terry's instability and worried that Emilie was suppressing nine-year-old feelings behind her show of strength.

I told him I thought that he and Maria had handled the situation as well as they could under the circumstances. Having the support of council obviously had empowered Emilie and helped everyone to say what they had to say. I suggested he and Maria prepare for some instability and change, after which all four of them might harvest new strength as they let go of the old patterns of family life. Besides reassuring him, I offered to help the family through the crisis by sitting with the kids, either alone or in a family council.

Both children did indeed have some hard times for the better part of a year. Terry pulled away from both parents, particularly Maria, and Emilie became even more of a "loner." But the family continued their weekly councils and, with a little outside help, kept current with each other about their changing family story. After a while, Terry and his father began to enjoy a much stronger connection than before. He and Maria established a new relationship that was loving in a less attached and intense way. Emilie continued to have a problem feeling comfortable in groups, but by the time she turned eleven, she had made a few close friends with whom she felt completely at home. She also developed into quite an artist, turning out both stories and drawings that amazed her teachers and parents. Strangely, Terry and she haven't materialized the closeness they both declared during that council. However, Dennis and Maria have no doubt that each of their children would go to the other's rescue should there be a real need. Dennis and Maria are doing fine, stronger than ever, and as far as I know, not acting out beyond the boundaries of their relationship in the same way they used to do.

Courage in breaking out of old patterns and commitment to being honest with each other in council changed this family's story. Sometimes "circumstance" takes matters into its own hands to help a family see their deep patterns and build a foundation for a deeper level of intimacy. Dennis and Maria felt they had little choice but to respond to Emilie's demand for an explanation. However, we do not necessarily recommend that parents always take such large risks in being honest with young children. The matter requires thoughtful exploration and judgment by each family, taking into consideration the developmental level of the children and the parents' preferences in order to establish the degree of openness that is right. In any event, however slowly or rapidly the family story changes, council is invaluable in providing the crucible in which transformation can take place. When it does, the shift in the Interactive Field of the family circle can be striking, as it was with Dennis, Maria, and their children. Their experience vividly depicts the four stages that often emerge during the evolution of family council:

- Family members are more or less caught in the family story both consciously and unconsciously.

- One or more family members awaken to the story, become witness to it and the possibility of change is initiated.

- All the family members begin to *see* the family story.

- Authentic communication flowers in the family circle.

Breaking Family Patterns

In part, parents define their parental roles through a combination of imitating their own upbringing and trying to avoid the kind of parenting they received as children. Additional important influences include values and beliefs incorporated from extended family, religious training, friends, "experts," and the culture in general. Mothers and fathers become attached to their roles in proportion to the amount of personal power and identity parenting provides. When awareness of role attachment is limited—that is, when parents function more or less "on automatic"—they rarely share their authentic feelings with their children.

In the story told in the previous section, Emilie's confrontation forced both her parents to let go of their normal parental patterns and become painfully real to both the children. Such an awakening of authenticity is ultimately nourishing, as long as the family is willing to go through a possibly tumultuous and unstable transition openly with each other—by practicing council, for example. When parents are willing to stretch beyond their normal roles and share themselves authentically, a family environment is created that accepts the children's struggles, doubts, and fears as well. When children are deprived of honest personal input from parents, they eventually hold back expressing their own feelings within the family. Then, if they do not have others outside the family with whom to connect deeply, perhaps act them out indirectly instead.

The discipline of council can also shake up the power balance in a family. When Emilie held the talking piece, Dennis, Maria, and even Terry had to listen. When Terry asked a difficult question, his parents could not hide behind the protection of their familiar parental roles.

Since everyone has the same opportunity to bring insight to the circle, council helps to dissolve family hierarchies. Emilie was the one to break a family logjam. When children feel empowered to speak "their truth," they become more perceptive—of their parents' relationship, for example. Family council may reflect aspects of family life that the parents haven't even noticed! "I never realized before how much the kids understand about how our family works—and doesn't work!" is a comment I hear often from parents after they practice family council for a while.

Finding one's voice in a family may be difficult. Shyness, fear of being teased, intimidation by older siblings, and skepticism about whether parents really want to hear their honest feelings are common obstacles children encounter in speaking authentically. As always, the primary ally in overcoming these forces is a commitment to the four intentions of council. It may take ten or fifteen councils to develop a safe and authentic environment. The challenge is to persevere through strong and uninspired councils alike, until the fire is permanently lit.

One of the ways to increase authenticity is for parents to use family council to discuss philosophical differences in what they see as the right way to raise children. Of course, it is wise for parents to council alone first in order to get clear about such differences. Issues that arise frequently in families include:

- The parents' struggle between protecting their children and encouraging them to be independent. For example, in one familiar family pattern, the father tries to compensate for what he views as the mother's overprotectiveness.

- Differences in the way each parent disciplines the children (withholding privileges, withholding attention or love, sending them to their room, spanking, etc.). Inconsistent or erratic discipline can be a major hindrance to children's moral and behavioral development

- Parents' attempts to present a "united front" to their children regarding values and behavioral limits. A united front is a fine idea if it is authentic. If not, most kids will soon uncover the hidden disagreements and use them to their advantage. Generally, when parents own their differences and *discuss them openly in council,* more *authentically unified policies* can be reached and the children's attempts at manipulation diminish.

- Being honest about the dilemmas and difficulties—as well as the joys—of parenting. Do your kids appreciate what it takes to raise them? Probably not, particularly during their adolescent years. Many parents feel that sharing the very real doubts and pains of child-rearing would be a burden for the children and undercut parental authority. But most children, at least by the age of nine or ten, are likely to be responsive when parents share their human side rather than trying to maintain the posture of "having it all together."

Facing these embedded patterns can be daunting at times and families need all the help they can get—including that of our old ally, Coyote. When a family has the ability to look at themselves playfully and with humor, emotional patterns ease, the witness state is strengthened, and heightened perception becomes a more likely reality.

EMPOWERMENT OF CHILDREN

The intimacy of family council offers children a fertile environment for self-expression, growth, and development. Although the following benefits can be harvested from any council of children, they are more prevalent in family councils where the circle is small and the issues often deeply felt.

Increased attention span. Practicing the four intentions of council can have a profound effect on a child's ability to maintain focus for an extended period. In particular, devout listening strengthens the ear/brain auditory linkage.[2] In the intimacy of family council signs of wandering attention (frequent eye movements, body restlessness, and lack of emotional involvement) are readily apparent and can be given immediate attention.

Learning to work with shyness. Council helps children face resistance to revealing themselves. When the circle is large, it is easier to "hide," since passing is always allowed in council. In a circle of four or five, however, the significance of each voice is greater and shy or resistant children are more likely to want to speak out, either because of the frequent invitation of other family members or by a compelling need to have their positions heard.

Learning to make and keep agreements. Invariably, a major focus of family council is the creation and maintenance of family agreements. Typically these involve chores, television viewing and/or video games, homework, maintaining good grades at school, communicating one's whereabouts when not at home, presence at meals and family events, and nonviolent ways to resolve conflicts among siblings and friends. The ability to make and renegotiate agreements when they are not working is a life-skill of immeasurable value. Council stimulates a co-creative path to agreements, rather than the authoritarian approach in which the children have little influence. As many parents have discovered, children are more likely to honor agreements when they have had a hand in their creation.

---

[2] See *The Conscious Ear: My Life of Transformation Through Listening*, Alfred A. Tomatis, Station Hill Press, 1991, and also Appendix I.

Conflict resolution. The process of resolving conflicts among siblings consumes a lot of attention in most families. Without support, children often feel frustrated trying to resolve disputes on their own. The simple form of council (or the fishbowl, for larger families) provides a way to air and resolve conflicts with the support and guidance of everyone.

Seeing parents more realistically. The practice of family council helps children get to know their parents beyond the identities as mother and father. Experiencing Mom and Dad as fallible human beings dispels idealized images and frees everyone. Recognizing their parents' human needs stimulates compassion and understanding in children; a greater sense of self-worth follows. In addition, seeing their parents more realistically gives older children useful information about what it takes to raise a family.

Acknowledging a larger context. Generally speaking, our culture and educational system encourage children to see their lives from an individualistic and secular point of view. Added to this cultural environment, the demands of ego development during the early years leave children few opportunities to become aware of "something larger" than the personal self. Exploring the subtleties of community life or being challenged to see the world from an interdependent perspective are rare experiences for many children. Family council is an excellent way to remedy this deficiency, since it provides a direct and intimate experience of family as community and, through the "voice of council," greater awareness of something beyond the secular world.

EMPOWERMENT OF PARENTS

A while back, a small group of parents asked me to introduce them to the basics of family council. After a daylong training session, they each initiated the process in their respective families. The following are excerpts from a council we convened six months later, for the purpose of comparing notes and evaluating progress.

Marion: Last week in our council I told John and the kids I felt like a short-order cook in a fast-food restaurant. We hardly ever eat a leisurely meal together. I had to say it a couple of times, but they heard me—finally. The discussion that followed has to be classified as a minor miracle. Jody was willing to commit to two dinners a week that would last at least an hour each. Her response inspired John. While she was talking, he stared at me as if my feelings were a complete surprise to him. Maybe I haven't expressed myself as clearly to him when we're alone as I did in that council. Mickey had the most trouble with the whole issue, but he finally agreed to Jody's plan and even offered to help with the cooking. I don't know what will come of our agreement, but it's a start. Whatever happens, I was glad to get the whole issue on the table.

    Bruce: My kids have been asking me to spend more time with them for years. I've always taken the position that my primary job was to provide for their mother and them, which didn't leave much time for anything else. Last week in council they really got mad and called me an "absent father." I called them "spoiled brats" in return and accused them of mouthing phrases they didn't understand. But this time they didn't back off. Mary supported them too, which made me really angry. Finally, as the stick went around for the fourth time, I heard what they were saying in a different way. I realized they actually missed me and wanted to be with me! I had always thought they saw me as a means of getting what they wanted. I've heard the words all these years, but I didn't let the feelings in until that moment. The whole council blew my mind.

    Nick: Our first few councils were awful. The kids squirmed like a bunch of worms. Austin yawned a hundred times each round. Madeline and I said we wanted our family to feel more like a community, with everyone supporting each other. Austin and Nicky glazed over whenever we talked like that. During the fourth or fifth council, I was about ready to throw in the towel when out of the blue Sam asked me, "Do you still have sex with Mom?" Madeline's face changed color. Sam's nine now and watches us like a hawk. When he gave me the stick, I told him, yes we do. "But we call it making love," I said. "Having sex doesn't do justice to what happens between us. We don't make love as often as we used to before you and Nicky were born, but it's deeper now."

I couldn't believe I was talking to Sam like that. The words just came out. Then I asked him what prompted the question. When he got the stick again he said, "You and Mom don't seem into each other like you used to be, so I just wanted to check it out." Madeline and I knew immediately he was on to something. We hadn't been very affectionate with each other lately, particularly in front of the kids. Our lives have gotten too busy. What really amazed us was how closely the kids watch our relationship. I always thought they were too absorbed in their own lives to notice what was going on with us.

Cynthia: Joe and I argue a lot about whether I overprotect the kids. He's always on my case about letting them make their own mistakes, earn their own money, and "heal their own wounds," as he says. You'd think they were in their thirties rather than fifteen and seventeen! During our regular council a few weeks ago, he was so hard on Seth I had to come to the rescue. I couldn't help it. But Seth had a big reaction to my stepping in. He told me he could handle his battle with his father by himself. I told Seth my response was instinctive and I knew he could take care of himself. "I don't believe you," he said when he got the stick again. "You act like I'm still twelve. I'm going to be driving in six months, you know."

"Driving has nothing to do with it," I told him. "There are a lot of men who drive who still haven't grown up. What's the rush? You'll be on your own soon enough." Mark got into it too. He's more tolerant than Seth of my need to protect them, probably because he's two years older. The council went on for over an hour. We didn't resolve anything, but during the next few days I found myself letting go a little. If only Joe would stop being so fierce, I could probably control my protective instincts.

Exchanging council stories helped these parents view their particular family dynamics within a broader context. It was reassuring for them to hear that they were not the only family struggling on the path to improved communication and greater mutual support. The teachings they received are familiar to those who regularly practice family council: learning to see other family members in a new light, the power of attentive listening to inspire productive family activities and deepen family ties, the importance of persevering with the practice until awakened by authenticity, and the power of honest communication to change family patterns.

FAMILY CEREMONIES

Council provides a context for intimate family communication on birthdays, anniversaries, holidays, and other family occasions. Coming together in a large circle transforms a family party into a "gathering of the clan," in which each voice has a chance to be heard and opportunities abound for authentic interaction. The council can be scheduled an hour or two before the meal is served or the rest of the celebration is to take place, so those who want to sit in the circle can do so by coming early.

Birthdays

Bailey tried to pay attention as his children spoke one by one. He had felt under the weather for a few weeks and less than enthusiastic about his wife April's idea for a birthday council before the party for him that evening.

"I give you the gift of having time to play softball every Saturday like you used to." [David was ten.]

"I give you the gift of not having to scold us because we're bratty." *[Josie was eight.]*

"I give you the gift of not asking for so many new clothes and tapes, so you don't have to worry about money." *[Jessica was twelve, going on thirty.]*

"Daddy, I want you to smile. I give you lots of smiles!" *[Becky had just turned four.]*

April's eyes began to glisten. For a while, she had a hard time speaking. "I give you the gift of gratitude for all that you bring to me and the children. I worry about how hard you're working. Maybe we need to make some changes in the way we live. I'm afraid the stress is affecting your health . . . I love you."

Josie wanted to give more gifts. She had council all year at school and birthdays were her favorite. "I give you the gift of not having to yell at me to clean up my room—more than once anyway," she said, taking the talking stick from her mother.

David couldn't help interrupting: "I bet you forget that gift by tomorrow."

"We're in council," April reminded him.

"Okay, okay. But we've all given our gifts. Billie's waiting for me to play."

"Oh, David," Josie groaned. "Daddy hasn't spoken yet. Give him a chance."

Bailey slowly picked up the "snake stick" he had carved on a camping trip two years before. The knot in his stomach felt better, but his head still pounded like a drum. "Thank you all for your gifts," he began. "I can remember when fifty seemed positively ancient, but here I am. David, I wish I could play ball again, but I've been working most Saturdays and my knees aren't what they used to be anyway. Josie, your gifts are great. I don't like to scold you about your room. Jessica, I love your gift. It's hard for me to say no to you, so your restraint will really help. Becky, just looking at you used to be enough to make me smile. I don't know what's happened this year.

Maybe I've forgotten how to smile. April, I don't know how you keep it all together. It's a miracle . . . But I've said enough! I don't want to cry on my birthday."

April took the stick from Bailey and wrapped it in the red and white cloth. It was Josie's turn to blow out the candle. The family held hands. David tried to scratch his nose against Jessica's shoulder. She shrugged him off and closed her eyes again. There was a moment of quiet before David exploded out of the circle.

Special Events

For several years now, Jaquelyn and I have called an extended family council (thirty-five or forty strong) on Christmas Eve and around the Summer Solstice. We started this practice with a little trepidation, not to mention eyeball rolling and groans from a few family members. Now almost everyone makes it to the council. For some it is a highlight of our gathering.

Many years ago, Mary Anne Dorward (formally a council leader at Crossroads) and I were asked to facilitate council for the annual gathering of an extended family that still regularly honors its illustrious eight-generation history. More than a hundred children and adults attend this five-day event, which includes a meeting of the directors of the family company and community service committees the family has established. Instead of the two of us introducing council to such a large group, we suggested the family invite ten or twelve key individuals to undergo a weekend training several months before the large meeting, so that council leadership could be provided from within the family rather than relying on outside facilitators.

Conducting a training with some of the most active and influential members of the clan turned out to be an illuminating exploration of family dynamics on a grand scale. Several months later Mary Anne acted as consultant to the newly trained leaders for the councils and other ceremonies at the annual gathering. The warm reception given council by even previously skeptical members of the clan exceeded everyone's expectations.

Marriage

I have a very part-time career performing marriage ceremonies for members of our family and close friends. In the past few years, most of them have chosen to include council as an integral part of their ceremony. The council, which usually takes place just before the exchange of vows, gives everyone the opportunity to add their voice to the celebration. In one configuration we've used effectively, people leave their seats one by one, spontaneously building a circle that includes the wedding couple. I begin with a few words about council and then the talking piece is passed from the previous speaker to the one just arriving in the circle. The interweaving of intimate stories, poems, and songs is always a strong part of the ceremony.

Wedding councils recall the spirit of traditional marriage rituals in many parts of the world. In the Judeo-Christian tradition, for example, the wedding is often -seen as a couple's initiation into the spiritual life of the community. The creation of a circle of family and friends around the wedding couple is a vivid reminder of this tradition.

A long time ago Gigi dreamed of a wedding council that would be led by a man and woman who fill the roles of high priest and priestess: This pair sit in the place of the North, while three other couples who have played an important role in the new couple's life take positions in the South, East, and West. Prayers and blessings are invited from each of the Four Directions, after which the voices of elders and children are honored. Finally, any and all of the gathered are invited to make offerings of words, songs, and gestures, as the talking piece makes its rounds. The entire circle witnesses and empowers the marriage after the leaders have guided the couple through their vows. In 2004, at the age of 54, she co-created her very first marriage ceremony with her partner Win. The celebration lasted for three days, the highlight of which was a ceremony that resembled her dream in many ways!

The Blessing Way Ceremony

The familiar baby shower is a social and practical way to help expectant mothers prepare for a growing family. Through the sharing of food and gifts for the baby, the shower primarily addresses the material needs of the expectant family. In the "Blessing Way Ceremony," however, the primary emphasis is on sharing nonmaterial gifts with the mother.[3]

The ceremony, which has its roots in Native-American traditions, is usually conducted for a first-time mother-to-be as a celebration of her transition from maiden and wife to becoming a caretaker of the next generation. With pregnancy she begins to embody—literally—the archetype of the mother, and her femininity blossoms in new ways that are uniquely associated with motherhood. In the Blessing Way Ceremony her women friends and family come together to honor the importance of this transition. The ceremony can be conducted in the span of a few hours, a day, or even as a weekend retreat, depending on the time available and how intimately the women know each other.

The group calls upon the ancestral mothers and grandmothers, whose strength and courage during birth have inspired the feminine lineage throughout the world since the creation. Then personal mothers and grandmothers are honored as the caretakers of everyone's lives. The circle calls upon all the female ancestors who have preceded the expectant mother to support her in this new phase of her life.

The celebration also focuses on how the expectant mother's spiritual life can be transformed through birthing and raising her child. The women who have gathered share their own stories and wisdom about the physical, emotional, and spiritual gifts and challenges of motherhood. The expectant mother is encouraged to acknowledge her fears, as well as the unique capabilities she brings to her new life.

These themes are explored in council, using the form which best suits the size and inclinations of the group. Generally, just moving around the circle is suitable for storytelling and exploring the spiritu-

---

[3] We are grateful to Sharon Gonzales-Aion for providing the following description.

al implications of motherhood. Interaction and discussion can follow by putting the talking piece in the center. If the group is large, use of the spiral keeps the council from going on too long.

Besides council, the ceremony usually includes the sharing of food, during which the expectant mother is fed by her friends and family in preparation for her new role as nourisher. Many activities that women share universally can be included—for example, singing, chanting, and caring for the expectant mother by brushing her hair and massaging her neck, feet, or entire body. Sometimes the women make a garland of flowers for her hair and dress her in new clothes. In the traditional Native-American ceremony, the expectant mother's feet are bathed in a mixture of oil and precious blue cornmeal, as a special mark of honor.

A ritual yarn-tying can also be added to the celebration. In this activity the women tie themselves together with a ball of yarn. Then each woman cuts the piece that is around her and attaches it to her own ankle, wrist, or waist, where it remains until the baby is born. Each time a woman notices the yarn, she offers a prayer for the expectant mother and occasionally calls her to see how she is doing.

Before closing the celebration, everyone offers to help after the baby is born by doing laundry, bringing food, baby-sitting, or running errands. This practice extends the circle's support by providing the rest and care the new mother needs until her strength is regained.

Rites of Passage

Several months after completing their council training at the Ojai Foundation, a couple came to me with an intriguing proposal. They had a twelve-year-old son who had several close friends of the same age at their local school. The Jewish families that composed the group had decided to forgo the bar mitzvah rite of passage and create an entire year of "transition into manhood" for their sons.[4] The group

---

[4] Diane and Mike Sanson initiated this yearlong rite of passage; Diane continues to lead similar ceremonies for groups of young men and young women. She has prepared a manual describing her work, *Adolescent Rites of Passage: A Family's Guide for Mutual Growth*, which can be obtained by calling (310) 457-9917.

wanted to use council as an integral part of their ceremonies. Our discussions led to planning the following ambitious program.

- Monthly council for fathers and sons with themes to include:

  Becoming a man in our culture;
  Heroes and myths about masculinity;
  Relationships to father, mother, women, community, and earth.

- Occasional councils for fathers alone.

- Several mothers' councils to explore the changing relationships with their sons.

- A yearlong program for the boys to include:

  Learning new physical skills;
  Making a strong connection with the wilderness;
  Community service.

- Developing a final rite of passage ceremony.

- Keeping a journal and recording dreams.

Most of the boys took up new athletic skills (tennis, skiing, etc.) in satisfying the fourth of these challenges; one became a carpenter's apprentice. Two challenging backpacking trips were planned for fathers and sons. The boys made a commitment to learn more about local ecology through hands-on activities that the fathers facilitated. Each boy found an agency in the community that needed young volunteers (for example, reading to the elderly and visually-impaired, working on cleanup crews, tutoring younger students, and raising funds for local charities). Dreams and journal excerpts were shared regularly in council. The final coming-of-age ceremony included blessings from the fathers, mothers, family elders, and mentors that had been instructing the boys.

Not surprisingly, rites of passage do not always go smoothly. More than twenty-eight years ago, in the winter of her thirteenth year, my stepdaughter, Linda, entered Heart-light, the small experimental school where I first explored council with children. By early March, it had become clearer than ever before that her priorities had little to do with academics. Social life came first, her appearance a close second, and schoolwork a distant third. But her disinterest in school did not entirely explain the discomfort in our relationship during those few months.

A day before the March full moon, at a time when Jaquelyn happened to be out of town, the dinner table conversation turned to the full moon council and meditation taking place at our house on the following night. I found myself telling moon stories, particularly those in which our lunar companion is identified with the feminine. Topics of this sort rarely interested Linda but, when I mentioned that one reason for the identification arose from the moon and menstrual cycles both having twenty-eight days, I had her full attention.

The next morning at school Linda's teacher took me aside during a break. "I wonder if you know that Linda started her period for the first time two days ago," Naomi said in a quiet voice.

I let out a long breath. "So that's what's happening."

"What do you mean?"

"It's a long story, but lately I've been particularly aware of Linda's rush into womanhood. The way she dresses and behaves . . . I wish her interest in school was even half as developed as—"

"She's testing her power to get attention, particularly from men."

"I'll say! I hope the world is ready. After this last month or two, I'm not sure I am!"

"So I've noticed."

That afternoon after school, I had a wild idea and went to find Linda. As usual, she was checking out her appearance in the bathroom mirror. "I'm in here," she shouted when I knocked. I stood in the bathroom doorway. "How do I look?" she asked. "I'm fixing my hair in a new way."

Her hair seemed to have been arranged by an egg beater. "It looks a little wild," I offered gently and changed the subject. "I heard today that you just started your first period." She turned and stared at me. "I think that's terrific," I added a little awkwardly.

"Why should my period make any difference to you?" she asked, returning her gaze to the sacred reflector. "Actually, it's a drag to deal with. I wish it hadn't started until I was older."

"We're having our regular full moon meditation and council tonight and I wondered if you would like to join us and celebrate your entry into womanhood. It would be appropriate, as you know from our conversation yesterday about the moon."

"You mean, actually be there and tell people I started my period? No way!"

"A personal ceremony would be powerful."

"No way will I sit with a bunch of people I don't know and talk about my period! I already know what I need to know. If you want to talk about women and moons, go ahead. I don't need to be there."

"You know some of the people who come," I persisted. "If you participated in the ceremony—"

"Forget it!" she said and dismissed me with a toss of her head.

Less than a dozen people arrived at the house that evening for the meditation—remarkably, all of them women! We were drawn outside by the unseasonably warm weather. After the group had finished meditating, I began the council by telling the story of my encounter with Linda. The women's laughter started a flood of recollections of their own first periods, some painful and poignant, others tender and joyous. What a blessing it was to witness a moonlit circle of women celebrating my stepdaughter's rite of passage—even without her being there.

Later I sat on the edge of Linda's bed talking about the evening. "You actually mentioned my name!" she said in mock horror. "Yes, and I told them how we've been getting on each other's nerves too. I think that has to do with starting your period."

"You're weird, Jack. What does our fighting have to do with my period?"

"Maybe I've been afraid to acknowledge that our relationship will go through changes now that you're becoming a beautiful young woman . . . But tonight, whatever has been disturbing me shifted. Each of the women talked about their first periods. Some of the stories were funny, some sad. A few remembered feeling very alone. Each story was a gift for you even though you weren't there. We celebrated your passage— and mine too! By the time the talking stick got around the circle I was loving you a lot—in a different way."

Linda smiled her child smile. For a moment she seemed innocent again as I said good night and turned off the light.

Celebrating the End of a Life

We gathered slowly in Donna's living room. Friends and family had come from all over the country. Many I hadn't seen for years; others were strangers to me. In one way or another we all had experienced Donna's free spirit, humor, and courage. Now she was close to death from a prolonged battle with cancer, a struggle that had lasted many years longer than any physician had dreamed possible. Donna wanted to have a council before she died to be with her friends and family one more time. Celebrating her passage this way seemed entirely in keeping with Donna's life.

We were already seated in the circle when she entered the room leaning on the arm of a nurse. Her eyes shone with a touch of the old vitality. She took her place in the council, propped up with pillows in a soft chair to ease the pain. She told us why she wanted to have a council before she died. "While I can, I want to hear from each of you about our lives together, what we meant to each other, our ups and downs. This doesn't need to be sad or solemn, but I want it to be truthful." She went on to describe her feelings about pain and death, and how her spiritual life had flowered in the past few months. At the end she said, "I feel enormously grateful today for what so many people have given me throughout my life. Your presence in this circle is a great blessing."

A small wooden figure that Donna loved started making its way around the circle. Considering the circumstances, the level of authenticity astounded me. Some of the stories of early childhood, star-crossed romances, ribald adventures, common work projects, angry battles, and loving friendships brought tears or raucous laughter. Strand by strand, the web of Donna's life was honored in the circle. By the time the wooden figure had gone around, she could barely hold up her head. She thanked us all and was helped from the room.

Donna died two months later. A traditional religious service honored her final crossing.

9
COUNCIL
IN INTIMATE
RELATIONSHIP

The first time was early in the morning
Heart to heart, motionless
Breath dissolving boundaries, minds silent
Touched by something otherworldly
Called by two bodies surrendered to each other

Then a month later on a Sunday
Our eyes were making love when a door opened
We didn't know existed
And we entered a realm where spirits play
With Sufi's worshiping their Beloveds

Who is that witnessing us—
Mentor, shaman, priest, priestess?
Who joins our councils
Opening a path through the litter
Of a lifetime filled with love, hurt, and other surprises?

All this time a temple has been rising, stone by stone
A hidden grotto silent mysterious
A forest shrine beyond the din of personal desire
Sanctuaries from worldly sensibilities
Ordinary stones, divine mortar

—A Brief History of Our Third, JMZ

FANTASY "TRIALOGUE"

"Matt" and "Katherine" represent many of the couples with whom Jaquelyn and I have worked over the years. Adjusting for roles, personalities, and other minor details—and with a little stretch of the imagination—the following "trialogue" might have occurred in the life of any of these partnerships—or in ours, for that matter!

Matt: I still feel silly sitting with you on these pillows in front of candles and flowers. This is our fourth or fifth council. How many more times do we have to do this?

Katherine: Jack and Jaquelyn suggested we stay with it to find better ways to talk to each other.

Matt: I don't have any trouble talking to you when we can find the time. Talking isn't our problem. It's that we see everything so differently. I don't need a stick in order to talk to you.

Maybe not, but you need one in order to listen!

Matt: Did you just hear something?

Katherine: Yes, distinctly.

Matt: We must be going crazy.

On the contrary. This is one of the sanest moments the two of you have ever enjoyed together.

Katherine: Who are you?

When the four intentions of council are practiced devotedly, the voice of the circle is heard . . . sooner or later. That's who I am.

Katherine: Maybe we're dreaming.

Not in the ordinary sense. But call me a dream if you like. I'm here to help you understand why sitting in council with each other is different than having a conversation.

Matt: Exactly my question. Why can't we just talk?

As I suggested already, because you don't listen to each other very well, even if the phones are quiet and the kids are asleep. Most of the time, talking doesn't move your relationship along.

Katherine: I had that exact thought the other day.

I know. That's one reason I'm here.

Matt: I hear everything Katherine says to me—well, almost everything. What makes you think we don't listen?

You start reacting to Katherine before the words are barely out of her mouth. Before she's finished, you've already prepared your response. She does the same. You're both predictable when you get into your disagreements. You start talking faster and louder, because you're afraid the other is about to interrupt— a justifiable fear, I'm sad to say. Frankly, compared to what's possible, the quality of your listening is mediocre.

Matt: I can usually tell what Katherine is going to say.

Katherine: Thanks a lot! You don't surprise the hell out of me either.

Patterned communication is rarely informative. That must get discouraging at times.

Katherine: Depressing, actually. I end up feeling alone sometimes, right in the middle of talking to Matt.

Matt: You never told me that. Why haven't you said something?

Katherine: I don't know. Maybe because I'm afraid you still wouldn't hear me and then I'd feel even more alone . . . How do we break the pattern?

Continue these councils and practice the four intentions diligently, particularly the one about listening from the heart.

Matt: It still seems ridiculous with only two of us here.

I beg your pardon. Am I chopped liver?

Matt: Sorry. I'm used to counting bodies, not phantoms. But I'm glad to see you have a sense of humor, whoever you are!

I get that from you. It's one of your more delightful attributes.

Matt: Come clean. Who are you—really?

First of all, I'm not a phantom. In fact, I'm a combination of your subtle bodies, which are quite real, even if you're unaware of them. Each of you is made of energy, only a portion of which manifests in solid form. The non-solid part of your being—your subtle body—is just as important.

Matt: This is beginning to sound like a physics class.

Yes, the physics of relationship. The subtle body can—

Matt: Spare me!
Katherine: Stop interrupting, Matt.

Thank you. As I was saying, I'm a combination of your subtle bodies, which you've actually sensed in quiet, attentive moments while holding each other at night or making love gently. Until you learn to pay attention, I'm a little indistinct.

Katherine: What is it like to be a combination of our subtle bodies?

At times, tense or tumultuous. But your subtle bodies can be full of sweetness and fire too.

Katherine: When we're making love, probably.

Matt: I've forgotten what that's like, it's been so long! You've been putting me off for weeks.

Katherine: Six days to be exact. We've been busy and I've had—

Matt: Yeah, I know, headaches.

There you go interrupting again.

Matt: I knew what she was going to say.

Perhaps to the end of that particular sentence. But if Katherine knew you wouldn't speak until she finished, you can never tell what she might have said next. Now it's too late. That's why I've come to support you doing council together at least once a week.

Matt: Once a week! We don't have the time.

I suggest you adjust your priorities and make the time. Council not only offers support for much needed improvement in your communication, but it also could provide something else this relationship needs right now.

Katherine: What's that?

Connection with spirit.
Matt: Heaven help us. We're getting religious!

I didn't say anything about religion. Listen more carefully. I said council can be a doorway for spirit to enter your relationship. Let me explain.

When two people are in a mature, erotically awakened partnership–and believe it or not, the two of you are–the interweaving of their subtle bodies becomes a lightning rod for Spirit. When you sit in council, I can give voice to this manifestation of Spirit. I embody and represent it. I can help you see what's best for the relationship, including how it serves others in the world.

My existence may seem strange to you, but it is familiar to many spiritual traditions. For example, councils of two are similar to what the Quakers call the "Third Way." When resolving conflict through dialogue, a Quaker says: "There is the truth you bring, and the truth I bring, and when we listen devoutly, we may hear the truth of the Third Way as well."

I am the Third Way in your partnership. I bring Third Presence. You can call me "Third" for short.

Katherine: Why do we need a Third to represent our relationship?

Because it's so difficult for the two of you to surrender most of the time. You judge each other as too imperfect to feel safe doing that. Yet relationship continuously requires greater surrender to "Other," if spirit is to enter and love to deepen. I represent Other in the relationship, the ineffable presence to which you both can surrender. I am particularly noticeable when you are being insightful or creative together, or at those sublime moments of lovemaking when the two of you become one.

Katherine: Are you just with us? . . . I'm not quite sure how to say this . . . Do you visit other relationships too?

I uniquely represent your–our–relationship, as other Thirds represent theirs. All Thirds "know" and support each other. We are always available to our relationships, but until called consciously, we can be elusive. We appear unpredictably, not only in moments of passion and co-creativity, but also at times of crisis and grief. I am here now to encourage your practice of council. I've attended all your previous sessions without your awareness, until today.

Matt: How have we been doing?

Pretty well, but I have a few suggestions that will improve your practice.

Make a commitment to hold council weekly. Call special sessions in-between times when issues arise that need immediate attention.

Take the time to create sacred space in preparing for council. Aligning yourselves with your surroundings calls me in. Creating sacred space supports the intention to communicate attentively and honestly.

Include a third pillow for me. The seat may look empty to you, but its presence will remind you that your relationship extends beyond just the two of you. You already know your children are a manifestation of your relationship. So am I.

When you start your council, bring your attention to the third pillow for a moment. Welcome me, invite me in, ask for my insights. When the going gets rough, I may be able to offer a different perspective. Or I might enter on a more challenging note to reflect your indulgence, self-preoccupation, or poor listening.

If you get stuck in your council, stop for a moment, move into silence and look at the third pillow. Imagine me. Put your talking piece on my pillow and meditate on Third Presence. As you get to know me better, that will be easier to do.

After listening for a while, compare notes on what you've heard. Each of you may pick up a slightly different message. That's all right. But, if you're listening attentively, the core of what you hear will be the same. If not, go back into silence and try again.

Once you become used to connecting with me in council, you'll be surprised how often I appear at other times of need or celebration.

At the end of the council, thank each other for sitting together and thank me as well. I thrive on recognition!

Matt: I don't mean to be disrespectful, but what are your credentials? How do you know what to teach us? Who guides you? We're supposed to surrender to you and serve you. Who do you serve?

I serve the two of you, as do the many Thirds that move in and out of the subtle realm we call the "Imaginal World."[1] As a group, we have our own

---

[1] See Creative Imagination in the Sufism of Ibn 'Arabi, Henry Corbin, Bollingen Series XCL, Princeton University Press, 1969.

spirit source, which you can think of as the "Divine Lovers." They are sublime spirit partners, unfamiliar to most humans. Although they have existed since the beginning, they will be making themselves known to more and more people in the near future, because the world desperately needs them. You might say the Thirds are advanced scouts of the Divine Lovers, each assigned to a relationship in which the subtle bodies have become sufficiently expanded. We all serve the Divine Lovers.

> **Matt:** Sitting in council with Katherine will be more exciting now that I know you might show up. I suspect with you around anything can happen.

Including letting go of the old patterns that have frustrated you both. Now close your council for today, thank me and each other, and blow out the candle.

> **Katherine:** Thank you.

> **Matt:** Thank you.

THE NATURE OF THE THIRD

An anthropomorphic depiction of the Third does not do justice to the *experience* of entering Third Presence. In our ordinary daily lives most of us function as if we were separate beings of finite dimension, living inside the boundary of our skins. But in a maturing, erotically alive relationship, it is possible to become increasingly aware of your subtle body as it awakens and interacts with that of your partner. The two subtle bodies interpenetrate to create a joint energy field that is particularly perceptible during intimate moments, such as prolonged lovemaking or in council. With increasing awareness of this field, in which you feel immersed in something that extends beyond your physical body and includes your primary other, your illusion of separateness dissipates.

Soon you learn to distinguish your own and your partner's subtle body in the joint field. In especially heightened moments something else is present as well, something at first mysterious and evanescent, that brings you a feeling of great joy and peace. In a moment of grace, you realize you are in the presence of an informed spirit that holds the full, undistorted potential of your relationship. We have seen how every council has an Interactive Field. *In councils of two ("dyadic councils") the Interactive Field is called, "Third Presence."*

The Third is not a dream, although it can also appear in the dreamworlds of both partners. The couple is unmistakably awake and in a joint state of heightened perception when entering Third Presence. Eventually a couple can evoke the Third through various practices of meditation, immersion in nature, dream sharing, conscious sexuality, and dyadic council.

But what of the "something else" that is felt in the Third's presence? With heightened perception, the partners sense this ineffable quality as extending beyond, and being "greater" than, their subtle bodies. Eventually, in a moment of exceptional relaxation and intimacy, they perceive a movement of energy that seems to arise from an even more refined, interior realm of being.

These finer emanations begin to create images of a dual-entity spirit in the Imaginal World. Jaquelyn and I have come to call the source of these images the *Divine Lovers*. Others speak of the "avatar couple."[2] We think of the Divine Lovers as embodying the collective ideal of relationship beyond the limitations of human thought. The Third is the partners' personal link to the Divine Lovers, guiding them into a spacious loving that fulfills the unique potential of their relationship.

---

[2]*The Time Falling Bodies Take to Light: Mythology, Sexuality and the Origins of Culture*, William Irwin Thompson, St. Martin's Press, Inc. 1981.

THE PRACTICE OF DYADIC COUNCIL

Since Katherine and Matt's Third has already provided us with the essentials of dyadic council, we need only add a few suggestions.

Inviting the Third. We call the council for two described in the trialogue the "Third Pillow Ceremony." Just the sight of the empty seat can transform the dynamics of the council. When the Third's turn comes around, the talking stick can be placed in front of the "empty" pillow and a few moments of silence observed. In the quiet of Third Presence, one or both partners may have insights that will refocus the Interactive Field in a productive way. Alternatively, when it is his or her turn, either partner has the option of moving to the empty pillow, if they hear the Third's message clearly. The other partner, of course, has the option of commenting on the stand-in's authenticity. With time, this practice enables each partner to distinguish a statement by the Third that has the "ring of truth" from one distorted by the conveyer's own agenda. With practice, distortion in the Third's guidance diminishes and the couple feels more and more at home in Third Presence.

Thematic material. Although councils of two can be left open thematically, it is sometimes useful to focus on a particular aspect of the relationship: sexuality, ways of expressing affection, competitiveness, conflicts in parenting, finances, and so on. In addition, dyadic councils can have broadly focused intentions, such as:

- Exploring shadows, in which each partner reveals something that bothers them about the other.

- Affirming the relationship, in which partners describe what they appreciate about the other and the relationship.

Special dyadic councils. There are occasions when dyadic council can serve a specific function. For example:

- *Clearing.* Calling a preparatory council before lovemaking is a good way to acknowledge and perhaps ease unresolved issues that might get in the way of sexual intimacy.

- *Visioning.* When decisions are pending as well as times of transition, it can be extremely helpful for partners to explore their fantasies, dreams, hopes, and plans for the future of the relationship in a visioning council.

- *Dreamsharing.* The container that dyadic council provides gives assurance that dreams can be explored without running out of time or being interrupted prematurely with associations and reactions from one's partner. And, as always, the Third is more likely to come forward with its special insights in the council environment. Many couples who enjoy dreamsharing choose to do so on a daily basis, by waking up a little early in the morning to tell each other their dreams of the night before—in the spirit, if not the form, of council. Reflecting on the dreams themselves is not the only purpose of dreamsharing. Partners can use the practice as a way to enter dreamtime together and, in this expanded state of awareness, explore their lives with greater clarity.

Witnessing. Sometimes it is helpful for a couple to invite a third person to join their council as a witness. This invitation can be motivated by the need for resolving conflict or simply to review the relationship's status. The witness can function in a number of ways, one of which should be agreed upon before the council starts.

- *Normal witnessing.* The witness listens until the couple finishes and then comments on the nature of the communication and the quality of listening.

- *Witnessing twice.* The witness offers reflections earlier in the process, after each of the partners has spoken two or three times. These comments can be utilized to focus subsequent rounds of the council. The witness also speaks after the final round, as usual.

- *Expanded Witnessing.* In this model, the witness is silent for a few rounds and then has the option of speaking in turn for the remainder of the council. This format enhances the role of the witness as a stand-in for the couple's Third. To fill this role effectively, the witness needs to avoid identifying with either partner and be skilled at entering the state of heightened perception. If either partner feels the witness' comments are not clear, he or she can say so, and the witness can check for distortion and return to normal witnessing when that seems advisable.

- *Multiple Witnessing.* A pair of witnesses can be invited, perhaps a man and a woman to provide gender balance. The pair can function in any of the three ways described above. Two people are desirable for expanded witnessing, since usually a fuller manifestation of the Third is achieved when a greater variety of perspectives are available.

THE CIRCLE OF LOVERS

The practice of dyadic council can be greatly enhanced when a group of couples is gathered with the intention of improving communication, expanding their erotic life, and entering Third Presence. This "Circle of Lovers" practice is a variation of the expanded witnessing form of dyadic council.

One of the couples takes their place in the center of the circle formed by the others. The two partners face each other and a third seat is set between them, slightly to one side, as in the Third Pillow Ceremony. The couple begins their trialogue with whatever issues are current for them, while the rest of the circle sets the intention to witness the couple's Interactive Field.

As the couple's interaction develops, anyone in the outer circle who feels so called can take the third pillow, wait for an appropriate pause in the interaction, and then allow the voice of the couple's Third to speak through them. Comments from the third pillow can be witness reflections, insights, or other statements that might help the partners see themselves more clearly. Identifying and labeling behavior or giving specific advice (as in conventional therapy) are less appropriate in this practice. In speaking for the couple's Third, brevity is important, and a detached, lighthearted touch often the most effective. On the other hand, Thirds have been known to become confronting when the partners' self-involvement calls for stronger measures. After making a statement, the stand-in for the Third returns to the witness circle and the process continues. When the couple feels finished, they leave the center and the entire group witnesses the process.

This practice can be surprisingly powerful when the circle has been together for a while, either during a several-day relationship intensive (such as the ones Jaquelyn and I have facilitated regularly at the Ojai Foundation, in Hawaii, Israel and elsewhere), or when a group of couples meets periodically over a long period of time. In the state of heightened perception evoked by this practice, insight flows, defensiveness dissipates, and humor can be a powerful ally. Many strong moments in the Circle of Lovers come to mind . . .

Didi's experienced tongue took Kenny to task for each one of his failings. Kenny began by directly defending himself, which only whetted Didi's appetite. So he switched to pointing out her shortcomings—particularly her unpredictable moments of anger and withdrawal. Finally, clutching the talking piece, eyes blazing, she said, "And where is your sexual passion? I want someone who can match mine and take me where I want to go." Kenny slumped on his pillow as Jaquelyn took the Third's seat. The rest of us waited expectantly.

"The woman's knife is sharp," the Third began. "She is very angry, and her rage turns constructive criticism into a weapon of destruction . . . The difference between an ordinary woman and a Goddess is not that the Goddess is able to destroy her man—any strong woman can do that. The difference is that the Goddess uses her power to help the man grow. When a woman uses her fire with an open heart, she serves the Goddess and her man as well."

Didi looked at Jaquelyn and felt a presence beyond the actual woman she had known for years, beyond the confronting champion of women who challenges patriarchal qualities in men, beyond the caller of women to own their power as initiators. Didi *saw* the Third of her relationship for the first time. She lowered her eyes and fell silent. Jaquelyn left the pillow and returned to her seat in the larger circle. Kenny and Didi continued their interaction surprisingly free of the adversarial and defensive qualities that had dominated it before.

A few months later, Kenny told Jaquelyn that her challenge to Didi had touched something deep in their relationship. "Thanks to you, we're doing much better," he said. Recapturing the power of that transformative moment in the group eluded Jaquelyn. After all, she wasn't the one sitting on the third pillow inside the Circle of Lovers . . .

Tim and Mary were about to move to a different state and start a community on a large piece of land they had just purchased. Witnessed by the circle, they debated how to spend the first year in their new home. Mary was concerned that Tim would continue living in his hyperactive "executive mode," leaving her struggling alone in his wake to contemplate the heartful core of their vision. Tim kept talking about guiding the community together with Mary, but clearly he was in a "Lone Ranger, full-steam-ahead" mode, designing structures, selecting teachers and planning retreats. The dialogue was heating up, when I took the Third's seat.

"The man and the woman say they want to build a community *together* that utilizes all their talents. If that is to happen, primary attention has to be given to their relationship. The community vision will grow out of the partnership. The man's challenge is to break old patterns and let my presence inspire his actions. I can help the woman break old patterns too, such as giving her man the role of primary articulator and manifestor. She needs to call him into the mystery of their relationship, so that a joint vision of the community can be seeded. Then, in due time, we three can give birth together."

There were tears in Mary's eyes before the Third's stand-in stopped speaking. Tim looked as if he had been hit by a truck. They both fell silent for a while. Then Tim picked up the talking piece slowly. "I get it," was all he said. I slipped away from the Third's pillow, feeling a little awed by the shift that had taken place in their Interactive Field. Mary and Tim continued their dialogue, agreeing to spend a lot of time together in their new home before beginning to create community. Later, the Third spoke again, through the voice of another stand-in, cautioning the couple that old patterns may not be that easy to break . . .

Patrick and Millie had been in an unproductive dialogue for almost fifteen minutes, during which the Third's pillow remained empty. Millie seemed to be "dying on the vine" for lack of attention from her partner. She talked on, words tumbling out of her vulnerability, and clearly feeling a little embarrassed about exposing her loneliness. Patrick responded briefly and without emotion. The rest of us grew restless, as we searched for a doorway through which their Third could enter. Finally, Robbie, the youngest of the men in the circle, filled the empty pillow. In an almost offhand, lighthearted way he said, "I wonder if the woman would be willing to look at the man without speaking for a few minutes. Perhaps then she would see him with new eyes."

As Robbie returned to his seat, Millie put the talking piece down in front of her and stopped talking. From where she sat (and several others of us as well), Patrick's head was silhouetted against the bright sunlight streaming in through the windows. Millie stared at Patrick for several minutes, squinting to make out his features in the glare of the light. Several of us did the same. Time seemed to stand still. Our restlessness dropped away. Millie finally broke the silence.

"You have a glow around you that extends way beyond the glare of the light. I see an old soul, a mystic, perhaps a monk from an earlier time. He has moved beyond words, finding them inadequate to describe what he has learned during his long life journey." (We found out later that some of us shared many of the details of Millie's experience.) "You are a beautiful old soul, a teacher, a wise and silent teacher, from whom I have much to learn. I have never seen that part of you before."

Patrick smiled but didn't respond. Millie spoke briefly one more time before they both left their place in the center of the circle. "A part of my heart has been closed to you all these years, because I haven't recognized who you are. I'm grateful to our Third for helping me to *see*. I hope this experience doesn't slip away, as we pick up the threads of our regular life together." A chorus of *Ho's* echoed Millie's prayer . . .

Sheila and Lindsay brought their long-standing debate about having a child into the circle. He was eager to be a father; at forty and in marginal health, she was ambivalent. The dialogue soon became an elaboration of how little their needs were being met in the relationship. Their Third—disguised as Jaquelyn—finally came to the rescue. "There are already two children here who need a lot of caring before another child can be considered" was all she said. Sheila and Lindsay's laughter shifted the level of their dialogue entirely. Although it took several more months, they finally resolved the issue.

By witnessing the process and standing-in for another couple's Third, each member of the circle develops the ability to enter Third Presence in his or her own relationship. The couple in the center receives helpful reflection to the degree that their witnesses are able to see the couple's Interactive Field. We often experience that stand-in's for the Third learn as much, if not more, than the couple in the center. The impact from a brief statement from one of these witnesses is often heightened by both the intention of the Circle of Lovers Practice to deepen relationship and the energetic support of the Interactive Field formed by all the couples present. Sometimes, when the magic is particularly strong, one can sense all the Thirds in a spirit ring around the circle.[3]

---

[3] A greatly expanded description of relationship practices that support the exploration of Third Consciousness can be found in, *Flesh and Spirit: The Mystery of Intimate Relationship*, by Jack Zimmerman and Jaquelyn McCandless, Bramble Books, 1998

10

COUNCILS IN COMMUNITY AND BUSINESS

We are the dance of the moon and sun
We are the light that's in everyone
We are the hope that's deep inside
We are the turning of the tide

—Chant attributed to Starhawk

THE WIND RIVER COMMUNITY

From the very first exploratory contact, many years ago, Jaquelyn and I were intrigued with the prospect of introducing council at Wind River. The core of this community consisted then of about forty staff, teachers and board members most of whom lived close to the community's land and meeting facilities in rural Washington. This group, plus several hundred more individuals who participated regularly in community activities, shared a common spiritual tradition and meditation practice. The teachers associated with Wind River still regularly bring this practice to meditation students from all over the country and abroad as well.

Having conducted residential meditation retreats for more than a decade at other centers, the community was ready to develop their own sanctuary and residential retreat facilities. Within a year or two many of the staff, and perhaps a few teachers, would be living on the rolling hills and shallow canyons that ran along the river of their seven-hundred-acre homeland. Some structures had already been built and the community had already launched a major capital fund drive that would complete the building program. On the personal level, several teachers and members of the staff and board were in the process of transforming their relationship with the charismatic woman who had been instrumental in starting the community, shaping the vision, and training many of the key people.

We were invited to bring the practice of council to Wind River at this important juncture in their development. Many community members wanted to improve communication among staff, teachers, and board members. They wanted to learn a form of group dialogue that was consistent with their tradition and spiritual practices. Council seemed a likely candidate.

We accepted the invitation, recognizing we had to avoid identifying with the many challenges Wind River faced which, at the time, were similar to those confronting our own community at the Ojai Foundation. The planning group for the weekend made it clear that they had a lot of business to conduct and issues to explore. Council was seen as a means to deal with these matters, not as an end in itself. Our challenge was to focus our teaching and facilitating skills on supporting their intentions. A touch of anxiety about my ability to serve a community of mature individuals with a well-developed spiritual practice and strong leadership was eased by knowing I would be working with Jaquelyn.

Their board, teachers, and staff had never before assembled all together for a weekend. The full schedule of meditation retreats they conducted each year placed a heavy load on the community. The board had been meeting monthly to carry out the implementation of their comprehensive vision, raise the necessary funds, and support staff and teachers. Many community members felt overworked and wanted more time to enjoy each other's company. In addition to all the other objectives for the weekend, they also wanted to have a little fun!

Our job as facilitators began several months prior to the weekend. Working closely with a small committee comprised of staff, board, and teachers, we devised the following simple questionnaire to be completed by members of the community:

- What are the main challenges facing your community?

- What do you see as the major obstacles in the community to meeting these challenges?

- What do you see as your personal obstacles to meeting these challenges and feeling nourished by the community?

- What decisions would you like to see made during the weekend?

We evaluated the questionnaires from teachers, staff, and board separately in order to search for common responses within each segment of the community. We found several:

"I don't feel like I'm part of the teacher community. I live far away and have other affiliations and demands on my time." [*Teachers*]

"Sometimes I feel unappreciated, particularly by the teachers." [*Staff*]

"I'm unclear at times how we can best implement our vision. It would help if we had closer and more continuous contact with the teachers." *[Board]*

"We have to support the staff in doing their practice, both individually and together." *[Teachers and Board]*

"How do I learn to say no to teachers or board members when I'm overloaded or think their requests are unreasonable?" *[Staff]*

"We need to add people to the board who are knowledgeable about raising money." *[Board]*

We also discovered that a great many concerns were shared by individuals in all three groups (those familiar with intentional communities will not be surprised by these):

"We need a better way of communicating among teachers, board, and staff. Some members of each group don't understand how the other groups function."

"I have to learn to set boundaries, so I can avoid burnout."

"Are running a residential retreat center and living as a spiritual community compatible goals?"

"Asking for money feels inconsistent with my spiritual practices. I know it has to be done, but I hate to do it."

"Are we biting off more than we can chew?"

"I just hope we can proceed slowly and sanely."

And, finally, we synthesized a composite statement from many similar responses:

"Although I feel overwhelmed at times, I wouldn't want to be any place else or work with any other group. I feel close to most of the people and nourished by what I do, much of the time. The practices and teachings that guide the community comfort and support me in many ways."

Although only two people mentioned it directly on the question-naires, we realized from discussions with the planning committee that the central teacher's strong influence in the community was an important issue that significantly affected the empowerment of board, teachers, and staff. However, we were unsure whether the community was ready to explore this rocky terrain.

In addition to determining common responses from the questionnaires to use as themes for the various councils, we listened to several tapes of teachers' talks, read vision statements, and perused a few books authored by their founder. Thus armed, we arrived in the community on a Friday afternoon, wondering how we were going to deal with the many serious issues that needed attention—and have a little fun at the same time.

After dinner we introduced council with a few words about its historical roots, a description of the basic form, and a presentation of the four intentions. This was followed by an opening council with the theme: "Share your desires and concerns about the weekend. Be honest about expectations and apprehensions. Share any dreams you've had recently that relate to the community." To our delight, a staff member had made a beautiful talking stick by adorning a piece of spruce wood from the land with small objects that were connected to the community's spiritual tradition.

In deference to this tradition, we had decided to begin (and end) each council with several minutes of silent sitting rather than drumming (which wasn't integral to their practices). This allowed community members to enter the circle (and leave it) in silence through the familiar door of their meditation. For a change of pace we did drum twice during the weekend. As it turned out, a large number of community members had brought various percussion instruments to the retreat.

At the opening council, excitement about finally coming together as a whole group dominated much of the sharing, although a few of the busier members of the community admitted being unhappy about leaving their families and professional pursuits for several days. A few expressed the fear that not enough of substance would be accomplished to justify the weekend. Towards the end of the round, people began to share inspiring or humorous stories about recent community experiences. The atmosphere grew more joyous as the group celebrated being together and saw we were there to serve the community rather than do a "council shtick." (A community member actually used this phrase later on in the weekend—without intending the pun—when confessing his initial apprehension.) At the close of the evening, we announced that a dream circle would follow sitting practice the next morning.

Because of the size of the group and the full agenda, we chose the simple form of sharing dreams (spontaneously, out of the silence) that we call the "Dreamstar." (see Chapter 4) Many dreams and waking visions were spoken, some of which related directly to the community.

Following the dream circle, we moved into a series of three councils using the fishbowl. Teachers, board, and staff each took their turn in the center while the other two groups witnessed. Thus each segment of the community had a chance to work on its own issues in full view of the other two. Before each group started, we offered a few themes based on the questionnaire responses, but urged members of the inner circle to pursue any topic they wanted.

The staff enjoyed the rare opportunity of holding center stage, which they used to deal with many personal and programmatic issues. The teachers were delighted to be all together in one circle finally and gave eloquent personal acknowledgment to how the core teachings they all shared had transformed their lives. Two spoke at length of their personal connection to the central teacher, which led us to believe the issue of her relationship to the community might become part of the agenda later on. Board members talked about the challenges they were facing, celebrated how well they worked together, and appealed for more expressions of gratitude within the community.

After each group had its turn in the center, we went around the full circle to hear witness comments. Many expressed appreciation for being able to watch other segments of the community deal with their issues, and a few astute comments comparing the dynamics of the three groups were offered.

The three fishbowls were followed by a silent walk to the sites of the future residential retreat facilities. Strangely, no one had mentioned the land in their questionnaire responses, so we decided to facilitate their connection with *place* as part of the weekend. Following the walk, we plunged into our first in-depth exploration of a community-wide issue. Because of the size of the group, we decided to use the spiral format.

We chose *money* as the theme of the first spiral. Talking about fund-raising or the cost of implementing various aspects of the residential retreat plan would have been premature. But the questionnaires suggested that the community would profit from relating their spiritual vision to personal experiences about money. We have often found that choosing a personal theme that underlies the concrete agenda creates a foundation for productive discussion later on. That is exactly what happened in this situation. The spiral on money and spirituality helped to set the stage for a lively discussion about fund-raising the following day.

Saturday night had been billed as the playful part of the weekend, so we planned a surprise. After a little informal singing, we divided the community into four groups, mixing teachers, staff, and board members all together. Each group had half an hour to prepare a five-minute skit on the ups and downs of community life. A trunk full of costumes was made available. (We were at a board member's home for the evening.) It took a few minutes for several people to overcome their resistance ("I can't believe they're going to make us work tonight too!" we heard someone whisper). But as the groups prepared their offerings, the laughter began. All the skits involved takeoffs on the woes of teaching meditation in the New Age. Teachers and students were treated with equal irreverence. We rolled on the floor, laughing so hard that tears came.

We combined Sunday morning's dream circle with a "weather report" that revealed a mixture of trust and concern about the community's future. Several people touched on the central teacher's role, and by the time the talking piece had gone around, I saw that the circle was ready to take the plunge. So we set a spiral with "leadership and community empowerment" as the topic. Four people leapt to their feet to fill the empty pillows. Soon it became clear that the leader also needed to be in the center, so that people could talk to her directly without having to turn their heads. She accepted the invitation readily. We adjusted the spiral format to allow her to remain in the inner circle as others entered and left.

What happened next paid tribute to the environment of respect within the community, the integrity of the leader, and the beauty of council as an art form. The leader received expressions of love, frustration, and admiration with equal graciousness. People spoke of being dealt with brusquely, ignored, and in one case, abandoned. Acknowledgment of her central importance to the community and concern about overdependence were both expressed. Many showed their love, respect, and gratitude for all she had given.

When it was time to bring the spiral to a close, she picked up the talking piece and, in a quiet voice, acknowledged the individual expressions of feeling and the need for movement in her relationship to the community. She unknotted a few misunderstandings with specific individuals and acknowledged her tendency to be abrupt. Having been through several difficult "leader-must-die" scenarios in community and family settings, Jaquelyn and I appreciated the compassion and integrity with which this process had unfolded.

Sunday afternoon was devoted to issues of personal commitment, fund-raising, and using the momentum from the weekend to establish improved communication within the community. Enthusiasm and trust that the plans would materialize in a good way prevailed. Several board and staff members expressed the desire to use council in their meetings. The teachers agreed to meet as a group within a few months, something many of them had wanted to do for a long time. The entire community committed to another weekend gathering in a year.

Jaquelyn and I left in a flurry of thank-you's, feeling good about the weekend. We had done what we came to do. The seeds of council had been planted at Wind River—and there were already signs of vigorous growth.

We returned the following year, and the year after that, to further deepen the community's ability to communicate and deal with the complex issues that were arising during their expansion. After our three years of close association with Wind River, other members of the Ojai Foundation's council trainers group took over serving the needs of their community.

CONTINENTAL COUNCILS

When Frank Nelson called me from his Lincoln Continental dealership in Florida, it had never occurred to me that the owner of a car dealership might be interested in the council process. But there he was going on and on enthusiastically about Gigi's and my council article in the *Utne Reader*.[1]

The article had intrigued Frank for many reasons. His sales managers deferred to his ideas so readily that he often felt alone in his weekly staff meetings with them. He wondered if they were ever completely honest with him—or with each other for that matter. He thought that council might be a way for these men to meet together, listen to each other attentively, and speak the truth. He had felt for a while that his salesmen could be more effective on the job and, just as important, that he could enjoy his time with them more. "Don't you think council would be effective in an automobile dealership?" he asked me at the end of our first conversation.

Over the next few months, we tried to answer that question by exchanging a lot of information. I learned that Frank meditates, attends ten-day silent retreats from time to time, and reads a surprising number of books about spiritual practice. I found out a lot about selling cars. Frank learned enough about council to invite me to Florida to introduce the process to his salesmen.

Although he was used to calling the shots, Frank felt nervous about how his salesmen would respond to council. He wanted to

---

[1] "The Council Process," Jack Zimmerman and Virginia Coyle, Utne Reader, March/April, 1991.

avoid losing their respect because he was "going off the deep end." On the way back from the airport, I reassured him we could introduce council without drumming, candles, or "spiritual language." For the talking piece Frank suggested the scale model of a classic Continental that had sat on his desk for years.

The next morning, Frank called in his five managers, each of whom led a team of six or seven salesmen. Since the team that sold the most cars in a month received a prize in addition to their regular commissions, there was a lot of competition among the five men and their teams. Three of the teams captured the prize most of the time; the team led by the youngest of the five men had never won.

Several of the sales managers did indeed look askance at Frank when he introduced me and heard why I had been invited. I explained council to the men as simply as I could. "When speaking in council, the intention is to be truthful and say what might be helpful to oneself as well as the group," I began. I told them the power of council arose from the careful listening encouraged by the rule that allowed only the man holding the model Continental to speak. I emphasized that council could be used when the whole group had important decisions to make.

The five men exchanged sly grins and said they were ready to try anything Frank suggested. They were used to his wild ideas for new advertising campaigns and other ways to improve sales. But this was a "whole new ballgame" (as one of them said to me later). Frank and I saw we were being humored, but I trusted that the magic of council would overcome even a car salesmen's skepticism. In setting up the first council, I suggested that they address several questions: "What changes would you make to improve your team's sales? Does the competition among the teams create too much personal pressure? What is it like to work for Frank?"

Frank had suggested the first two questions himself, but I surprised him with the third. The five sales managers were particularly delighted with that question and gave it a lot of attention. "Sometimes, I have trouble keeping up with your new ideas," one said. "Your mind works so fast, I have difficulty understanding what you mean," another agreed. At first, Frank was a little uncomfortable with the men's honesty, particularly since he had to remain silent until it was his turn to speak. But, by the end of the meeting, he realized that their outspokenness was just what he wanted and thanked them for being so candid.

Despite their skepticism, the sales managers had a great time. They teased Frank about not being able to interrupt them when they were holding the talking piece (as apparently he had often done during their regular sales meetings in the past). When the younger sales manager told us how bad he felt always coming in last, the other men expressed a degree of sympathy that surprised me. They also gave him a lot of advice, both about the salesmen that worked for him and the way he led them. I began to see that the five men were good friends as well as competitors. When we finished, everyone said they wanted to have another council the following day. One of the men suggested we use a tennis ball for the talking piece, since the Continental model was too heavy and cumbersome to pass around.

The next day, after the yellow ball went around the circle once, the men came up with a plan for how to continue. Each time someone finished speaking, whoever wanted to speak next was to raise his hand and the ball would be thrown to him. Soon the ball was flying back and forth with talk about the challenges of being salesmen. They explored the destructive as well as the constructive forces of competition. They gave each other a lot of advice and spoke even more honestly to Frank than they had the day before. By the end of the second council, Frank told the five men he had been thinking about giving them more responsibility in running the dealership. The managers asked me to introduce council to each of their individual teams before I left for home—which I did with similar success.

Over the next few years, I returned to Florida several times to help Frank and the five sales managers refine and expand their use of council. On my third trip, I asked Frank about the women who worked in the dealership. (All the sales people and maintenance staff were men.) "The women take care of accounting, advertising, and the telephones," he answered. It was already clear to me from wandering around the dealership that the women did not enjoy equal status with the salesmen. I suggested all the women have a council—without Frank—to find out how they felt about working in his "store." "I think the women are happy here," Frank told me, "But go ahead and meet with them if you like."

The women took to council immediately. I even described the practice of saying *Ah-Ho*, which I had not mentioned at all to the men. Their circle was full of fire. Several women said the salesmen treated them like second-class citizens by asking them to run errands, fetch food, and do other chores that were not part of their job assignments. Others said some of the men offended them with suggestive remarks and uninvited physical contact. One salesman in particular was accused of sexually harassing several of the women. When I asked them why they hadn't spoken to Frank, one woman replied, "Most of us are used to that kind of treatment. That's how men behave in places like this, although most of them would never get away with treating their wives the same way. So we didn't think Frank would take our complaints seriously. Besides, Frank and many of the men are basically kind, so we're better off here than in most other jobs we've had." Several women shouted Ah-Ho when she finished speaking.

I told the women that many of their concerns might be eased, once Frank and the other men knew how they felt. I encouraged them to share their feelings more openly in the future. Then I asked their permission to tell Frank in general terms what had taken place in the council. (We had agreed at the start that what they said individually would be held in confidence.) The women gave their "okay," although they were skeptical that anything would come of it.

After hearing my report, Frank immediately called in the five team leaders and Maria, the woman who ran the accounting office. They decided to hold a council, which I offered to witness if Frank would lead. He agreed, although he didn't feel quite ready. At first, the five men thought the women were making "mountains out of molehills," but listening to Maria's passionate description of how she felt about working in the dealership changed their minds. They agreed to speak to their men. Frank said he would personally talk to the man who had been accused of harassment. At the end of the council, I congratulated everyone on the quality of their listening, applauded Frank's leadership, and emphasized the importance of keeping the lines of communication open with the women.

Exhilarated by our successes, Frank decided impulsively we should hold a council for all the men in the maintenance department. Then he started thinking about it a little. "They may think I've gone bananas," he said. "I can't even imagine a suitable theme...These guys may be more of a challenge than the salesmen." I suggested that he first give a short description of council, including what it had accomplished in the dealership so far, after which he and I would guide the circle together.

I still hadn't come up with a theme as we gathered in the conference room. But listening to the men's shyness in the way they joked with each other and with Frank gave me an idea. "I'd like to suggest a theme," I began after Frank had finished his sales pitch about council. "Some of you may have hobbies or outside interests that you haven't talked about with many people at work—perhaps not with anyone. If the idea appeals to you, this council might be a good opportunity to share that part of your life." Some of the men looked a little startled, so Frank decided to start the circle himself, which he did by sharing his interest in meditation. Only a few close associates at the dealership had heard about this important part of his life before. His openness broke the ice.

Many surprising and moving stories were shared in that circle. One man spoke of his recent wedding and described what being married meant to him. Another told us of his passion for fishing and sitting quietly in his boat connecting with nature. One man admitted he had no life outside of work except downing a few beers with friends. Several men said their family life kept them very busy at home, so they didn't have much time to themselves. Many acknowledged that Frank's "store" was a great place to work. After the council, the maintenance department manager said to me, "Now I have a way to meet with my men when problems arise."

After I stopped visiting the dealership, formal council was used primarily for important decision-making and brainstorming sessions. Nevertheless, the spirit of council remained strong at Nelson Continental. Frank and the salesmen listened to each other more respectfully at their regular meetings, the women noticed a definite improvement in the men's behavior and— after an investigation—the salesman who had been accused of sexual harassment was asked to resign. A year later, the sales manager whose team had never won decided he was not cut out to sell cars. After he left, Frank gave the other four team leaders the opportunity to become financial partners in the dealership.

OPENING THE DOOR

Commenting on the Wind River and Continental dealership experiences will give us the opportunity to make a number of general suggestions for transmitting council to institutions, communities, and places of business.

Getting to Know the Organization

In the two cases described above, we did a lot of homework before council training actually began. We learned about the tripartite structure of the Wind River Community and became familiar with the language of its spiritual tradition. We actually practiced the form of meditation the community teaches for a while prior to the weekend retreat. We heard a lot about the challenges facing the community and designed the questionnaire.

Since I knew little about the workings of an automobile dealership, there was much to learn in that situation as well: automobile jargon, the highly competitive nature of the car business, and the "team" structure that dominated the salesmen's daily lives. Interestingly enough, the dealership turned out to have a tripartite culture as well: salesmen, maintenance personnel (all male), and an office support group (all female).

Suggestion. Get acquainted with the organization beforehand. Learning its idiomatic language, internal culture, and idiosyncratic ways of functioning facilitates transmitting the experience of council in a more indigenous manner. Maintain a witness perspective during the transmission process. Find ways to involve the organization in exploring the issues that led to your invitation *before* you arrive. In this regard, don't forget that every organization has shadow aspects. Be alert to such patterns as: unacknowledged animosity between two executives, hidden inconsistencies in the treatment of male and female employees, and denial that the company's products or services are no longer in demand. Otherwise these shadow patterns may arise spontaneously and dominate the agenda.

Getting to Know the Values

In broad terms, Jaquelyn and I were familiar with the way people in intentional communities tend to view the world, but the same was not true for automobile salesmen. On several occasions, I had to bite my tongue to avoid getting into philosophical arguments with the five team leaders. For example, all but the least successful sales manager believed unequivocally that competition was a natural and necessary part of the human condition, that it "built strong men," and that it was the "heart of the American Way." Having worked with students most of my adult life, I have serious doubts about the validity of this perspective. However, my challenge was to work *within this competitive world view* and not fall into a judgmental and polarizing position during the councils. I was not entirely successful in accomplishing this goal.

As we have said repeatedly, council is not only a context for communication but also a spiritual practice. As a result, experienced practitioners of council tend to develop values about individuality, interdependence, authority, and hierarchies that differ from those of the mainstream. (This important issue is elaborated in Chapter 12.) The carrier of council has to be aware that such values may *or may not* be shared by members of the organization. In the case of Wind River, council harmonized beautifully with the community's spiritual practice and value system. But this was less true at the Continental dealership. Nevertheless, the salesmen developed a respect for the council process and were willing to reflect on their previously held positions about competition, individuality, and leadership. Indeed, progressive members of the business community have been among the most active explorers of unfamiliar group processes such as council. As a result, we have found that many in the business community have an increasing openness to the values that council and similar processes naturally encourage.

Suggestion. Be sensitive to significant differences between your personal values and those of people in the organization. When such differences exist, set the intention to suspend judgment when selecting themes, leading council, and acting as witness. If your primary purpose is to transmit the practice of council, avoid editorializing about the organization unless specifically asked to do so. Let the councils speak for themselves. Of course, in some situations sharing your personal perspective will not only be appropriate but exactly what you are there to do.

Finding Partners

We worked closely with members of both organizations over a period of several months before the council training actually started. In the case of Wind River we were guided by a small planning group that included the executive director and representatives of all three segments of the community. This committee kept us well informed (by telephone, fax, and mail) about both the enthusiasm and resistance to our plans for the weekend. (The central teacher was not involved in the planning.) As a result of these interactions and the questionnaire, we felt in touch with the community before we arrived. Except for the surprise agenda for Saturday evening, the committee knew what we were planning to do.

During the weekend we conferred with the executive director between sessions to adjust schedules, shift themes, and select the appropriate forms of council to use. Since members of the planning group had limited experience with council, they chose not to co-lead the circles during the weekend. However, co-leading councils with Wind River community members was appropriate when we returned the following two years.

I was also in close contact with Frank Nelson for months before my first visit to his Continental dealership. Being invited by him gave me all the authoritative support I needed. However, rather than implementing council by edict, he chose to play the role of a council salesman (appropriately enough for the group at hand) and asked me to do the same. He and I essentially "sold" council to his organization during my early visits. Of course, we might not have been as successful as we were, had the owner not been on my "team."

During the early visits, Frank didn't want to co-lead council, even after participating in an intensive training with Gigi and me. He declined a leadership position because he wanted to sit in the circle equally with his subordinates to allow his role as CEO to be freely discussed. Eventually, he did co-lead the maintenance department's council and led one or two others alone, during which I played the role of witness. Between my visits, he led council regularly.

Suggestion. Whenever possible, work in partnership with members of the organization during the transmission of council. In order to avoid getting caught up in local politics, find out as much as you can about individuals or factions in the organization that are resistant to council *prior to arriving.* Do the organization's leaders know that council is to be introduced? Are they supportive? Generally speaking, the more foreign the notion of council is to the business or community, the more leadership support one needs in carrying out the transmission. Ideally, at least one member of the organization should participate in formal council training before introducing the process.

Understanding the Hierarchy

In both instances the central person's relationship to others in the organization became an important issue during the transmission. With Wind River, we knew that in advance; the question was how to deal with the issue. At the dealership, I deliberately chose to make the owner's management style a topic early in the game. There were two primary reasons for doing this: I didn't think his subordinates would bring it up on their own, and I knew he wanted to move away from being so controlling but wasn't sure how to go about it. I also trusted that he would respond constructively to whatever the men had to say.

Over the years, we have learned that when an organization is drawn to council, there is an excellent chance that some transformation in its hierarchical structure is in the offing. The reason is not that mysterious. Council can be thought of as a "horizontal" context for communication, in contrast with the "vertical" or hierarchical structures so familiar in business, education, and government. Because of council's intrinsic non-hierarchical form, authority is shared by everyone in the circle. Beyond that, council participants eventually discover that the true authority of council resides more in the whole circle than in any portion of its members.

Suggestion. Be sensitive to the nature of the relationship between members of the organization and its leadership. Exploring this relationship may be an important part of why you were asked to introduce council in the first place.

Choosing the Talking Piece

Rather than bringing one of ours, we suggested that Wind River choose a talking piece for the weekend. They went one step further and created a beautiful instrument, using elements from the land and their spiritual tradition. As a result, the community was able to identify with an important part of the council process at the outset.

The spruce-wood stick was initiated during our visit and remained at Wind River to be used at board, staff, teacher, and community-wide meetings.

The choice of talking pieces also played an important role at the Continental dealership. We began with a familiar icon, the classic model car, and then switched to an object that helped the men express their resistance to council in a playful way. The tennis ball also allowed for a bit of physical movement during the meetings. Obviously, introducing council at the dealership with a rattle or crystal would have been inappropriate.

Suggestion. Whenever possible, use an "indigenous" talking piece, ideally one that is created by members of the organization and provides some connection to the place or to the theme of the council. However, come prepared with a few pieces of your own, just in case.

Irreverence

When first introduced, it is often the carrier of council's presence that empowers the process, not the forms and accouterments of council. It takes a while for the source of empowerment to shift to the practice itself, at which time the carrier can shift further into the role of steward and guide. Therefore, in the beginning, a certain amount of irreverence about the form need not be counterproductive, as long as there is a sufficiently safe container in place by the time people want to share more deeply. A way to look at this particular aspect of introducing council is that the organizational novitiates get to play the coyote role, even before they know what council is about. Entering through "coyote's doorway" is a powerful way to learn council. That was an important part of what happened at the Continental dealership.

"Losing one's cool" in reaction to irreverence can transmit attachment to the form rather than the intrinsically open and accepting spirit of council. By the time a leader has become an effective carrier of council, a strong irreverent response should be a rarity. However, if irreverence gets out of hand or turns hostile, the carrier can step back from the proceedings, still maintaining the state of heightened perception. "This is not council," the carrier might say, acknowledging the truth of what's happening. "When you want to begin again, let me know."

Suggestion. During the early stages of transmission, a certain amount of spontaneous irreverence can actually help maintain the integrity of the circle. An experienced carrier's personal sense of reverence is usually sufficient to maintain the necessary balance.

Brevity and Simplicity

Remember that the council process is primarily characterized by silence. The spirit of council is transmitted as much in the spaces between the words as in the words themselves. Of course, the choice of language is still important. Despite the community's sophistication, even at Wind River, esoteric explanations of council would have been ill-advised. We also had to avoid the temptation of explaining council by making analogies to the spiritual practices of their community. Doing so might have offended some people as well as limiting opportunities for members of the community to realize their own connections to council. On several occasions prior to the weekend, the planning committee reminded us to keep our introductions "generic" and let council speak for itself. It was good advice.

At the Continental dealership, I was challenged to find a way of talking about council that allowed the men to trust me and become interested in what I was "selling." In other words, I had to gain their respect as a salesman. So I "pitched" council, emphasizing that it helped to build trust and effective communication among members of the circle, qualities they already respected as professionals. A skilled salesman knows not to talk too much, instead drawing out his customers as much as possible. I had to remind myself of that principle frequently.

Suggestion. Keep verbal introductions as brief and simple as possible. Refinements can be introduced as they become relevant to what is actually happening. If the organization already has a well-defined set of mores, let the members decide how council relates to these practices and ways of operating.

Assorted Offerings

We conclude with several suggestions arising from our consulting experience with a variety of organizations.

- *Be flexible.* Schedule and plan the sessions in advance, but be willing to drop your preparations and reshape the program "on the spot" to reflect what is actually happening. Include open spaces in the schedule. Often, in the desire to cover a lot of ground, too much is planned. Leave space for the spontaneous—the unplanned.

- *Stress the importance of confidentiality.* Offer an agreement for the circle's consideration or facilitate the group coming to one of its own. Review and refine the agreement periodically.

- *Vary the pace and nature of the activities.* Singing, movement, and walking can be a productive part of the transmission process. If you do not feel equipped to lead such activities, ask someone in the circle to do so. In the case of movement, for example, there is usually someone who can lead stretches or knows yoga. Almost anyone can dance—if you find the right music—and a walk outside serves many purposes.

- *Frame the council themes in a personal way.* Avoid stating them abstractly or philosophically, particularly in the early stages of transmission. Intellectualizing often limits the power of council. Select indirect themes that penetrate the issues most troublesome to the organization without confronting them head on. Turning into the skid doesn't mean driving into a brick wall!

- *Don't be rigid when evaluating an organization's "council behavior."* For example, don't assume that specific behaviors, which were inimical to council with other groups, are necessarily unacceptable in the current one. Just as certain conduct can be considered positive in one culture and negative in another, so each organization can have its own set of acceptable manners and patterns of behavior. It is the intent behind a particular action that greatly determines how much in tune it will be with the purposes of council in a particular organization. In some companies or political institutions people may be accustomed to addressing each other formally, which may not be a sign that the desired openness and honesty of council are being resisted. Referring to a person as "Mr. Samuels" or "Mathew," rather than "Matt," may be just as much "from the heart" in such an organization as in another where first names are the custom. Subject to satisfying the basic intentions of council, "when in Rome, do as the Romans do."

- *Remember to "turn into the skid."* If the transmission isn't going well, reflect on why (hopefully in a state of heightened perception) and deal with whatever is in the way. If you are unable to discern why the transmission is stymied, ask members of the organization to help you solve the problem. Without an explicit invitation, they might be reticent to do so. Being willing to deal with your own or anyone else's shadow material from the start can actually enhance the introduction of council.

- *Pay attention to everyone's dreams.* Listening to dreams that relate to the organization or individuals present may guide you and others during the transmission.

- *Remain aware of the importance of witnessing.* Stay close to the witness state yourself and become a formal witness if possible. Ask others in the organization to witness when that seems appropriate. Although formal witnessing may not be familiar to many people, it is essential to the council process.

- *Do whatever you have to do personally to remain in a state of heightened perception.* Stress arising from over-scheduling, eating poorly, or insufficient exercise may inhibit your capabilities in a significant way. Draw on your own personal rituals to stay centered, healthy, and connected to place.

- *Have fun yourself.* Being asked to transmit council is a sacred process, but that doesn't mean you have to be solemn or serious all the time. If you're not enjoying yourself, members of the organization probably are not either.

- *Suggest ways the organization can continue learning about council with or without your assistance.* Gently challenge the circle to take responsibility for developing the practice further on their own. Be alert to the organization becoming dependent on your presence for council to "work."

One evening as I was leaving the Continental dealership during my second visit to Florida, Tim, the young manager whose team had never won a sales competition, came up to me. "I want you to know how much today's council meant to me," he said. "I've never felt safe talking the way I did today—except at home with my wife. Being able to reveal so many of my feelings in front of the other managers felt great—and started me thinking about my abilities to lead other men and my whole career in sales. I don't know where it will all lead me," he concluded as he waved good night, "but it sure felt good to be honest and not get put down by the other guys."

"*Ho!*" I said silently, as I shook his hand goodbye.

11

EMBRACING THE WAY OF COUNCIL

One planet is turning on its path around the sun
Grandmother is calling her children home
The light is returning
Even though this is the darkest hour
No one can hold back the dawn
Let's keep it burning
Let's keep the light of hope alive
Make safe the journey through the storm

     –Chant attributed to Charlie Murphy

We have held the dream that the Way of Council will find growing acceptance in our culture for many years now. In our vision, increasing numbers of primary and secondary schools adopt council as an integral part of their curricula; families use council as a way to develop clear communication between the generations; couples commit to the practice of dyadic council as a way of bringing spirit and Eros into their relationships; and communities and organizations discover that council builds trust, improves productivity, and leads to a respectful relationship with the earth.

Some significant progress has been made in recent years towards fulfilling this vision—particularly in regard to the spread of council-based programs in schools. The Council Practitioners Center at Los Angeles Unified School District has the District's support to bring council to as many Los Angeles primary and secondary schools as possible (see Appendix I). Some 40 schools–both public and private—in the LA Area now have council programs. A second frontier of growth involves the council programs that have and are being introduced in Europe, Africa and Israel. Gigi and I have been particularly active in supporting council abroad these past several years.

In the long run, the acceptance of council by business and governmental organizations is central to fulfilling our dream. We believe that if the way of council were embraced by a large number of our society's more hierarchical organizations, the culture would enter a period of transformation and growth. How might this unfold?

We have already mentioned the way in which council can be seen as a horizontal form of communication, in contrast to the vertical hierarchical structures that currently dominate business, educational, and government institutions (and many families as well!). Carriers of council often face the challenge of interweaving the horizontal and vertical forms as they bring the way of council into organizations and communities. To accomplish this interweaving, an organization first must develop an appreciation of council as a viable—even preferable—process for making decisions. When members of a community, business, or educational institution come to trust council as a context for decision-making, introducing the spirit of council into the organization as a whole becomes more feasible.

DECISION-MAKING AND COUNCIL

Based on our experience at The Ojai Foundation and with other organizations that have asked for our assistance, the many ways of using council to assist in decision-making fall into two basic categories.

Individual leadership. In the spirit of "serving the larger circle," one person is empowered by the organization to take responsibility for making the decision. He or she calls a number of councils to gather information and explore a wide range of views. Knowing they will be truly heard, members of the organization usually feel better about this way of making decisions than in the traditional hierarchical system.

Circle leadership. The organization selects and empowers a circle to make the decision. (Usually one, but preferably two, individuals are asked to shepherd the process and report the results.) Generally, decision-making in council involves the following steps:

1. Members of the chosen circle (and others) gather the information needed to make the decision from appropriate sources within and outside the organization.

2. If a sufficient number of alternatives have yet to be identified, a vision council can be conducted to focus the creative talents of the group. The visioning process continues, with time off for "sleeping on it," if necessary, and for gathering more information, until a number of viable proposals have been formulated.

3. Next a council is held, during which members of the group present their individual views on the matter. (If the deciding group is large, a spiral format can be used to allow fewer, self-selected voices to speak for the entire circle.) Representatives of other parts of the organization who have a stake in the decision can be invited to the

council as witnesses. In addition, one or more regular members of the circle can volunteer, or be chosen, to witness this exploratory council.

4. Assuming one round fails to produce substantive agreement, the talking piece is sent around again or is placed in the center. If the group is experienced in the way of council, it may not be necessary to use the talking piece formally at this point. Alternatively, it can be left in the center in full view as a reminder of the commitment to the four intentions of council, while the discussion proceeds more informally. However, if members of the circle start interrupting each other or there is other evidence of insufficient listening, formal council can be reinstated by anyone at any time. In some situations, the leader (or anyone in the circle) can suggest a theme for the new round, with the intent of moving the discussion "beneath" the level where the confusion or disagreement exists to search for common ground. Witnesses can be particularly helpful at this juncture.

5. If strong personal differences arise that interfere with the decision-making, a fishbowl can be called to identify and deal with the personal aspects of the conflict. Alternatively, the council can be adjourned while the two find a witness outside the circle to sit with them and explore the situation. When movement towards a decision seems to be blocked for any reason, taking time to sit quietly as a group (or individually) to focus on how the obstacles might be overcome can also be extremely helpful.

6. The process continues until consensus (if that was the agreed upon decision method) has been reached or it becomes clear that time is needed to sleep on the matter and make the decision at a subsequent council. Consensus does not necessarily mean that everyone is in

agreement. One or more people can register an opposing view, while still choosing not to block the action desired by the majority. If there is extensive opposition to the majority view, or it becomes clear for other reasons that the decision is not ready to be made, steps one and two can be repeated, time permitting. If the decision method is simply majority rule, council can still be used in the process leading up to the final vote.

This sounds a little pat. What's to prevent the process from going on forever?[1]

Theoretically, nothing. However, these steps only describe the skeleton of decision-making. As always, what makes council work is the collective awareness of the circle.

I assume you'll elucidate.

The heart of the process is contained in the fourth step. Clarity about the decision emerges when enough people have found their way into the state of heightened perception and see the truth of council.

Great! But if people are that clear, who needs council? Any group in that state can make a good decision.

That's exactly the point. The group uses the process of council to evoke a state of perception in which the right decision can simply be seen. This means members of the circle may still hold, but are no longer attached to, their positions, have circumvented the effects of personal antagonisms and, most importantly, have been listening to each other attentively. Because council encourages these conditions, right action becomes a more likely reality.

Touché. One point wasn't clear to me in the fourth step. What exactly do you mean by choosing a theme that goes "beneath" the conflict to "search for common ground?"

---

[1] Questioning and critical voices are always welcome to the circle!

I'll answer that question with an example. Suppose a community is trying to decide among three designs for a large residential structure. After several hours, the circle is no closer to making a choice than when they started. At this point, there are two basic possibilities: (1) none of the three designs is appropriate, or (2) the structure is not ready to be built yet. The first of these is easier to handle, since the design committee can always be asked to bring in more designs. But a blocked council may mean the residence is not ready to be built. The question is *why?* Is it lack of money? If so, that should be apparent and would not restrict the Interactive Field.

Something even more basic may be in the way. Maybe the group is not sure it wants to live together in a single communal residence. That may have been the vision originally, when the design process started (probably a long time ago). But alternatives such as separate dwellings or living off the community's land in conventional homes may be more fitting now. Perhaps disagreement, or at least confusion, has arisen about the community's vision. In this case, a good council leader might say: "Forget the design of the house for a moment. In fact, forget houses altogether. Let's go back to our basic purpose for existing: the service we provide others, stewarding the land placed in our care, and what we learn by working together. How do you see living here in a way that is most consistent with these basic purposes?"

So a blocked decision process suggests the frame of reference has to be revisited.

Exactly—and perhaps new kinds of questions asked. When the truth of council is "no decision is possible now," the decision-making circle, and possibly the entire organization, has some creative thinking to do. Of course, the circle needs to understand the consequences of not reaching a decision in the specified time. Issues of control may be involved. Not reaching a decision may mean the circle is giving up some control to other parts of the organization (or to an outside agency). That may lead to a strong teaching. The need to maintain control by making a decision willy-nilly is based on an adversarial model of the situation. Council teaches us that all interested groups are part of a single interdependent system. That often allows us to relax our need to control, sometimes with amazing results. We've found that even governmental bureaucracies can be seen ultimately as cooperative members of the circle.

You sound idealistic. The world rarely works that way.

That's true. Nevertheless, we can move in that direction one little step at a time. The way of council leads to a less adversarial, more creative way of functioning.

OK, OK, but who has the time to do all this?

When that question arises, as it often does in modern and survival cultures, we ask people to factor in the time that resistance or even revolution takes if the leader moves ahead without truly listening to the voice of the people she or he is leading. In some situations it's the preparation time in council that makes the difference when a difficult decision has to be made.

Gigi was put the ultimate test of how real making decisions in council has to be when she was Co-Director at The Ojai Foundation during the winter solstice fire in 2002. Over a period of three days the fire alternately approached the Foundation's land or seemed to be of little threat, as the direction of the wind changed. She walked the land, met with the fire marshal and talked with the guests (who did not want to leave). She checked in continuously with the staff, which feared for their homes and were ready to leave, but only if necessary— all the while watching and listening to the fire. She was literally in continuous council through a twenty-four hour period with the question, "What is best for us to do now?"

When the fire took a sudden and unexpected turn towards the Foundation's ridge, everyone was ready to leave, although still no one really wanted to. Her decision to clear the land was immediate, fully heard and acted upon. The community evacuated literally in minutes, safely ahead of a seventy-five mile per hour fire wall. As they

all waited, safely nearby, everyone felt they had taken the right action, by wetting down the buildings, protecting the land—and leaving.
When they were able to return just six hours later to fight the residual
fires, much of the Foundation, its trees and gardens was amazingly
untouched. The damage that did occur made it clear how dangerous
the fire had been.

That's an amazing story about the Foundation but do you really
think council could be adopted by a sufficient number of organizations to
make a difference in the world?

We do, indeed, and have experienced enough success with business firms, schools, and communities to take every opportunity to
recommend it strongly. If you look at the big picture, there's a lot at
stake, even the possibility of refining the democratic process.

Now you're getting grandiose.

Perhaps, but there is an important point to be made here. People
often ask us if council is democratic. Strictly speaking, it's not, at least
in the usual sense of "one person, one vote." As we've seen, decision-
making in council is not based on majority rule. It has more to do
with listening with equal attentiveness to every voice and providing
an equal opportunity to be heard than with equal voting power. This
takes the usual democratic process to a deeper level.

And what happens in council can also be influenced by "absent
voices." When someone who normally holds a strong seat in the circle is not present, the Interactive Field obviously changes because an
important point of view missing from the discussion. However, more
often than not, others can express the missing person's position ade-
quately. More subtly, the Interactive Field also changes because those
present are aware of the person's absence, which in turn can alter the
circle's collective state of heightened perception in a significant way.
Then finding the truth of council or searching for the right decision
is done in a different state of consciousness than if the person had
been present. In this respect, council is analogous to a silent prayer

circle. Even though no words are spoken, the presence or absence of a single individual may subtly affect the nature of everyone's praying.

I hope you're not suggesting that council is a religious activity.

No, but when it is practiced devoutly, council is an accessible *spirit-based* process that can be a catalyst for transformation in an organization. It may take a while, but I've seen the practice of council bring important changes to schools and businesses as well as communities, families, and primary relationships. The changes are subtle at first, but clearly detectable. When council takes hold, one could say that decision-making and other interactive processes *become democratic in a more awakened way.* This statement deserves elaboration.

AWAKENING AN ORGANIZATION THROUGH COUNCIL

For the past thirty years, we have been experimenting with the integration of council and hierarchical authority at the Ojai Foundation—and helping other communities, business organizations, and schools implement similar intentions for more than half that time. The major challenges in establishing a viable council practice have included clarifying the organization's vision, maintaining clear operational goals, and learning to balance the use of council with individual responsibility and accountability. As a result of these efforts, the spirit of council has gradually found its way into a variety of organizations, bringing with it the following tangible changes.

- Members of the organization listen to each other more carefully and greater personal honesty is fostered.

- Members become more patient.

- Members find it easier to acknowledge personal conflicts and do something constructive about them.

Hearing each other's stories and sharing feelings more readily fosters greater trust and intimacy in working relationships.

- Members are less likely to impose their ideas on others.

- Members are more respectful of what has been accomplished in the past when offering suggestions for change.

- Agreements between members are made more consciously and, therefore, honored more consistently.

- The need to "gather around the water cooler" (and thus encourage "talking in the bushes") decreases, because this innate desire for personal contact is satisfied by integrating council into the organization's daily operations.

- There is less free-floating personal anxiety, since council offers a safe place for dealing with concerns and problems honestly. As a result, actions and behaviors based on fear and anxiety diminish significantly.

- General feelings of personal well-being are generated through the opportunities for positive feedback and acknowledgment in council.

- Being less fearful, members are able to risk being more innovative and creative in doing their work.

- Decreasing fear and increasing trust leads to less stress.

- The increased attentiveness that occurs in council during the decision-making process easily compensates for the additional time spent in the circle. Fewer decisions have to be made more than once. The experience of being heard and the strong connection with the group that results from this way of operating increases individual participation and creativity in implementing decisions.

- Learning to listen to the voice of council helps members understand the goals and purposes of the organization. Individuals see more clearly how their activities relate to the overall scheme of things. Thus the alienating feeling of working in isolation diminishes. Seeing how they "fit in" also increases member's capacity to take greater responsibility and pride in their work.

- Sharing dreams and plans for the future on a regular basis increases member's capacity to vision together. This, in turn, enriches long-term planning.

- Through council, the organization's leadership continuously undergoes "in-service training," since they work less in isolation and receive more honest feedback. Leaders who do not listen well are encouraged to change their ways. A leader's tendency to over-control becomes more apparent.

- Over a period of time, council helps develop the sense of collective awareness that is possible in groups that share a common vision. As a result, there is a greater sense of the organization as an "evolving organism" rather than as an entity fixed in time and space. Members become more flexible and innovative about the organizational structure itself.

- With more room for authentic personal interaction, the feeling of separation between home-life and work diminishes.

- Since council leads to a greater understanding of the principle of interdependence, greater sensitivity to environmental issues develops, including an increasing interest in sustainable systems and products.

We would be remiss if we failed to discuss the many challenges that can arise when introducing and using council in organizations. We have observed the following dynamics during various stages of the process.

- Some members resist the challenge of becoming more involved in the life of the organization.

- Those who need to be told what to do with regularity become anxious.

- Some council practitioners cling to the verbal practice of council and forget to work creatively with music, movement, and silence. Forgetting about the variety of forms possible, some members feel stuck in the "going around the circle" format and complain about the lack of direct dialogue.

- Some members indulge the increased opportunity for personal expression and test the patience of others. Those for whom patience is not a virtue have a hard time.

- Members who feel unable to express themselves well are inhibited at first and, perhaps, withdraw for a while. In order to break this pattern, council must be imaginatively facilitated.

- Some leaders believe that sitting in the circle with "subordinates" threatens their authority.

- Executives who are accustomed to more controlled meetings feel frustrated when a council does not resolve the issue at hand. As a consequence, they feel momentarily less effective as leaders.

- To some, the process seems inefficient at first. They protest, "Too much talking, not enough doing!" The third intention of council is particularly important in organizations, but learning to be lean when speaking is difficult for some people.

- Some use council as a place to "hang out," an escape from work, or as a way to avoid needed alone time.

- Some members become so attached to the form of council, perhaps even dependent on it, that they fail to listen to the immediate needs of the group. They hold on tenaciously to council format, when actually the spirit of council would be better served if they let go of it for a while and gave others a chance to introduce different ways of interacting—for example, the town meeting format, or the traditional way of the Quaker meeting, or the unstructured and leaderless "dialogue process" suggested by David Bohm.[2]

The notion that the organization is an experiment unfolding is unsettling to some people. However, with effective council leadership, their source of security can shift from reliance on familiar ways of doing business to trusting in the effectiveness of "good process." In time they come to trust themselves and their circle of cohorts as they experience the power of listening and speaking from the heart. Gradually the experience of being part of a dynamic and evolving organism furnishes the security provided previously by the organization's hierarchical structure.

---

[2] See "Quantum Leap: An Interview with David Bohm," by John Briggs, New Age Journal, September/October, 1989.

RESPONDING TO THE CALL

For a few people, the familiar hierarchical way of running a school, business, community, or government office has seemed alien since birth. For an increasing number of others, the sense of separation from the prevailing power structures of our society increases daily. Once a person experiences the power and wisdom of the way of council, there is no turning back. When you know what is possible, it is difficult to settle for something less. This is one of the reasons why we continue to believe in the dream of a culture that embraces council.

Another is that the changes taking place in our lifetime demand that we recognize the *principle of interdependence* that is such an essential part of the way of council. We are reminded of this teaching whenever others in the circle articulate what we were unable to express. Or, listening to the voice of the circle, we see that, together, all of us make a whole that is clearly greater than the sum of its parts. Awakening to the reality of interdependence usually involves taking greater responsibility for our bodies, our children, our mortality, and our relationship to the earth. We are all beginners in this awakening, struggling along, often unable to grasp the big picture. But, as the Buddhist teacher Thich Nhat Hanh (and so many others!) remind us, the journey is not about arriving at the North Star, but heading in that direction.

For us, the challenge has become one of living the way of council and daring to initiate it in places we never imagined possible. Generally we follow the principle of going where we are invited. There have been enough missionaries! Yet sometimes we also look beneath the surface to see what is truly wanted—and then dare to offer it. In that spirit, carriers of council have been drawn to help heal many of the polarizations in our culture: body and soul, mind and heart, work and family, male and female, youth and elder, rich and poor, ill and healthy, Arab and Jew, Black and White.

At the Ojai Foundation, for example, council grew out of the intention to bring many different kinds of traditions and teachers together: Aboriginal, Native-American, Tibetan, Judeo-Christian, and leaders in the natural sciences. Joan Halifax, the Foundation's founder, had been inspired by her years in the civil rights movement, her medical anthropology travels and her research with Joseph Campbell. Joan called many councils of elders together in the Foundation's early years, some lasting for as long as a month. She still offers council at her Zen Center, Upaya, in Santa Fe, New Mexico, today. As have so many other communities and individuals, we have come to appreciate that learning to embrace differences is essential for our survival.

Sitting in council with people already committed to the practice helps us develop the skills for living an interdependent life and models the practice for others. But it is clear that the spirit of council is being called for in new situations throughout the culture. We invite you to listen for these opportunities and respond when you hear the call. We urge you to continue being a student of the practice as a way of being, living, and working in the world.

The way of council is very new and very old. We find that the practice invariably feels familiar to those who are open to the experience of interdependence. The simple form of the circle and the practice of attentive listening continue to manifest in cultures throughout the world. When all is said and done, we are only naming and bringing attention to the ancient "circle wisdom" inherent in the survival of our species. Often carriers of council talk about "remembering council," as they introduce the practice to a new group of people.

In closing this chapter we offer four stories that suggest council can be an agent of cultural transformation. In each situation the cultural gap between leader and circle started out wide, but the power of the practice was sufficient to bring a small measure of healing to the circle. We hope these stories will encourage you to share the way of council, even when the likelihood of success seems small and the personal effort great.

Honoring the Old, Welcoming the New[3]

Two hundred Mentors of a well-established, international path of healing had gathered together to discuss the issue of lineage. Once again the age-old question of community—who's in, who's out—was the focus of their agenda. Over the years, I had heard many communities debate the issue in one form or another. I knew from these experiences that each group has to find its own way.

But how were these two hundred people from different backgrounds, economic classes, and countries to find consensus? My partner, who was on their advisory board, had dared to suggest council might provide a means of reaching common ground. Despite one skeptical board member, I was invited to introduce the practice. As I listened intently to the passionate opening discussion, several questions emerged:

- Do we establish a standard of excellence and respect for practitioners of our healing path? If so, how?

- What if a Mentor misuses his or her power?

- What about people who say they are Mentors, but have not been initiated according to the traditional teachings?

- If all who claim to be Mentors are accepted in the community, what is the purpose of a professional association?

Many people emphasized the need to honor tradition. If certain standards were relaxed or changed, the power of the healing practice would diminish, they argued. In support of this position, case histories were described in which members of the community had been judgmental of a professed Mentor. Some argued that the judgment showed discernment, others contended that it revealed arrogance.

---

[3] Gigi is the storyteller in this and the following two stories.

I was introduced by the board and asked to speak. Though I felt officially invited, I knew this was a risky venture. The leader of the Mentors was present and had told the board he was open to exploring the issue, but not everyone had had their say about inviting an outsider into the circle of Mentors. In the moment before speaking, I saw questions about my presence reflected in many faces.

I dove in, trusting my call to carry council and the ability of the practice to support a community searching for its truth. After talking about the power of listening and heartful expression, I proposed a wisdom circle through which the community could seek guidance. "We might not find answers to all our questions, but at least we'll open ourselves to greater understanding and new insight," I said.

I suggested a fishbowl format, in which several of the oldest initiated members of the community would take a seat in the inner circle. If this group were able to put aside their personal positions, they could become a "council of elders." I emphasized that these individuals should listen deeply and express their truth in the spirit of service to the community.

My suggestion met with many nods of approval, but the very nature of council challenged the community's more traditional hierarchical approach. I could also hear the silent voices of the lineage: "There is nothing to discuss. Our leader and all that has gone on before will continue to guide us in what we do."

A woman spoke up: "We can't call a council of elders with an outsider in the room. We shouldn't have shared as much as we have already. No one besides our initiated members can talk about our secrets and symbols."

Another added more fuel: "Is this woman a Mentor? Why is she here? I like what she has offered, but it doesn't feel right to open our circle in this way."

Others begged my forgiveness and urged me not to take these statements personally. I sat quietly and practiced mindful breathing. When someone asked me directly whether I was a Mentor, I took the question deep within. "I do not know," I answered finally.

At this point the leader of the Mentors commanded everyone's attention by rising to address the group. He honored the concerns of the individuals who had spoken but demanded that the community "live by the truth of the present moment and not by the rules of tradition alone." He was in favor of conducting the council and having me present. "If Mentors can be recognized only by certificates or the color of their clothing, we must be blind and need to look more carefully!" he said.

His support together with the board's created a sufficiently safe climate in which to continue. My presence and the possibility of a council had brought the issue of the community's openness to a head. A new sensitivity was needed in order to embark on the critical discussion of lineage and authenticity. I suggested that each member of the group ask herself or himself the question, "Will what I say serve myself and serve the circle?"

The seeds of an elder's council were planted that day. As the process unfolded, I suggested the fishbowl be opened in the future into a spiral to permit others to learn from sitting in the elders' seats. I encouraged the group to seek guidance and let go of the expectation of reaching an immediate decision. I supported their commitment to finding right action and took the risk of suggesting that greater awareness of the issue would serve them better in the long run than a new set of rules. I left the journey of discovery to them.

In the months that followed, many members of their community joined our council trainings and subsequently brought the practice into their personal and professional lives. The board member who seemed most skeptical at first became a carrier of council in her own unique way.

The elders' council was put on call, learning to offer their wisdom in the spirit of service. However, as far as I know, the spiral format has never been utilized to cycle people in and out of this circle. Centering authority in the hands of more than a very few people continued to be a controversial issue in the community.

Beyond Boundaries

For many years, I had been leading ten-day wilderness journeys designed to accommodate diverse groups of people from different countries and cultures. The core of the journey is a four-day fast for each person alone in the wilderness. On these trips we explore the wilderness as an immediate physical reality and also as a metaphor, a way of learning how to relate to that which is wild in our ordinary lives. We find that nature serves as a mirror for the wilderness within each individual, as well as reflecting the untamed nature of our relationships with others. My Godson put it well after his journey the year before: "The fast and the time out alone opened and challenged me, of course, but the most surprising part of the journey was relating to the stories from people and places completely foreign to me."

This particular journey into the high desert of Central California included people from Germany, Holland, Switzerland, and America. During our preparatory councils, I could feel an undercurrent of tension that swirled around one participant, Ted, from Holland. Finally, after everyone had completed their four-day fast and we had gathered again, the source of the tension—and its healing—emerged clearly. Sitting around the council fire on this final evening together, Ted, began to speak in a strong and clear voice:

"This trip has served me well. I have faced the dark of the desert night and looked at myself in the light of the noonday sun. I have questioned my life as a man, husband, lover, father, and healer—and emerged stronger than ever. But the most dangerous part of the journey was being in council with all of you Germans. Your passion, manner, and even your voices have frightened me most of my life. It's not just the stories from World War II. I have met you and you *are* different. Your way of looking at the world is different. I have often felt small and overwhelmed in your presence, as our country literally was, and still is, in some ways. Yet after this journey I can listen to you and be in ceremony with you. I can laugh and cry with you. Something has shifted and healed. There is room for us all. I have come to love each of you and for that I give great thanks."

Ted's honesty and compassion were the harvest of sitting in council with those who "live across the circle" from us, beyond the boundaries of our culture and the world of familiar experience. The common call had been to be on the land, to fast in the wild, to deepen the understanding of self and to connect with the earth. Answering that call had drawn each individual into instant community with people from other countries, social classes and belief systems. And, once again, council had helped us all to awaken the spirit of interdependence.

Council Among Strangers

The message that the doctors had given my grandmother twenty-four hours to live brought us together hurriedly to honor the passing of our matriarch. Both childlike pleasure and awkwardness marked the gathering in the sun room of her Connecticut house. Many of us had not seen each other for years. One by one, fifteen of her living legacies visited her in the hospital to share last words. It took the immediacy of Nana's death to accomplish her lifelong desire to bring us all together.

She didn't pass that night or the next. I began to wonder if we were here for some other reason. We talked about celebrating as if it were Christmas. Although Nana could not leave the hospital, she was with us in spirit. I felt that the proximity of her death was giving our stiff New England clan the opportunity of being together in a new way.

On the third day of wondering what to do, I saw an opening. My cousin Sean had talked to a few of us about his approaching marriage. Others discussed it more extensively when he wasn't around. The comments ranged from solicitous to nasty: "Aren't you worried? He seems confused to me. Do you think she's right for him? She seems to be more interested in his money than anything else." No one shared these latter feelings directly with Sean. I became increasingly uncomfortable with the lengthening shadows and thought of calling a council.

We had often congregated in the sun room to eat, talk, laugh, and (in true Connecticut mainline fashion) drink and smoke. My openhearted, truth-speaking Mormon relatives were among the few of us over sixteen that had not surrendered to this life style. They might hear my call, but otherwise introducing council in Nana's sun room would be like trying to get someone's attention on the New York Stock Exchange floor.

I took the plunge: "Hey, you guys, I have a family exploration to propose." A ripple of surprise and fear passed through the room. In forty-five years, I had met few New Englanders who were big on rocking the family boat. "It's pretty clear Nana is not going to die right now," I continued. "Everyone is beginning to think about returning to their families and jobs, but I feel we have an unexpected opportunity here." I didn't wait for encouragement or questions. The die was cast. It was sink or swim.

"Nana's always wanted us to get together. I suspect she's so happy with her success now that she's going to stick around a little longer." (Just that morning the bewildered doctor had told us she would be able to come home in two days with around-the-clock care.) "Maybe there are other reasons for our gathering. Nana's passage may be in the future, but Sean is facing a major life transition right now."

"What do you mean?" someone dared to show interest.

"During the last few days," I went on, "many of us have been talking about Sean's engagement and approaching wedding. He's told me directly that the marriage proposal was such a big deal for him. So, suppose we give Sean a chance to say what's on his mind and then ask everyone here, old and young alike, to ask questions, offer reflections on relationship, give blessings, or whatever else comes up."

"There are a lot of old marrieds in this room with years of experience as well as a few spinsters like me," I added, trying to lighten the mood. "Wouldn't it be wonderful to honor the importance of Sean's decision by sharing our own experience about what's valuable in a marriage partnership?"

To this day I'm not sure I received a yes from everyone in the sun room. But Sean was more than game. He jumped at the idea, like a thirsty man being offered water.

The next two hours were passed in the true spirit of council. Most people followed my suggestion and also added personal comments about the upcoming wedding. Though Sean was nervous at first, he soon relaxed and began accepting the many gifts the group offered. Without an official talking piece, I played road chief like I never had before. Somehow it all came together. My sister and her husband spoke of their marriage with such authenticity that I saw the strength and beauty of their relationship in a whole new way. Many other truths were offered compassionately. Most important, everyone listened.

Despite a lack of ceremonial formalities, my family had created a stronger experience of council that afternoon than I imagined possible. Amidst cocktails and overstuffed baby hot dogs, we touched the magic of the circle. We listened to Sean's dreams and worries. The mother of the groom unburdened herself of the feeling of heaviness she had been carrying for months. Our elder's call had created an unexpected and powerful rite of passage for the family.

A few days later, Nana heard the story of our gathering. A few months after that Sean decided to cancel his wedding plans.

Council With the Forgotten[4]

It felt like a big risk to convert the informal rap sessions at the youth shelter into councils. Most of the kids presented a tough exterior to the world and were skeptical of anything "groupy" or New Age. But council seemed like the perfect format. The polarization between the ones who never shut up and the ones who hardly spoke was huge. I hoped council would close the gap.

Our circle met weekly at the shelter's day center, during the late morning, against a background of ringing phones and continuous comings and goings. The kids were not used to sitting still for very long—unless they were exhausted—and then they would sleep through most

---

[4] This story has been adapted from the unpublished journal of Elissa Zimmerman, MFCC, who led councils in homeless youth shelters in Los Angeles for many years.

of the council. When we first started, if they felt restless or bored, they would just get up and leave, no matter how many times I reminded them to come on time and stay until everyone had spoken. Holding the spirit of council in that circle took everything I had—and more. On the days we had council, I often left the shelter on the verge of tears.

I brought a large quartz crystal to use as the talking piece. By offering something that was valuable to me, I thought the kids would feel my trust and care for them, both of which deepened as the weeks went by. They always showed interest in the crystal, both in the metaphysical sense and because the common street form of speed is called "crystal." Comments like, "We're always 'shooting-it-up' in council," brought many laughs. At first, I had trouble with the word *Ho*, which, on the street, means whore. After a lot of giggling, several of them decided to clap instead.

The circle was made up of older street kids and shelter kids under eighteen, who had been homeless for shorter periods of time. Some had run away from home to "make it" in the city; others had escaped disinterested, addicted, or abusive parents. Some had left their families rather than disclose they were pregnant or gay—or were thrown out after their parents had found out. There were always a few whose backgrounds seemed indistinguishable from those of the young people I had sat with before in more familiar settings. I often wondered what had led the shelter kids to the streets and not the others. Some hated being homeless, but many who joined our councils were proud of living by their own wits and felt they had learned a great deal from their homeless life.

I was surprised to find out, not only how deeply religious a lot of them were, but, considering their youth, how many religions they had explored. Usually, there were a few fundamentalists in the group and now and then a devil-worshiper, which made for some lively councils! I was impressed by those who said they had gotten something useful out of every religion they had tried, but the real challenge was to create a unique spiritual path that worked for them.

We also had some strong councils about love. When Pierre, nineteen, began one of those with, "You have to have respect, honesty, and trust, if you're going to have love," he was greeted with derisive laughter. But we stuck by the intentions of council and soon got into a long discussion about how much their parents really loved them. Many agreed that mothers and fathers can verbally and physically abuse their kids in the name of love. They were experts at mimicking parents who say, "This hurts me more than it hurts you," and "It's for your own good." They seemed to really understand that being told you're no good while growing up leads to feeling bad about yourself and having difficulty loving others in later life. The idea that abused children become abusive parents made Autumn (young and pregnant) very angry. "That's just shit," she said during one of our councils on love. "I'm tired of hearing about it. My parents didn't have to act that way just because they were abused. I'm not going to abuse *my* kids."

There were times I left the shelter feeling helpless and wondering whether council would make any difference in their lives. One of those times was the day Jesse finally said he was ready to talk. For weeks he had insisted he was only interested in listening, but that day the floodgates opened, releasing years of pain, hurt, and anger.

"The worst part of being on the street is being pushed into prostitution and doing drugs," Jesse began. "It's the only way you can get by. I've been on the street for eight years—since I was thirteen. After that long, you don't worry about it anymore..." He went on to tell us his story for almost half an hour. His mom was an addict when she was carrying him and during his early childhood. Because he was identified as a "hyperactive" baby, she felt justified in putting vodka in his bottle to quiet him down. At the age of six, he began to be attracted to men and at twelve, not knowing it was "wrong," told his family he was gay. They disowned him and he started life on the streets, firmly entrenched as an alcoholic.

"I've slept with people fifty years older than me," Jesse told us. "Isn't that sick? I know it sounds crazy, but I still say that I've never turned a trick. I was so lonely; I told myself I was making love every time. I never had a puppy—or a dad—but I've had plenty of step-dads. My mother doesn't even know who my real dad is. I've never had anyone, even a friend, tell me they love me—and really mean it." His voice was full of pain, but surprisingly free of self-pity. "I tested HIV positive a year ago," he went on. "But I haven't told anyone until now. I knew the guy I got it from. It was my idea not to have safe sex. I see now how that was my way of committing suicide—the slow way. I didn't have the guts to actually do it the fast way, although I tried."

Jesse started to cry as he talked about his three suicide attempts and that put him over the edge. "I'm sorry I spilled my guts," he sobbed. I tried to help him see that his rush of feeling was a natural part of finally telling his story and would help his recovery. But he was too immersed in his grief to see that anything good could come out of having spoken so honestly. He finally calmed down, but it took sitting with him an hour after council was over. I left the shelter feeling the enormous risk he had taken in opening up—and the promise. I didn't know which way he would go. I wondered whether there was something else I should have done.

The following week, he was the first to show up for council. He said that after spilling his guts, he had slept better than he had in a long time. He told us, proudly, that he had been reaching out more to friends and the shelter staff. He said that speaking in council had been just what he needed.

12

THE IMPLICIT
VALUES AND
SKILLS OF
COUNCIL

" . . . In the primordial forests of the first living creatures there was no speech, no spoken symbols systematically arranged into significant expression. But there
was communication. Before linguistics, before the
literal link of language, there was listening . . .
Listening . . . perhaps . . . is just a mind aware . . . "

Hannah Merker in "Listening"

We have spoken a lot about the practice of council and shared many stories . . . A few years ago, I wrote a piece about council for educators, entitled, "The Implicit Curriculum of Council." The idea was to touch on the more subtle aspects of council that (fortunately) often grace our experience and add immeasurably to its magic. Re-reading those words made it clear that I had dropped into the witness voice—in fact at different times from each of the four directions. It seems appropriate at this point to share my reflection on what has been already written in the previous chapters as a way of probing more deeply into the unbounded possibilities of the practice.

It is important to explore these more subtle implications to remind the practitioner that something happens in a circle of people who are deeply listening and speaking authentically to each other—beyond words, topics, stories, the decisions being made and the conflicts being explored—that can have lasting implications for those present and for their community, even for the culture. Moreover, exploring the implicit dimensions of council is good preparation for responding to the often asked question, "What actually happens in a council that makes it so compelling for people? What's the big deal? Why can't people just talk to each other?"

The implicit aspects of council can be divided loosely into four overlapping categories:

- Those that arise simply from the call to gather and the very nature of the circle itself

- Those that arise from the four intentions of council

- Those that encourage the expansion and maturing of human intelligence

- Those that arise from our history—from tradition, from our "ancestors" and the roots of human experience

To some extent our exploration will be subjective because of the nature of the implicit landscape—even though we have sat in thousands of circles and talked with many hundreds of council leaders over the years. New practitioners will soon find their own language to witness these subtler, and yet so apparent, dimensions of the process.

THE CIRCLE AND THE CALL TO GATHER

Let's start with children. Young students get the message about the importance and purpose of going to school usually by the end of Kindergarten or First Grade. We all go through the process. Most of us are told that we are in school to learn and become more skilled, so that each of us can have a good life, make a living and become a productive member of society. These values are stressed directly and implicitly in many ways that soon become second nature to virtually all students. The possible value of a completely different kind of education—without four-walled schools and even teachers as we commonly know them—doesn't arise for most children until later when they might be lucky enough to read such novels as "Green Mansions," "The Island of the Blue Dolphin" or experience the wilderness directly in one way or the other. Only then do we begin to realize the extent to which we have taken on a set of values during our early educational years (we might call them "urbanized/pragmatic values or perhaps, more currently, internet/pragmatic values") that are not necessarily a self-evident part of our DNA. Since most of us live in an urban environment, reading or experiencing the ultimately mysterious qualities of nature may stir a part of ourselves that we didn't even know existed when we were young.

But, in one way or another—and sooner or later—most of us awaken to the realization that the values we assumed to be universal in the first part of our lives are not the only ones we might have chosen. Other assumptions about the nature of reality might exist that could have—and still might be able to—shape our lives, perhaps in an equally or even more productive way, were we to have experienced them with the same regularity as those that are so familiar. It has become clear to many of us that this awakening can come from the way of council.

Take just the "call to circle"—that is, setting the intention to gather a group of students and teachers for a weekly circle, lasting an hour or so, to share each other's personal realities. Or a community of health practitioners deciding to conduct monthly councils to deepen their practices and support each other. Gathering for these purposes implies that there is something larger than our individual goals and reasons for being in school or practicing some form of medicine, something that has to do with communing with others that can produce a wide range of experiences from joyous to solemn, from comforting to challenging—and from uneventful to exciting .

We value this coming together intrinsically for the purpose of connecting, even without knowing how the experience will actually turn out. (We might use the phrase "the pull to community" to describe this intrinsic instinct to gather.) Our lives are filled with comings together for a variety of purposes: to eat, work, gather with neighbors, witness sporting events, worship, to listen to a speech and—in school—to learn. In council the purpose of gathering can have similar aims . . . and yet there is another more hidden purpose to gather that, although not unique to council, occurs there with remarkable frequency.

We gather in council in order to experience the wisdom that is greater than the sum of the individual experience and knowledge brought by each members of the circle. This "synergistic wisdom" arises in large part from the deep listening that occurs in council.

This shift into collective awareness can be disorienting, even a little threatening, to some at first, since we live in a culture that venerates independence and individual achievement so strongly. In council, however, it is often the strength of the circle and the rich diversity of views expressed that we sense as being so powerful, even when there is significant disagreement within the group. Something happens in council that is often missing in a free-for-all group discussion, particularly when the topic is controversial. Part of this "something" arises from the very shape of the circle itself: nonhierarchical, without beginning and end, and with the possibility of everyone making eye contact with each other.

One less abstract name for this sense of synergy is "mutual endeavor." Using such a term brings the mystery of council a little closer, since most of us can accept the importance of mutual endeavor in the work place, in our families and in schools. In council mutual endeavor is given special emphasis by the shape of the circle, the intention to listen to each voice attentively and by the possibility of hearing the voice of the circle—the collective wisdom that is an ultimate harvest of accomplishing something as a group.

Just accepting the value of mutual endeavor is a step in the right direction. When we experience our commonality (rather than the more familiar feelings of individuality and competition that are so common in our culture generally), we are well on the road towards understanding ourselves—and others—more realistically. Even when there is disagreement, we can still recognize—and even embrace—broad mutual concerns underlying and beyond the issues about which we are at odds. This awareness of mutual concern even in the face of disagreement is often what is sadly lacking in organizational meetings, legislative bodies and even family conversations. Sitting with each other, making eye contact with the intention of deeply listening, starting the council with a dedication—all of these aspects of council, and many more, help us to remember that ultimately we are all on the same team, facing the same challenges of creating an interdependent, mutually supportive life together on "satellite earth" (as Bucky Fuller used to say).

For intimate partners the mutual endeavor is, fundamentally, the relationship itself, which many mature couples experience as having a life of its own, as we described in Chapter 8. As that relational "we" becomes stronger, the couple's ability to communicate, collaborate and be compassionate with each other (the three "C's" of a good relationship!) expands and deepens. In a family, it is implicit in the family "We," such as when a member says, "We always celebrate birthdays in a special way" or "We never turn anyone away from our door when they are hungry." Between friends, the mutual endeavor is the ongoing existence of the friendship itself, which can be prospering even if the two friends are both suffering and, conversely, can be suffering even if the two friends are individually in fine fettle. The friendship has an existence all on its own that is, paradoxically, deeply connected to the two people and yet not totally dependent on them. In council we learn to listen for the voice of the circle, even when it is not spoken explicitly by any one individual. Sometimes the wisdom carried by its words—or its silence—can take our breath away.

Achieving a direct experience of mutual endeavor in a school, community or place of business is often quite challenging, even with council. For example, how often do parents, children, teachers, administrators and counselors sit together to even acknowledge, much less experience viscerally, the awesome undertaking of educating young people in the Twenty-First Century? How often do people living in urban neighborhoods even know each other, much less gather together to discuss concerns of mutual interest? Even in more intentional communities, the process takes enormous patience and perseverance, as our Wind River story in Chapter 10 revealed. Despite the enormous benefits that can be harvested from such pursuits, many of us rarely persevere to create such "full community processes."

THE VALUES THAT FOLLOW FROM THE INTENTIONS OF COUNCIL

The implications of the four intentions of council are more self-evident than the subtleties explored in the previous section . . . and we still marvel at the powerful ways the practice of council draw us into exploring deeper levels of these intentions. In council it is clearly not as easy to hold back the truth and compromise ones authenticity as it is in ordinary conversation. When we are being witnessed attentively, there is a palpable, almost magnetic, call for greater honesty, self-revelation and vulnerability—not the more superficial or self-justifying version of "truth" that often takes over ordinary conversation.

The guardians at the gates of the ego seem less attentive in council. The old adage: "Truth will set you free," becomes a direct experience. Council allows each person in the circle to approach that state of freedom at their own pace and in their own way. A council-mate may challenge us to go further or question whether we are telling the full or real story, but in council even this challenge tends to feel more like an invitation than a judgment. As we go deeper into the circle process, we know that harsh judgments tend to be witnessed in the reflections of others and so, over a period of time, we sit less in the judgment seat and become more naturally empathetic. This kind of maturing is primarily experiential and usually happens slowly over a period of time . . . An old story comes to mind.

I remember a time many years ago when a first grader at Heartlight began to share dreams in the morning circle. It was clear to the rest of us that his ˋdreams' were being made up on the spot so he could have something ˋsignificant' to say. A few of the older kids would smile when he began to tell his stories and occasionally one of his friends would say, ˋyou're just making that up,' when they got the talking piece. However, the dreams kept on coming, along with protestations of their authenticity, until we began to realize—children and adults alike—that Martin was speaking a ˋtruth of his own' and needed to do exactly what he was doing. His dream-story creations really harmed no one and took only a little council time now and then.

After someone had challenged Martin one day, an older friend of his explained to the circle, ˋWe make up the dreams we have anyway, so Martin is just making his up in a different kind of way . . . It's actually quite creative.' That comment led to a remarkable council on the nature of dreaming and a subsequent council on the subjectivity of honesty. After a few months, Martin stopped telling us his ˋdreams' and then several weeks later shared one that felt quite authentic. The tone of his voice and the way the story flowed were different than before. We all felt good listening to him that day, good about ourselves for having been non-judgmental, and pleased that Martin had begun to remember his dreams."

Obviously, honesty is not a simple matter. It is significant that the first intention of council grew to be, "speak from the heart," rather than, "tell the truth" or "be honest," even though those words were and are often used in explaining what the first intention actually means in practice. In choosing words to explain the intentions of council in those early years, the children faced the challenge of being honest by placing the focus indirectly on what seems at first a metaphor, a metaphor that connects truth and love. We now know that the heart has a neurological dimension as well as its familiar function as a pump for the blood system and so there is actually a way that "speaking from the heart" can be taken quite literally.[1]

The implications of the second intention also take us into the subtleties of authentic communication—in this case the nuances of listening. Sadly, the process of listening seems to be increasingly less well understood in our mainstream culture. The era of sound-bites, MTV and kids plugged into Ipods and Gameboys makes it difficult for most of us to understand much less experience (as author Merker points out) that listening is a comprehensive experience of the entire human condition that goes way beyond hearing words.[See "Listening," by Hannah Merker, Southern Methodist University Press] Those two strange looking objects that stick out of the sides of our heads send messages to the brain—even during silent moments—that are integrated into the full sensory awareness of the central nervous system. In council we get at least a chance to break out of our limited experience about listening and begin to have an inkling of how devout listening actually can encompass the full range of human emotions. Just as our eyes can be blind to what we are not accustomed to seeing because of the way the optic nerve and brain are connected, our ears cannot truly hear another person's story unless the "ears of our heart" are also awakened. That the children made up the phrase, "listen from the heart," to describe this kind of listening thirty years ago, can only be described as intuitive wisdom.

---

[1] See for example, "Heart-Brain Neurodynamics: The Making of Emotions," by R McCraty, HeartMath Research Center, Insitute of HeartMath, Publication No. 03-015. Boulder Creek, CA, 2003 and "The Biology of Transcendence," by Joseph Chilton Pearce, Park Street Press, 2002

The complex connection between the physiological and psychological aspects of listening has been studied by many researchers, including French physician Albert Tomatis. His research has led to the development of a comprehensive process for dealing with learning disabilities and brain-body coordination in children and adults that focuses on reawakening and re-sensitizing listening capabilities. The Tomatis Method also provides a comprehensive framework for understanding communication, language, and the nature of learning through listening.[2]

Tomatis notes that "interconnected with several different levels of the brain, the ears act as a double antenna receiving messages from both the body and the environment. They are a link between the world within and the world without."

Tomatis practitioners have shown that by learning to "focus the ear," one can more effectively integrate the sensations and perceptions of the inner and outer worlds and, as a consequence, become more responsive, creative, and productive. This process provides a physiological basis for attentive listening. The Tomatis method provides specific physical exercises (called "Earobics") for improving focusing skills that have met with considerable success, particularly with children. The practice of council is also profoundly earobic.

When we start to listen attentively in council—really attentively—our hearts are stirred, often palpably. This in turn allows us to listen still more empathetically, with the ears of the heart, which then opens the heart still further. The effects of this biofeedback loop eventually changes the way we relate to people and the way we feel about ourselves. This kind of listening also can improve students' academic performance, as the WestEd quantitative evaluation of the Palms Middle School Council Program demonstrated some years back.[3] The earlier in life we begin to have these kinds of listening experiences the better, since the ear-brain neurological system is fairly well established by the end of adolescence.

---

[2] *When Listening Comes,* by Paul Madaule, Moulin, 1993. See also, *About the Tomatis Method,* edited by Timothy M. Gilmore, Paul Madaule, and Billie Thompson, Listening Centre Press, 1989.

[3] "Palms Council Project Evaluation: Final Report," WestEd, by Barbara Dietsch, August 31, 2001

The third intention of council—to be lean—is a "sleeper." For a long time at Heartlight we thought of it as a practical guideline that allowed councils to proceed in a timely fashion and not have the talking piece end up halfway around the circle when the bell rang (not a happy situation!). Speaking in a lean manner tends to avoid those agonizing times when someone goes on and on with a story that's not relevant to the topic or when you know as a facilitator that, unless you interrupt, time will run out before everyone has a chance to speak. As we said in Chapter 2, when the Heartlight students made up the intentions many years ago, they said simply, "Be brief," but we changed the word because we didn't want to shut down longer, more moving stories that really needed to be spoken.

With the change to the word lean, we evoked the implicit teachings of the third intention.

The meaning of "lean" tends to be more subjective than that of "brief." A lean story needn't be short and a short story may not be lean. Leanness has to do with what is essential to the story and is the mark of a great storyteller. Even though creating great storytellers is not a main purpose of council, it doesn't hurt to pick up a few leanness skills in one's life. They go a long way in improving social interactions and can play a major role in intimate relationships, not to mention public speaking.

When we launch into a story in council keeping the third intention in mind, we are more likely to pick up the Interactive Field of the listeners and have that awareness shape the way the story is told. We can feel "people leaving us" as we go on, even if we haven't been speaking for a long time. As we get more sensitive to the field of listeners and respond to it naturally, it can be a great teacher, reminding us that we're telling the story or making the statement as a contribution to the circle, as well as satisfying our own personal needs for expression. Any interaction with others has the potential of teaching us the same lesson, but in council the teaching is transmitted more often and more powerfully.

Leanness has a lot to teach us about impatience as well. Sometimes, a person needs to go on a while in order to discover how she or he feels about an experience. Giving voice to these feelings in council may be providing the first glimpse of what really happened for the speaker and so becomes an adventuresome plunge into the unknown. This aspect of the Third Intention teaches us tolerance and how to distinguish the search for meaning from the sharing of something whose meaning has already been grasped. The tolerance comes from learning to listen, even if someone seems to be lost in a search for meaning by shifting from needing to be entertained into being supportive of someone else's process. Needless to say, this lesson is an important one in all our relationships and lies at the heart of relating empathetically. Being able to step out of one's personal needs for a moment, shift focus by perceiving what someone else is trying to do, and then become interested in supporting them by listening more attentively, is a great ally in battling our culture's narcissistic tendencies.

Finally, the third intention can also challenge the skills of even experienced council facilitators. When is it appropriate to interrupt someone who is going on and on, seemingly off topic and obviously creating restlessness among many members of the circle? We have already explored this issue at length in Chapter 5. Suffice it to say here that such decisions are intense teaching moments for facilitators—and others in the circle as well.

The challenges council participants face fulfilling the fourth intention are legend. Being truly spontaneous is one of the greater challenges of the human condition. Considering how hard it is to train our minds to be still, this is not surprising. As the talking piece approaches, even the most seasoned council practitioners experience thoughts, feelings, stories—perhaps as well as songs, gestures and also the option of silence—as possibilities for offerings to the circle. A still mind is hard to come by at any time and in council, with often so much going on, it can be quite a daunting prospect. Devout listening, of course, is an ally of spontaneity. The second and fourth intentions are inseparable, even symbiotic. As we have said before, if you are really listening, you can't be preparing and, if you are preparing, you can't be listening very attentively.

But if—just if—as the piece comes closer, we manage to sufficiently still our anxiety, excitement and mental activity about what we are going to say, then, when it becomes our turn, that stillness can take us into an expanded state of consciousness that is intrinsically spontaneous. In this state we often discover that we have more authentic creativity and insight then when our ordinary mind is running the show. Being spontaneous allows us to hear new voices from our inner council that sometimes we didn't even know existed. Again and again, council facilitators have the experience of watching young and old faces alike light up with amazement as they discover they can be creative, insightful or empathetic even with people they don't get along with very well.

Thus the intention to be spontaneous can guide us into the same terrain that we explore during meditation or when experiencing a place of natural beauty without being distracted with a flood of busy thoughts. The basic practice is simple, even though each of us may have a unique way of staying focused as our turn to speak approaches: take a breath, go deeper into listening to what is being said; let go your thoughts, particularly those that keep returning . . . Then, finally, even let go of thinking itself . . . Forget to think! When this happens and then the talking piece appears in our hand, we're not sure which member of our inner council is going to show up. Sometimes, the surprise is delightful . . . and sometimes it can be startling to discover who does!

Obviously, long-held, deep personal patterns can be an obstacle to spontaneity. Yet, without any patterns we would have to make up who we are in each moment, which sounds like a lot of work. In council the guardians at the gates of our ego-identities can become more interested in what is actually going on with others than in keeping something new from passing through their portals. Then we soon find ourselves discovering a new voice in our inner council and so take a step further towards knowing who we really are. When we hear another person say something that would normally produce a familiar response and, instead, something entirely new comes out of our mouths—perhaps even silence—we feel freed from the bondage of our old self-definitions, at least temporarily. At times, this shift can be truly transformative. These moments of "council realization" can become part of a new way of speaking or reacting to others that we carry onwards into our daily life.

I remember a time long ago at Heartlight when two boys who fought with each other verbally on a daily basis fell into their usual dance in council:

Richard set the bait, not at recess or between classes as he usually did, but this time when he had the talking piece in our morning council. He described an interaction with Billy the previous day that made his "friend" look like a jerk. The story was funny, vivid and painted a pretty bad picture of Billy. Although he could hardly contain himself, we were in council, so this time Billy couldn't immediately respond. His whole body went into a silent spasm that communicated quite clearly how he was feeling. I held my breath to see if he would break council . . . but he didn't say anything. As it happened to be that morning, Richard was sitting across a circle of 18 students from Billy, so there were eight children that would have a chance to speak before he would be able to tell his version of the story. I doubted Billy could wait that long, but I underestimated the "power of the process" to transform a patterned situation. Several of the intervening kids commented on the way the two boys argued day after day. Others spoke of what was uppermost in their minds and hearts—which had nothing to do with the familiar Richard-Billy interaction.

All the intervening sharing began to have an effect on Billy. I watched a change come over him slowly as he took in the witnessing of his relationship with Richard and, despite his upset, let himself get interested in what the other kids were saying. As the talking piece come closer, his body relaxed noticeably, and by the time he began to share, I realized that he had actually forgotten what Richard had said. Their relationship pattern had been identified by a few of the other students as boring and tiresome, and Billy had taken those reflections to heart. The energy fueling his usual emotional reaction had been redirected into hearing about the lives of other classmates and so he "chose" not to respond to Richard in the usual way, or even say anything at all about the previous day's interaction. It was a breath-taking moment for a few of us—and it changed Billy and Richard's relationship forever. Council had offered Billy the rare opportunity of being released from a long-held pattern and he made full use of the opportunity. I felt enormously grateful.

THE VARIETIES OF HUMAN INTELLIGENCE

Many educators have come to recognize that the standard curriculum in US public schools (and many independent schools as well) has been primarily focused on only a portion of human intelligence. The evaluation of students, teachers and even schools themselves is increasingly based on standardized testing that primarily measures linguistic and logical-mathematical aspects of intelligence. It turns out these are but two of the seven intelligences explored by many researchers over the past thirty years, including Howard Gardner, Daniel Goleman and Rachael Kessler.[4] The remaining types of intelligences are: intrapersonal, interpersonal, kinesthetic, musical and spatial. Despite the growing awareness of the importance of these other five kinds of intelligence, most students are still evaluated primarily on the basis of their linguistic and logical-mathematical capabilities and so end up thinking of themselves as successful or not, depending on their linguistic and logical skills. This self-identification usually extends into adulthood and can limit our sense of self in profound ways.

Obviously, the practice of council also values linguistic intelligence through its emphasis on verbal expression and authentic communication. Logical-mathematical intelligence comes into play (perhaps to a lesser extent) with both students and adults through exercises and council themes that explore what results from making certain as-

---

[4] See, for example, "The Soul of Education," by Rachael Kessler, CES National, 2002; "Social Intelligence: the New Science of Social Relationships," by Daniel Goleman, Bantam Book, 2006; "Multiple Intelligences," by Howard Gardner, New Horizons, 2006

sumptions about the issue at hand. These assumptions are often tied up with our chosen system of values in ways that can be unconscious. Illuminating this complex thought process is analogous to the way students study the implications of certain axioms in their study of Geometry. It was his exploration of "undeniable assumptions" (again, often made unconsciously) that the physicist, David Bohm, used in developing his "dialog" approach to conflict resolution and decision making. Bohmian Dialog and council have many similar intentions, although the practices unfold in quite different ways.[5]

It is also clear that council provides ample room to practice "intrapersonal" intelligence—the ability to access personal experience in forming a cohesive story about one's life (as was emphasized in Chapter 7 and elsewhere). Council helps us to see our whole life as an unfolding story much in the same way that collectively we create our cultural mythos. Most of all, council provides endless opportunities to develop our "interpersonal intelligence"—our abilities to listen empathetically to the thoughts, feelings and stories of others.

In recent years the network of CCT practitioners has broadened its capability—both with young people and adults to encourage "kinesthetic," "spatial" and "musical" intelligences. For example, in Chapter 4 we described a variety of councils "without words," all of which stimulate kinesthetic intelligence. Beginning a council with movement, shifting into a physical mirroring exercise, or playing "Simon (or Simona!) Says" when verbosity has "clogged the field," brings balance to the circle.

A certain kind of spatial intelligence is encouraged in council through the ongoing, invitation for everyone to learn to "read the field." The longer we sit in circles, particularly in the facilitator role, the more adept we become in taking in the full emotional and visual aspects of the circle (including ourselves!) and so learn how to adjust our listening and speaking accordingly. Spatial awareness can also be stimulated in council through the use of such spontaneous art exercises as the drawing of "life picture maps" that describe visually the

---

[5] *On Dialog*, by David Bohm, Edited by Lee Nichol, London:Routledge, 1996.

emotional, physical, mental and spiritual aspects of our basic personalities and the way we live. Another council exercise that works well with young people, and is sometimes of great help in adult circles as well, is to use clay to form an object that represents our current mood or state of mind.

Stimulating musical intelligence is one of the consequences of using sound councils (described in Chapter 4) to shift the emphasis from verbal communication about "content" to the more right brain, interactive aspects of what is going on in the circle. Sound councils often delightfully remind us how much communication can occur without words. Of course, beginning a council with song or drumming provides a direct stimulation of the kind of intelligence that is rooted in music.

Gardner also suggests the possibility of an eighth type of awareness that he calls "moral," and which he says arises as a combination of logical, linguistic, intra- and interpersonal intelligences. Council is fertile ground for enhancing moral intelligence through its use in exploring and resolving conflicts, deciding what actions to take when difficulties arise in the group and going deeply into the differences people exhibit in how they decide what is right and what is wrong. An excellent example of the latter is a set of "lessons" on values clarification, developed by Bonnie Tamblyn in recent years for the Eighth-Grade Council Program at Crossroads School. This council curriculum takes several weekly councils to implement and is one of the more comprehensive exercises and activities in the school's overflowing "Council Treasure Chest."[6]

---

[6] For further information about the Values Clarification Curriculum and other council materials, contact Sheila Bloch or Adam Behrman at Crossroads School, 1714 21st Street, Santa Monica, CA 90494

IMPLICATIONS ARISING FROM THE TRADITION OF COUNCIL

As we have emphasized throughout the book, it is important that council in general—and particularly council programs in schools—be offered in an eclectic context, as a universal practice unattached to any particular culture or tradition. When someone asks where the practice comes from, we often begin our response with, "council belongs to all people." At the same time we acknowledge as "ancestors" the many manifestations of council in traditional cultures (particularly those rooted in Native American practices) and part of the inspiration for remembering council in a contemporary setting. Holding the practice respectfully in this manner by expressing gratitude to the long line of practitioners to whom we are indebted has a subtle effect on all of us who lead councils and, therefore, also on the people we facilitate—even if we never speak of this lineage explicitly. At a moment of particular intensity in council, some of us have had the feeling of "remembering"—a sense of knowing that we have done the practice before, a very long time ago. There is a "Field of Council" embedded deeply in the human condition and, although the practice can be forgotten for generations (as has happened in the West), it re-emerges again from this Field, reborn and compelling to those that feel its call.

Just a song or a few words during the brief ceremony that starts a council can open the door to this lineage connection. The form of the circle itself and restating the four intentions can be enough to induce a feeling that the practice has been handed to us from those who have gone before—as if council itself is an invisible talking piece being passed from generation to generation. However, honoring our lineage is not a common experience for many of us in Western Culture, in part because of the Mainstream's focus on youth and the accelerating pace of technological innovations. To put it another way, the Mainstream lacks a coherent vision of elderhood. The wisdom of elders often is unappreciated and so not utilized. We tend to think of getting older in terms of aging rather than in terms of becoming "wisdom keepers," as was—and still is—the case in many traditional cultures. Sadly, many of our elders accept this model of aging and fail to appreciate their own gifts. When this happens, retirement can become their goal rather than playing a significant role in the culture during their final vital years.

Council practice tends to counter these mainstream tendencies in many ways, most directly because the elders in traditional cultures often utilize some form of council as their way of meeting and decision-making. Just the ongoing use of simple ceremony and the emphasis on storytelling connects us with the past. In a council circle telling a story can take on a slightly bigger than life quality, relative to sharing the same story informally over a meal or as part of casual conversation. The active listening empowers the storyteller to go a little deeper, choose language a little more boldly and see the bigger picture inherent in the story more clearly. This is how myth is created, slowly over time, through the telling and retelling of the stories of life in a context that embraces deep listening.

Particularly before they reach adolescence, most children come to a sense of the passage and continuity of time without having to understand the process consciously. One important reason for exposing students to council in elementary or at least by middle school is so that tradition can have a place in their time-consciousness. Without exposure beforehand, by eighth grade, physiological changes and the desire to "be cool" make it more difficult for students to participate in the creation of personal myth through the process of "talking story" (the traditional Hawaiian expression for attentive conversation and story-telling). If children don't grow up with a deep exchange of stories as part of family life or as an integral part of their community, then it is even more important to introduce this life-affirming practice in their schools through council. We have initiated students successfully to council at the eighth-grade level and later—with perseverance, patience and the use of appropriate lead-in exercises. But when a circle of eighth-graders has already had council for several years (as is the goal of LAUSD's Council Practitioners Center), the difference can be quite remarkable. By then, the implicit meaning and skills of council can have entered their bloodstream sufficiently for the practice to actually become part of what it means to be cool!

We don't mean to diminish the natural and even necessary rebelliousness of students, particularly during pre-adolescence and adolescence. And, of course, coyote can be very present in adult councils as well. Dealing with this energy in circle is a familiar experience for all of us who facilitate councils in schools. In the vast majority of situations, the council process is strong enough to handle rebelliousness and, in fact, grow from it. We're already talked about "coyote presence" in Chapters 4 and 7. Coyote tests how strongly the group holds the intentions and how the facilitator can bend with the wind like a willow tree without breaking. A circle without coyote's presence over a period of time can become quite flat. On the other hand, too much irreverence can break the integrity of the circle—at least temporarily. All of us have been through such difficult moments and lived to tell the tale. Usually we end up being stronger for it, primarily because council has a long history, has survived greater challenges than we can imagine and lives in the core of human experience. We wouldn't be surprised if some day geneticists discover one or more genes for council!

When irreverence and playfulness are given their seats in the circle—authentically—rebelliousness is less likely to take on more violent and destructive forms. As we all know, having something urgent to say and no place to say it is a main source of rebelliousness and why, historically, rebellion has been necessary at times in order that much needed change can take place.

Challenges to Council Values: "Council Fundamentalism"

Although many people support most of the values discussed in the previous sections, certainly some do not. So it behooves us to comment on how one can handle conflicts of values when they arise. We also feel obliged to alert (particularly new) practitioners to the pitfall of getting so enthralled with the possibilities of council that the practice is used in a way that might be inappropriate in their particular setting. This is particularly true for school council programs.

Council's innate egalitarian context for communication and the inevitable expansion of honest, authentic interactions that takes place in council can become threatening to those community and business leaders, school administrators and teachers who feel such a level of openness is not appropriate. For example, a teacher might say (and more than a few have over the years), "After all, the primary goal of a school is to deliver a successful academic program, not exchange a lot of personal information." Most council facilitators who work in schools understand this traditional perspective and have learned to deal with it. Fortunately, with time, many of these teachers and administrators have come to see that council has its place in a curriculum and, moreover, can actually enhance the delivery of academic programs, as we have already emphasized in earlier chapters.

However, by no means does everyone "come around" to embracing council. There are still those educators who disapprove of taking an hour a week away from academic studies and a (very) few who seem quite adamant that council has no place in primary and secondary education. At a public school in Los Angeles many years before the Council Practitioners Center was created, one administrator's strong antipathy for council and the less than enthusiastic support from the Principal, finally led to the termination of the program after a few years, even though the students were enthusiastic, the several trained teachers were deeply committed and a group of enthusiastic parents raised most of the money to support the program. (Many years later, after the administrator left, the council program was reinstated by the still committed teachers.)

In such cases one invariably speculates that the disapproval may be for more personal reasons rather than conflicts of educational philosophy or a missed hour for the standard curriculum, however the objections are stated. Encouraging deeper relationships among students and teachers may be threatening to "teacher-authority" for some members of the faculty. On a more personal level, the idea of being openly honest about one's feelings in a circle of peers, much less students, can feel so foreign (for cultural/ethnic reasons perhaps) and/or frightening to some adults that they end up making judgments about council's appropriateness.

To whatever extent these explanations may be true at times, it is simply not possible in the busy life of a school to sit with a person who holds antipathy towards council long enough to (possibly) help them through their reactions, particularly if they have not the slightest interest in doing so. So, in the case just mentioned, we let the program go and focused our energy on schools that were inviting us to start new programs. We felt sadness for the students, the few teachers that had been involved in the effort and the parents who had worked so hard to keep the program going, but there seemed ultimately no point in trying to "push the river" any longer.

The reality of meeting resistance to council in starting a program—whether it be in a school, community or place of business—offers a special opportunity to those involved. In the business context, for example, corporate leaders sometimes fear that incorporating a process like council will take time away from more directly productive activities and perhaps even "cool the aggressive edge" needed to be competitive in the marketplace. Our story of the Continental Dealership in Chapter 10 reveals how limited this point of view can be but, nevertheless, we have talked with many business leaders who need a lot of convincing (and some direct experience!) before they get the message. What works is to be in the spirit of council during these kinds of exploratory dialogs. The guiding facilitators of a new program need to live the practice of council in every preliminary meeting and discussion with the leaders of the community, business or school (including parents and students in the latter case). A council program works far better in any setting when those who lead the program "walk their talk" and live the values we have been discussing.

Sometimes this fails to happen when practitioners get so enthralled with council that they polarize with those who find it inappropriate or unsuitable and fail to see that this divergent point of view needs to have its seat in the circle as well. All voices are welcomed in council. It is a profound challenge to stay open in this way, particularly if the very life of the program depends on it—but that is our challenge in bringing the practice into any organization, particularly if it has a long-established structured style of operations. The personal guidance we offer facilitators in these situations is to first come to terms with your own way of understanding council's implicit values and then hold these values fluidly in the spirit of council with those that challenge you. We might say, hold council and its values as you would hold a much-loved child—with the balance of firmness and gentleness that arises from deep caring and understanding.

This is also good advice in combating "council fundamentalism." By this we mean pushing the use of the practice in situations that are, in fact, inappropriate under the banner that "council can handle every human interaction better than any other means." This is simply not the case. Even in traditional societies whose ethos supports a "culture of council," we find certain situations that were and are still best handled in other ways. Furthermore, the basic forms of traditional council practices vary considerably, particularly in regard to the level of authority given to the council leader(s). For example, in the traditional Hawaiian practice, "Ho'o Pono Pono," the clan elder plays a far more active role in shaping and directing the proceedings than a council leader does in the way we have been implementing the practice at the Ojai Foundation and in the CCT Network. In the Hawaiian tradition the role of the leader can be described simplistically as a cross between a council facilitator and a traditional elder ("kapuna") or even a shaman ("kahuna"). Obviously, having facilitators play these kinds of role would not be easily embraced in some settings.

In addition to being clear about appropriate limitations of the leadership role, there are a variety of situations for which council is generally inappropriate, whether the context is community, school or business. These include:

- Doing interactive, therapeutic or psychological work with a single member of the circle

- Discussing feelings about an individual familiar to the circle when that person is not present

- Creating an opportunity in council for the circle to make decisions about some aspect of their collective life without appropriate leadership having delegated such authority to the circle

The first of these applies to virtually all council settings, except those that are specifically meant to focus on personal therapeutic work. The second is universal; when it happens, the effect on the circle can be quite damaging.

The last of these situations is a particularly interesting one in a school setting. We have on occasion used council to create a mock decision-making process about some aspect of student life—such as how to discipline a student who has broken a school rule or policy. This can be a powerful experience for a group and stimulate a deeper understanding of the need for clear rules and appropriate consequences when the rules are broken. On the other hand, if it is not made entirely clear that such an exploration is being conducted as an exercise and will not necessarily have any effect on school policies (if this, in fact, is the case), then there is a risk that the students will feel understandably let down if they come up with what they think is a great process for disciplining students and nothing comes of it.

Some years back we did conduct an exercise of this kind and came up with such a clear and useful way of handling disciplinary matters that the facilitators and students decided to make a formal proposal to the faculty based on what they had discovered. To our delight, the faculty responded favorably and initiated the process as part of school policy. The process that was finally implemented actually involved councils of students, teachers, administrators and parents and has worked well now for many years.

A Final Story

Our exploration of council's implicit values and the skills it helps to develop has taken us along a winding path strewn with many words about the human condition. In the spirit of the third intention of council, we end this chapter with a familiar short story about geese that, in its own way, says it all.

"Next fall, when you see the geese heading south for the winter, flying along in a ` V formation,' you might consider what science has discovered about why they fly that way.

As each bird flaps its wings, it creates an uplift for the bird immediately following. By flying in a ` V formation,' the whole flock adds at least 71% more flying range than possible were each bird to fly on its own.

"When a goose falls out of formation, it suddenly feels the drag and resistance of trying to go it alone . . . and quickly gets back into formation to take advantage of the lifting power of the bird in front. When the head goose gets tired, it rotates back in the wing and another goose flies point. Geese honk from behind to encourage those up front to keep up their speed.

"Finally—and this is important—when a goose gets sick or is wounded by gunshot and falls out of formation, two other geese drop out with that goose and follow it down to earth to lend help and protection. They stay with the fallen goose until it is able to fly or until it dies. Only then do they launch out on their own or with another formation to catch up with their original group."

13

THE NATURE
OF COUNCIL

Air moves us
Fire transforms us
Water shapes us
Earth heals us
And the circle of the wheel goes round and round
And the circle of the wheel goes round . . .

Source Unknown

RETURNING TO OUR ROOTS

A thread runs through much of what we have shared with you on this council journey that touches both the primal roots of the practice and informs our present capacity to live council fully. This thread has to do with the inseparability of council and the setting in which we do the practice, the timeless quality of what happens in council, and the core values of earth-cherishing cultures—most simply, *council and nature*. My earliest experiences of council were in the Sespe Wilderness of Southern California. I felt council for the first time sitting on the earth, many miles from any structures, with a fire to warm us and light the way. My earliest experiences of council with children, which were with the Heartlight students in the early Eighties, involved the natural world in an intrinsic way. At Heartlight all the kids participated in two nine-day retreats each year that included alone time in the Sespe Wilderness, a stone people's lodge at the Ojai Foundation—and a lot of council. The Crossroads Mysteries Program included five-day retreats at the Foundation, starting in 1983, the first year of the program; the Palms three-day student leadership retreats at the Foundation followed suit, starting in 1992. Since then, many of the schools that have ongoing council programs include retreats in nature, either in a wilderness setting, in the Foundation's semi-wilderness environment or at a similar location. Part of The Foundation's mission statement is to . . . *strengthen individuals, families, schools and communities by teaching ways to listen and speak from the heart, to honor life's passages, and to express our connection with nature by deepening relationships with each other and the earth . . .*

In this chapter we take a deep look at the marriage of council practice and nature, particularly in the context of rites of passage. The interweaving of these threads sheds light on council in schools, in homes, in communities—and in the city. Nature is present where council is practiced—and when those in the circle are conscious of this reality, the practice has boundless depth. Gigi has walked the path of council in nature in a profound way—since her childhood, as you will soon see— and brought the wisdom of this path to everything she does as a trainer, facilitator and circle participant. The alliance between council and nature has shaped her "call," as she would say, motivating how and where she brings the practice to the world. It is more than fitting that I pass her the talking piece to tell the story of, "The Nature of Council."

THE BEGINNINGS

Often people ask me when and where I learned council. What was my first council? To answer I go back to my earliest memories of childhood, times when I felt alone and lonely, and not a part of a neighborhood with other kids. We were driven to school, so the friends made there were left behind once the bell rang at day's end. I took refuge in the woods and there, in the seemingly infinite forest behind our suburban New England home, I found and made community. Old boards and bottles formed the inner shelves of my sanctuary. Rocks, branches and other local "trash" made my tables, benches and living area. I designed and decorated, sang and sat—and then waited for who would show up: a robin, a chipmunk, a neighbor's Lab, and one memorable day even a skunk. These friends formed my first councils which were filled with endless conversations with myself and with them. Each creature had a message, a place, and a role in the journey, a journey that has continued for years, living council with "all our relations."

I must have been around five years old but I can still remember what might be called my first council with people. It happened in that kindergarten activity Show-and-Tell. From my wooded sanctuary I brought an old bottle, worn down to a musty deep blue color, beautifully shaped, and perfect to pass around for everyone to hold. The bottle served as a kind of talking piece and held everyone's attention. Wow, I actually felt seen and heard! I was able to tell my story; others joined in once it was their turn to hold the bottle. I brought them into my world and, through the field that was created, I was able to communicate in a new easier way. In Show-and-Tell we shared what we cared about, what was special to us, what was sacred. I remember how interconnected everything felt; I remember the power of listening, of telling stories, of speaking spontaneously from the heart. I remember in those early experiences what I have come to call "*the nature of council.*" It is a world that is whole, truthful, and carries respect for all beings—a place where everything, not just the human, is a part of the circle. It was the chipmunk that visited each day who helped me open the gate of loneliness, and that old friend, my genie in the bottle, that gave me the confidence to speak in "public."

As I sit in council today with people of all ages, I often ask them when and where in their lives do they remember an experience of council. Many at first say, "No, oh no, there was none of that in my family or school." But then gradually a few stories emerge.

"I visited my grandparents every Sunday and it was so comforting when they would stop everything and for hours the world would slow way down. Not that it was a formal council, with a talking piece, a dedication or anything like that, but the spirit of council was there. My Grannie would notice everything about me that had changed from the week before—my hair, my new shoelaces, the band-aid on my finger. She would follow every story I told with one of her own so that the hours together moved into a sort of timeless dream. That was the time in my life I first felt seen and heard; that was when I felt a love and connection that I know now to describe as unconditional."

Often there are stories of pain and loss, followed by memories of a place—a rocky outcrop at the end of a beach—that served as a rest, a home, a meeting place for a six year old, or places where the animals became the confidantes, the healers, and the community for many in the city as well as those on the farm. What is exciting about these memories is that they are our own, not taught or given, but a natural part of being human. These experiences are cross-cultural and emerge beyond religious and national boundaries. They remind us that the experience of council is familiar and available to all of us.

LEADERSHIP TRAININGS
IN THE WILDERNESS

Council immersed in the natural world is one way I know to ground people in the nature OF council. As our native elders so beautifully remind us, we are not separate; we are part of the great circle, the great mystery. This perspective is a little different than the New Oxford American Dictionary's definition of nature: *"the phenomena of the physical world collectively, including plants, animals, the landscape, and other features and products of the earth, as opposed to humans or human creations.* There is a consciousness we have inherited from our ancestors, that is formed and evolves from deep dialogue with a wider circle, the circle of "all our relations." This reference to and inclusion of the natural world has become essential to my way of understanding the fullness of council and my guidance as a council carrier.

A few times a year I offer a five- to eight-day intensive course for council leaders, during which each participant is focused on council in the natural world, and the circle is seen more clearly as far more than human. Every day includes time alone on the land, as well as together in the circle. On the first day we focus on our listening and connection to water and, on the second day, to the earth. On the third day we climb up high to be fully with the air, and on the fourth day we build the fire and then greet the sunrise. Each participant brings a story back from these solo journeys with the four elements to enrich the council.

"As I sat up high on the ridge for my time in the north focused on the element air, I looked out over the valley and asked what I needed to learn. What was my work now as a council leader? I waited for an eagle or a hawk—some wonderful messenger bearing news. As the hours passed and none showed, I looked down at the ground, feeling a familiar place of doubt and self-pity creeping in. There at my feet was a whole world I had barely noticed: a small pink cactus flower growing out of the rocky outcrop; a colony of ants carrying their sticks across the uneven terrain with unending tenacity, rows and rows in formation. What were they building, and how did they carry loads that were twice their size? Watching this world I was moved to revisit mine and look at my work in a new way: many sticks, much rough ground, lots of helpers, a flower able to bloom even in an area where there appeared to be no life at all. I would return to the classroom, I would call on the support of my community and I would dare to introduce council in terrain that seemed barren and unfriendly. A breeze came up as the afternoon sun dipped in the sky. It brought me down the mountain in gratitude with—well— what I called a fresh breath, my second wind."

Near the last day of the training participants have the opportunity to go on a longer solo, and take the time to confirm their work and their paths as a carriers of council. We have found that the confirmation and empowerment that comes from this experience is one that really lasts, helping to offset the inevitable doubts and ego wrestling that come with leading council. As a carrier, it is important to be free of the need to be a "good facilitator," a star in one's circle. To receive the call and confirmation in nature in this way, without the dependence on being liked or confirmed by others, is deeply supportive. Although it may be best, as in the old traditions, to be confirmed by our elders, we live in a world where that is not always possible. As we seek to re-create councils of elders and rites of passage in modern times, we can also turn to other elders, ones that are not human, not so evident perhaps, yet always available. For example, we are blessed to be able to visit the ancient Bristlecone forests, not far from our home in Big Pine, California. They are the oldest trees in the world.

The magic of council emerges as we gain deep understanding that we hold but one seat in the circle and are only a part of the unfolding story. This lesson is confirmed daily in the natural world, through the dimming twilight, the power of a lit candle, the direction we choose to sit in, the storm thundering outside—all of which affect what happens in council. When we're in wild nature, this awareness tends to arise quickly.

"I was crying and asking for help, feeling tired and overwhelmed, lost in the story of abuse that had happened to me as a child. Not knowing what more to say, I suddenly felt raindrops falling gently on my hands and head. It seemed to be a blessing, a cleansing, somehow part of a healing that was quietly unfolding."

Many of us have the challenge of bringing these teachings of the natural world—vividly and fully alive—into our offices and classrooms. I ask leaders to remember this connection with nature, and find ways to elicit and offer direct experience of it in the circles they facilitate. One way is to let the talking piece serve as a reminder of other natural forces at play.

"A stone from our home, our land, allowed the kids to think about ancestors in a new way. They looked at the fossil embedded in the rock and it drew them into another time and place. The experience opened a door for us to talk about our relationship to homeland and truly explore our common ground."

There are many ways to become aware of our connection with nature. Perhaps the most direct experience is to participate in the kind of rite of passage in the wilderness that I describe in the next section. Some students are fortunate enough to have access to outdoor educational programs that incorporate sensitivity to the connection with nature. However, in general our contemporary Western culture tends to see and describe nature as something "other," something we visit or use for recreation. The strongest message I hope to share—one carried so beautifully by earth cherishing cultures—is that we are never separate from nature. We *are* nature. The opportunity to listen to "all our relations," not just the human ones, exists wherever we are. How-ever, since not everyone is able to journey in the wild, we need other experiences that can create the inspiration that nature provides. So before we describe rites of passage in the wilds, I want to offer a few examples of topics, exercises and activities that can serve this end.

SUGGESTED ACTIVITIES, EXERCISES AND COUNCIL TOPICS FOR YOUTH WHEN WILD NATURE IS NOT AVAILABLE

Ask your students or any young person, "When in your earlier child-hood do you recall an experience of council?"

Ask if they know or can imagine any council or circle gathering that are part of their ancestry . . . Ask them to tell the story.

Send your group out for a walk alone in silence for two hours with a topic or question that is current in their lives. When they return ask them to tell the story of what they did and what they saw. Ask them how that provides information about or an answer to their question.

Invite your group to find a place in the natural world that calls them and where they would be comfortable. Ask them to spend at least an hour there and return with a story about the place and their experiences.

Spend a classroom period outdoors and ask the students to see if they can find any circles or spirals in nature. Ask them to bring the story of that exploration back to the circle. (This is quite possible to do even in the inner city.)

Ask members of the council to bring a talking piece from their home, land, or environment and use it as part of their sharing in council. Ask them to explain why the piece is appropriate or meaning-ful to them, and how it relates to the current theme in the circle.

Hold a thematic council and ask everyone to be particularly mindful of sound, movement, and changes in the environment during the council—especially when it is their time to share. If a cloud comes over or a siren goes off on the street, ask them to weave that into their sharing—possibly giving it meaning as a part of their story.

Ask the students what they know about the Four Directions, and to name some qualities or characteristics they think are appropriate for each. Ask them to sit in that direction and take on the quality in some way when they speak about a given topic. (For example: East is the sun rising, light, inspiration; South is the midday sun, the place of the child, and trust and innocence; West is the place of the setting sun, the Grandmothers and introspection; North is nighttime, the fallow period and the place of knowing.)

Create a 'council of all beings' in the spirit of John Seed and Joanna Macy. Listen to what nature has to say.[1] List the ways nature and council are similar and a mirror for each other.

RITES OF PASSAGE FOR YOUTH

One of the deepest experiences of council I know for youth and adults is to give themselves the gift of joining a wilderness quest. For youth this experience is extremely valuable as the kind of a deep initiation ceremony that is so needed in contemporary times. The journey is inspired by the initiation rituals in many ancient cultures and, as with council, the call for it seems inherent in all of us. I remember wondering as a child what Jesus was doing during his forty days and nights in the desert, and what Buddha was doing sitting for so long under the Bodhi Tree. My curiosity led me to spend time each year seeking guidance in the silence and solitude of the wilderness. Like many young people I sought connection, understanding, meaning, purpose, a sense of accomplishment or recognition, communion —no one word can de-

---

[1] *Thinking Like a Mountain,* by John Seed, Joanna Macy, Pat Fleming and Arne Naess, New Society, 1988

scribe it. In 1980, when I met Steven Foster and Meredith Little, their vision of the Vision Quest articulated the call very well.[2]

There is a natural longing to push against the boundaries of our humanness, to face death and, in so doing, reclaim life and hopefully find our own wild place, both within and without. In the search for the "edge," this leads many to take risks in nature, to go on modern walkabouts, to join gangs, or to experiment with drugs and sexuality. There is a natural— and I would say universal— need in young people to test themselves and then want to sit in council with elders in order to be seen, heard and finally recognized as capable, self-realized adults. The rite of passage for youth that we offer now at the School of Lost Borders incorporates a mental, psychological, physical, and spiritual testing of self that includes a three-day solo time of fasting in the wilderness. The young people return to base camp after the solo-fast to tell their stories. The days and nights, rocks, trees, stars, wind and sun all become their teachers.

"I was missing my father, now perhaps more than ever. He left before I was born and my stepfather spent many months working overseas far away from home. I wasn't really sure what it was I was missing but there was a big loneliness that even having the best mom in the world didn't fill."

Four days later this young man returned from his solo fast with a remarkable story about a fly that visited him the first day and then kept returning, reclaiming its territory by chasing other flies away.

"By the third day the fly had become my buddy, my ally, my friend. You may laugh but I know this was the same fly and he was there for me the whole time."

Although a father can never be replaced, this young man had found his emptiness filled by one of nature's most common creatures.

---

[2] *The Book of the Vision Quest*, by Stephen Foster and Meredith Little, Simon and Schuster, 1992

He was fascinated and fully engaged in the ease of creating a relationship with a stranger in the wild without being preoccupied with his usual Ipod activity. The experience created a beautiful metaphor for the possibility of having an extended family in the future. Hearing his story reminded all of us of the relationships available to us each day—if we are open and attentive to the present moment. In telling his story he created council with his peers, his elders, all his relations, and most particularly his stepfather, who sat in the welcoming circle with love and admiration.

During this kind of wilderness journey, the ability to speak truthfully and heartfully often comes more easily. The need to be better, cool, or different quickly falls away. In the natural world, without day-to-day distractions and routines, the experience of connection is amplified. This feeling of interrelatedness extends to the community of peers, youth and elders, to the natural world, and often to that which is bigger than life: the Divine, Spirit, the Mystery. No one is directed toward any belief. Rather they are given an opportunity to deepen and explore their own existing values, beliefs, and sense of the sacred. The shift in individual consciousness is supported by the rapid bonding of the group as together they face the authentic need for safety and cooperation. The freedom of inquiry, speaking one's truth, and the direct experience of heartful communication and interrelatedness often informs their future explorations and relationships.

In the councils, where everyone's stories are honored, peers are no longer the subject of the usual judgments and comparisons, and elders are no longer authority figures to be resented or resisted. Individual responsibility takes the place of hierarchy and the equal voice and value of each person becomes a vivid reality. Both the wholeness of the circle and the beauty of differences are celebrated. Facing difficulties together becomes an integral part of the experience, much like a passing storm, to be lived fully. Fears definitely arise—both because of the challenges of the wilderness and the deep inner work being done—but can be greeted as allies who help to keep us awake while we walk the edge.

"By the end of the story council, this time together has offered me a safe haven, a refuge, a place inside and out I had longed for, a place I could finally relax and be myself."

This is what we hear, year after year—and what we learn sitting with youth. They show up a hundred percent, given the chance. No pain is ignored and no happiness is seen to be 'better' than the pain. An inner city kid, who's hard life includes sleeping on the street in his car, hears the suffering of a wealthy "valley girl" whose cuts on her wrists accompany her sobbing plea to be more than a materialistic, superficial blonde. The young people release their old stories of life and step into the dreams of what they care about and who they really want to be. Each has a chance to let go and leave behind that which no longer serves. Each has a chance to wake up, a little more than they have before, with the dawn, reborn, ready to return with "gifts for their people"— most importantly, the gift of themselves. Usually they return from the mountain more at peace, expressing greater understanding and acceptance of who they truly are. With the community support they have been given and the sense of accomplishment under their belt, life appears a bit more livable and their future even exciting.

"I know I will get depressed again. I know I will have bad days with my friends, with my parents. But now, I have a sense I can move through them in ways I couldn't before— singing, writing, walking up a meadow or screaming at the stars at night."

With quest and council, young people can create a foundation, a touchstone, to take on the challenges of being an adult in a difficult, ever-changing world. Though they may never return to a similar wild place nor see any of the people in the circle again, they know what is possible and what living council with oneself, with others, and with the natural world, can be. Of course, they are not healed forever nor do they come back without many of their old flaws and challenges.

However, they are now grounded in the seasonal nature of growth and change—and in the deep knowledge of a circle way of thinking, working and living. The lessons nature teaches are hard won; how they faced their fears can guide them in the times to come. What they have accomplished is with them forever. On the tough days simply a tree, a rock or a star can remind them of who they really are.

It is both the council before they go out on their solo and the one after they return that help to give their journeys deeper meaning. The youth listen to each other's pain, challenges, frustrations and dreams—and realize more than ever that they are not alone. They have been held in a council of elders (those of us holding base camp), each one listened to and mirrored. Their story is reflected back to them both as a mythic journey and a deep personal experience. With all three phases of the Vision Fast completed—severance, threshold and incorporation—the council recognizes and welcomes each one into adulthood. As more youth discover and carry the way of council into their schools, churches, homes and hearts, they are able to live more openly, honestly, and in a way that is true to themselves. They have become initiated adults who, knowing more about their own strengths, weaknesses and gifts now, have a better chance to act in harmony with what they deeply care about in this world.

FOR ALL AGES

We encourage everyone we meet to mark the many passages in life, and include and honor elders, parents and younger siblings in many of our youth quest councils. Just this last year I heard a child give one of the most beautiful blessings for a mother about to give birth that I have ever heard. A few months later I watched that same child sit with unusual presence and love as she bore witness to the death of one of her teachers. Both of these experiences took place in council, under circumstances that some might worry would be too hard for a child so young and, consequently, disruptive for the adults. Just the opposite was true. In my experience, if we respect children and give them a role in the council, they respect the process and all those present in return. And when so-called disruptions do occur, they are quite often just the sign from nature that we need—the "wild card"—the action that surprises us, turns everybody upside down and keeps us awake.

"I came in to lead the group that evening tired. I had no theme in mind and no talking piece in hand. I sat down, carrying the weight of the world, only to be thrown, fortunately and quickly, off that pedestal. Sandy, age four, came into the room half dressed, with a larger than usual twinkle in her eye. She asked me if she could pick a talking piece and begin the council. I surrendered and suggested she do so and then pass the piece to me. I had a partner, a co-leader, just when I needed one. The sleeping doll she offered fit the mood of all of us and awakened in me the truth-telling with which we needed to begin. The theme became clear: what do we feel tired from and how do we need to take care of ourselves this month? Once again I was reminded of the infinite possibilities of council and the need to not have to do it all myself. I had been led by a precious four year old who we had thought did not even know what a talking piece was."

Weddings, births, deaths, divorce, illness and other times of significant change are all transitions when we can include children in the circle. These natural passages are often a time when the greatest learning happens. Council offers a way for us to be there together, each fully who we are—parent, friend, daughter or mentor—and to share from this perspective. No one needs to be left out—not the black sheep, the one who is too shy to speak up, nor the one whose anger reminds us of our own.

The dynamics of a family, community or a business organization are given an opportunity to shift and grow each time a council is called to offer a ceremonial marking of change. For many years we offered family quests during which the kids supported the parents going out and fasting in the desert. We were motivated by people's feelings of separation when either the parents or the kids came home from a transformative experience for which the other had not been present. On the family quests the kids did their own guided journeys in the wild and made gifts for their parents while they were away.

"I was scared to go out on my own but somehow knowing everybody else was out there made it OK. With our guides, I decided that nine hours was good for a nine-year old. I thought the time would never end until I found some beeswax type stuff dripping all over a log. I made a picture in it for hours I guess, pushing and molding it into a creature-friend. Then I noticed the sun going down and left my mark, my name, there, so relieved to return to my family below. I was glad that I knew a little something about what others had been doing out there and excited that I had been on my own journey."

The children felt their own empowerment as part of the story council, and were able to hear and honor their parents in a way that is unfortunately rare in most people's lives.

YOUTH AND ELDERS

Any opportunity to bring youth and elders together through council is to be encouraged. Yes, there are many wonderful youth trips with excellent young leaders and times when young people need to be learning entirely on their own. Yet given a society when the over-fifty crowd is growing larger, we have a great opportunity for the baby-boomers and young people to sit together—to offer an option other than retirement to those who have been so active throughout their lives and a voice to those who will now carry the responsibilities. In this way many stereotypes of both old and young can be dispelled.

I had the honor of helping catalyze councils between the "13 Indigenous Grandmothers" from around the world who were meeting in Dharmsala with the Dalai Lama, and the "Bioneers" who were gathered in San Rafael, California.[3]

Each night five of us from a larger council of a hundred that had met in the afternoon gathered again in the evening to speak and pray with the Grandmothers over a live satellite link. This extraordinary use of technology created a special form of council. No speeches were prepared. The themes were introduced: healing ourselves, healing our relations, and healing the planet. We all listened and spoke together in council for two hours over a distance of twelve thousand miles.

Needless to say, the highlight of the councils was witnessing the young people speak from their hearts and listen deeply to the wise ones. The connection was palpable when one young man asked about how he could reconcile the discovery that he had inherited land stolen from the Cree People. One of the grandmothers responded with great love and presence:

"The past is the past and we must go on, finding a better way, together. Find some way to use the land now to serve the people."

The courage it takes to name a wound and own the pain, to remember a crime, to forgive and start again, all touched us with just these few words exchanged over a great distance. We need the youth and the old ones to sit together; we need women . . . men . . . people of different faiths, races and species . . . to convene in councils of diversity. And we need public political voices that are real, truthful, and speak from the heart. Council is a training ground for such future leaders.

---

[3]"Bioneer"—from biological pioneer— is a neologism coined by filmmaker, author and eco-activist Kenny Ausubel. According to the *Utne Reader*, a bioneer is "a biological pioneer, an ecological inventor who's got an elegant and often simple set of solutions for environmental conundrums."

Many of our leaders have been lacking that voice. There seems to be little relationship between what some of them say and the expressions on their faces. The talk in council rarely suffers from such disconnection. What if the microphones of the world became talking pieces eliciting authentic, heartful speaking and deep listening?

A few years ago, before deciding to make a film about one of the youth quests, we had some concerns about recording a council ceremony. Would participants be shy or tend to perform in front of the camera and not be fully themselves? As it turned out, the kids loved it and used the opportunity to great advantage. They took the filming seriously, feeling it was their chance to truly be heard.

Now, as my colleagues and I continue to support indigenous elder's councils, we are also initiating cross-cultural youth councils to provide a place where young people can share their visions, dreams and prayers for the world. We hope to film these councils in a variety of countries and when possible bring more young voices from other countries into U.S. classrooms. Through this "Beyond Boundaries Initiative," we are hoping to create new opportunities for reconciliation and healing.

The elder and youth councils are significant steps towards an even broader vision. We envision councils in which there is room for all, perhaps, most importantly, the voices of those that have been least heard on our planet—the young, the old, the refugees, the impoverished, the oppressed, the animals, and the earth itself. Council is one place where we might truly learn how to do it together.

The nature of council is a call to the widest of circles, to all peoples, to all beings. Council is not a solution to all of our challenges, nor a course or a technique. It is a way, a path, a journey that we can choose to take together. The nature of council has much to teach us: wholeness, shared experience, interdependence and the natural creative circle of life.

At the last minute I had been asked to lead a closing of the Bioneers conference after an afternoon of workshops. We began with thank you's as we all gathered together around the straw bale outdoor stage. Then I dared to pass the microphone out into the crowd, asking people to share a few words that would help to close the circle. The spirit of council was palpable. A young man bore witness to how his life had been changed over the three days of the Conference . . . A women offered a poem that creatively captured the story of our time together and another suggested we share a song. After several more people spoke, I could feel peoples' nervousness about the council getting out of hand with endless personal sharing and so go on forever. When the woman asked if we could sing one more verse of the song, I suggested that we take the next verse out with us to sing to others after we leave. Then I asked for a few moments of silence so we could listen again to see if anything else was needed to honor the beautiful time of learning we had shared at Bioneers._

We waited together . . . A few moments passed . . . There was such a stillness and a feeling throughout the group that was hard to describe with words . . . No words were needed . . . The geese, who had been sitting around the council tent for days—the geese who fly with such awareness of each other—lifted up in formation through the sunset and flew directly overhead. We all looked up and knew that the conference was complete.

EPILOGUE:
THE NEXT ROUND

*"Empathy strikes me as the most
important quality that we need in America
and around the world."*

—President Obama

*We've been waiting, waiting
We've been waiting so long
We've been waiting for our children
To remember to return*

—Chant attributed to Paula Wallowitz

Suppose that the vision we elaborated in the previous
chapters comes to fruition—whatever the path of manifestation. Imagine what would take place in a culture that
embraces the spirit of council! Even the most formidable challenges
that confront us now—widespread hunger, militant nationalism, violent ethnic adversity, the growing rent in the ozone layer, the dying
oceans, the urgent need for clean and renewable sources of energy,
and the disposal of nuclear waste—might be manageable.

Imagine that it is the year 2012 and we are preparing a third edition of *The Way of Council*. Rather than retelling the tale of the pueblo elders that inspired my interest in council, the new introduction
might begin with a different story . . .

Gigi and I felt honored to have been invited to the gathering of Atomic Energy Commission members, state officials,
members of the nearby chamber of commerce, and Native-
American leaders. The focus of the meeting was the AEC's
proposal to build an underground nuclear waste storage facility at this remote portion of Federal land that borders on the
state's largest Native-American Reservation. We assumed our
invitation had something to do with all the councils we had
led over the past thirty years as this issue began stirring so
much debate.

It was good to be back in this part of the world. The desert
stretched for miles to the east beyond the large meeting tent,
towards the base of the bluffs that shone deep red in the late
afternoon sunlight. Our group of thirty or so had decided to
assemble on the proposed site rather than in Washington D.C.
or the state capitol. Now the beauty of the land had drawn us
outside to open the proceedings. A hundred yards from the
large tent someone had started a fire, anticipating the chill of
the desert evening.

Gigi and I were filled with a hundred silent questions.
What could be done to resolve this deeply troublesome matter? Since the beginning of the new millennium, two nuclear

waste dumps in other parts of the country had been leaking badly. Fear and outrage dominated public reaction. Now recently developed technology promised that a safer underground/overground storage facility could be built that would also serve as a research laboratory and shrine to our previous unconsciousness in dealing with nuclear materials. But no one was sure. The proposed site was remote from the populated portion of the reservation and other communities, but geological problems still existed. The local business community felt ambivalent. Some anticipated the commercial possibilities of a five-year major construction project in the area. Others saw the likelihood of a long-term decrease in property values and business opportunities after the hazardous material arrived at the site.

What could this diverse, intercultural group possibly accomplish in just a few days? Many years of debate, political maneuvering, and animosity characterized the relationships among the organizations represented. Would these people be able to bridge the enormous differences that separated each group's official position? Simultaneous with our trepidation, we felt hopeful, as if wrong action would be unlikely in a place of such beauty.

Just as the sun disappeared behind the mountains to the west, a woman from the chamber of commerce called the group together. "I would like to offer a song to this land that my grandfather taught me many years ago. I want to sing it in Spanish the way I first heard it as a child." Her voice was strong enough to still the desert wind and the rustling in the mesquite near the tent. Again and again the phrase "*despenaderos rojos*" (red bluffs) rang out in the evening air. Soon we all caught on to the chorus and joined in:

"Despenaderos rojos han hablado a nestros abuelos y abuelas atravez el alba del tiempo."[1]

---

[1] "The red bluffs have spoken to our grandfathers and grandmothers since the beginning of time."

When we stopped singing, a Native-American leader offered a prayer for the land, which he repeated several times while walking around the fire. In the silence that followed, we all sat down without anyone saying a word and formed a circle around the fire. A fair-skinned man from the AEC told a story about the first time he had visited the red bluffs before beginning the feasibility study. He had felt a strong presence when he walked the land, which he didn't understand at first. "Now I realize that initial experience has influenced everything I've envisioned for this place, right down to the detailed design of the facility," he said.

The prayers and stories continued into the night. Our ordinary sense of time dissolved, expanded, reformed, and dissolved again. Even the many thousands of years that the nuclear waste would likely take to decay into harmless matter seemed like a brief moment under the desert stars. No one spoke of the issues directly or called for decisions as we drew ourselves closer and closer to the fire.

Gigi and I exchanged a silent acknowledgment of what was happening. People shared their stories and songs in three languages; the vast silence of the desert dominated the spaces between the words; we were all rooted in the place as if we had lived there forever; no one was leading the group; there was no talking stick—none was needed; no one had to express the intentions of the meeting or how to conduct it. The spirit of council abounded in this place of wild beauty.

The circle slowly found its voice, song by song, story by story, silent moment by silent moment. The men and women present all heard the voice and would be open to its guidance later in the discussions. The circle was filled with grace. Could this actually be happening? The gathering was a prayer answered, a dream fulfilled. We had all entered Dreamtime together. We might even survive the terrifying legacy of our past unconsciousness . . .

And we continue to dream . . .
That children everywhere will have the time,
support and guidance to sit in council . . .
That indigenous ways will be honored
and the old wisdom carried forward . . .
That the voices, ideas and energy of youth
will be heard, respected . . .
and enter the mainstream . . .
That, as one of many species, we will adapt,
evolve and awaken . . .

Written on the inauguration day of the
new president, more than thirteen years
after writing the original Epilogue.

)(

APPENDIX I
SETTING UP A
SCHOOL COUNCIL
PROGRAM

*"When adults in a school trust and value what
students have to say, plenty is said . . . Schools that
encourage students to help govern are democratic.
Democracy is not only a topic that's covered in these
schools—it's a way of life."*

Barb Aust and Wendy Vine,
"The Power of Voice in Schools" ASCD Publication Vol. 7. No. 2, October 2003

"In a school where the council process is deeply rooted, the school site is the nexus, the hub and the heart of the community . . . The school is ideally the location for this work because it represents, quite literally, the reason and purpose of all community activity: the education, health, well-being and sense of efficacy of this generation and the generations to follow."

Joe Provisor: Coordinator of the
Los Angeles Unified School District's
"Council Practitioners Center."

I deally, the decision to initiate a council program should involve members of the administration, faculty, parents and students of the school. Council can change the atmosphere in a school; the "air" the students and teachers breathe is healthier when students sit in council each week. The curriculum is transmitted through a different lens when the *personal* voices of students are deeply heard by the faculty and administration. If council is truly embraced by the school and practiced authentically and regularly, the school may undergo a transformation over time that is akin to what happens when a tree is watered slowly and deeply in nourishing soil. Growth happens.

How a council program is started in a school has a lot to do with the quality and success of the program many years later. In this appendix we will share some experiences in starting council programs in elementary, middle and high schools, both public and private since 1980. During these almost thirty years, our community of "Center for Council Training" (CCT) practitioners has been involved in initiating more than fifty school council programs in California, Arizona, Colorado, Washington, New York and Israel among other places. Many of these programs are ongoing, some are not. We have learned a lot about increasing the viability of council programs in schools—and we still have a lot more to learn. The birth of the Council Practitioners Center (CPC) as an integral part of the Los Angeles Unified School District (LAUSD) in 2006 was a major step towards bringing council into the mainstream of the country's second largest public school system. Besides CPC's role in expanding council in LAUSD and Southern California generally, we expect to initiate school programs in Hawaii, Africa and Europe, as well as other parts of the US over the next few years.

In what follows we will outline the steps we feel should be taken in starting a school program to give council the most fertile environment in which to grow. Much of what we have to say holds for programs at all levels: elementary, middle and high school. Where there are issues to address that are unique to any one of these settings, we will point those out.

THE BEGINNING

Now that the acceptance of council in schools has been growing for almost thirty years, the conception of a program often starts with a member of the school community hearing about council from a friend, colleague or student from another school. Sometimes the first seed is planted by someone who has participated in a council at a school that already has a program. Then the word gets around over a period of time, the period depending on the what's happening in the school community. If the school is facing the challenges of dramatically improving students' academic performance, reducing fragmentation and hostility in the student body or dealing with faculty and/or administrative turnover, this incubation period may be brief. Unlike the early years, when those of us carrying the council vision knocked on the office doors of many school principals with only limited success, we now experience a surge of interest as educators realize something qualitatively different has to happen if the challenges they face are to be resolved productively. The era of simply fine-tuning the curriculum, changing an administrator or a few teachers, or easing parents' concerns through better public relations is past. Educators are increasingly more willing think out of the box and try something "new" to improve the quality of students' performance and their sense of well-being in the school community. Of course, the existence of district centers such as the CPC in Los Angeles accelerates this process significantly, since its primary focus is to initiate council programs in LAUSD.

It is obvious that convincing a school to start a program is more likely to result in a successful program that is ongoing in proportion to the number of influential members of the school that are turned on to the idea. Therefore, the first challenge for whoever is carrying the flame is to build authentic interest in their school before trying to initiate a program. Of course, there are teachers we know who took it upon themselves to start doing council in their own classroom after getting a less than positive response from their colleagues or administrators. Some of the more persistent of these "council guerillas" have been successful in finally getting a program started—and others have given up the ghost after a few years of struggling.

Sometimes it is a passionate parent or two who lights the fire. This has been the case in schools, such as those in the Waldorf System or a new charter school, where parents tend to be more deeply involved and there isn't a large administrative hierarchy that has to be convinced of council's efficacy. Obviously, a good first step for the inspired parent is to bring the idea of starting a program to his or her parent organization and generate a few allies. Since council is more difficult to describe than practice, the best way to get others interested is to invite them to a council presentation that includes participation in an actual council.

On occasion it is a student who has experienced council (say, in middle school) that starts the ball rolling when he or she moves on to a high school without a program and misses the opportunity to share deeply with others.

More often, however, teachers or administrators are the ones who get interested in council and want to see a program start at their school. If a nearby school has a council program, a good first step is to expand the initial "interest group" by inviting a colleague or two to witness a few councils with you. After several people have become interested, then it is time to plan an introduction to council at your school for as many faculty and administrators as you can gather. Naturally, it is wise to invite experienced carriers of the practice—for example, members of the CPC or council carriers from the Ojai Foundation—to make the presentation. It's a good idea to invite school counselors and members of the parent organization to the introduction—and in the case of a middle or high school possibly a few students as well. Members of the Center for Council Training have been conducting such introductions for many years. These events are often a powerful experience for those attending and create the necessary fertile ground out of which a viable program can grow.

The introduction usually consists of four parts:

- A brief verbal description of council, its roots in many cultures and its broad appeal to children and adults. This includes how council can strengthen a school community, improve student self-esteem, deepen student/faculty relationships, and the how and why council can improve academic performance.

- A brief review of the kinds of programs schools have started, particularly those that have been facing the same kinds of challenges as the school hosting the introduction.

- A "live" council with such themes as:
    - "What are the issues and challenges facing your school?"
    - "What are the changes you would like to see take place in your school?"

- "What do you think the obstacles would be to setting up a council program in your school?"
- "Do you see a process such as council being of benefit to you personally?"

• A discussion about what a council program might look like, how and when it might start, what training for teachers and assistance from outside consultants would be needed and how it might be funded.

At the end of the meeting, it is important to identify the individuals at the school and from the presenting group who will follow up on starting a program and clearly define the next steps to be taken.

Sometimes, additional meetings with other members of the school community are necessary before a program can be initiated. It is important to take time during this early stage to prepare the soil for what is to be planted later. Rushing the preparation often leads to challenges downstream, such as involving segments of the community that felt left out or unheard. At Palms Middle School, for example, it took four large-scale introductions and several other smaller meetings over a period of seven months before we were ready to launch the program. At the Highland Hall Waldorf School in Los Angeles, we spent a year meeting with faculty and parents before the school was ready to launch a council program.

Most schools that have been operating for a while have a hierarchical structure that needs to be informed about what it takes to start a council program. Finding an influential individual at the school who might champion the program is a useful step, even if it takes a while to convince him or her (for example, by visiting ongoing councils in other schools, talking to administrators in these schools and/or reading inspiring material about council). This "ally" might be an assistant principal, senior teacher, magnet supervisor or the head counselor. Building a cadre of people who know how to answer questions from parents, teachers and students, as well as respond to concerns about council, goes a long way in providing a solid base for the program.

In a new, small or charter school there is the opportunity to introduce council to the entire school at the same time. This highly desirable situation starts everything off on the right foot and can set a precedent for the ongoing training of the faculty in the council process. We have worked with schools in which almost the entire faculty, administration and key parents were introduced to council at the same time, then underwent council training as a group, and eventually participated in creating the program at the school. At the Open Charter Magnet (Elementary) School in Los Angeles, for example, the core faculty, interested parents and the principal followed this path. For the first few years of the program, these members of the school community gathered annually at the Ojai Foundation for a few days to strengthen the school community, deal with current school issues and receive additional training in council.

FINDING AN EFFECTIVE WAY TO LANGUAGE THE INTRODUCTION TO COUNCIL

It is important for the program initiators to find effective language to describe council, particularly during the program formation period before most people in the school have had chance to experience the practice directly. One basic challenge arises from the fact that sitting in council can lead to profoundly moving experiences that are similar in nature to what some people might associate with the word *spiritual*. Indeed, in its traditional context in many cultures— the Native American, for example—council is an integral part of the spiritual life of the community. The way we have introduced council into schools (as well as in business, government and many communities) respects this ancestry and yet presents council as a universal form of communication free of any doxology or connection with an existing culture or religious practice. Sometimes, when people who have been deeply touched by council share their experience with others using spiritual language, the communication emanates a missionary quality that can be off-putting. The choice of words is important, particularly in a school setting where the sensitivity to such matters is appropriately heightened.

If someone we don't know very well asks us, "Is council a spiritual practice?" and we don't have time for a length explanation, we might answer, "It certainly can be a spirited practice when there is enough trust in the circle for participants to be open, honest and listen from the heart, but the way we practice council is better described as a universal form of communication that allows people to know each other more deeply and completely." In our culture, the meanings of the words spiritual and religious are not well differentiated and it is important to avoid giving the impression that we want to introduce a religious practice when talking to people about council for the first time.

In a school environment, we suggest describing council as a form of group communication that has many uses and leads to a variety of experiences rather than trying to describe or characterize these experiences as spiritual, secular or in any other way. The fact is that council can feel secular when it is used in a meeting to make financial decisions whereas, when personal stories are shared, council can lead to a level of easy intimacy even when people in the circle have not known each other for a long time. Council can lead to playfulness or grief depending on the topic and the circle. Once the majority of people in a school have experienced council a few times, the question "what is it really?" usually diminishes and even disappears.

Emphasizing the uses of council often helps those introducing the practice to find effective language. It is good to point out that council can be used to share stories, brainstorm, explore conflict, make decisions, debate complex issues and get to know each other—all situations that arise naturally and often when groups of people go to school together. Any one of these experiences, when handled in council, can produce a range of experiences from the mundane and boring to the profoundly moving. It is usually enough to leave the introductory words to that. To expand on the utilitarian value of council in schools, some of its primary uses in the educational setting are to

- Build individual self-esteem, through expanding authentic self-expression

- Improve the listening skills of those involved

- Improve academic skills, particularly those basic to English and Social Studies

- Improve the level of understanding among various cultural elements in the school

- Improve the level of understanding between the genders

- Provide opportunities for students and teachers to deepen their ability to accept a wide variety of "others" with a certain amount of grace

- Appreciate that each person has a unique story to tell

- Provide a direct experience of building trust that affirms what is possible among people

- Discover humor and playfulness as ways to bring people more closely together

- Build a strong, more cohesive sense of community in the school.

The choice of which aspects of council to emphasize and what words to use in describing them depends on the age of the children who will be served, the level of familiarity with council that already exists in the faculty, parent body and administration, and the issues that led to the interest in council in the first place. When they are grounded in the kinds of goals listed above, the experiences in council that go beyond the secular are not threatening and are embraced as a natural harvest of good communication.

Training Teachers and Other Facilitators

By the end of the introductory phase of starting a council program it is essential that the school understand the need for formal training in council and agree to have as many of their teachers and administrators trained in the process as possible—at least enough to support the pilot program being considered. Many schools also include parents and other community members in the group to be trained (for example, grandparents, social workers who live in the district and local business people). In Appendix II we describe the council training process at some length. The two most common alternatives for a school starting a program are:

- Having a training at the school, when there are enough members of the community to warrant that (usually twelve or more). Such trainings are a primary offering of the Council Practitioners Center (CPC) at LAUSD.

- Sending those to be trained to a Center for Council Training (CCT) "Introduction to Council" in their area. This is usually the most efficient option when the new program is small and only a few teachers are to be trained. These trainings are offered several times a year in Southern California, either through the CPC or the Ojai Foundation. CCT trainings are also offered in other locations both in the US and abroad in response to demand.

Ideally, all those who will be involved in the new program should complete their training in advance of starting the student program but not more than four or five months before that time. The impact of the training experience is usually strong and generates enough momentum to help trainees face the challenges of sitting in council with students. If too much time elapses between the training and beginning the program, a portion of this momentum may be lost. For example, if a program is to start in September, a good time for the training is in the late spring or early summer.

The initial two- or three-day training experience is only the beginning of the process of learning how to facilitate council. CCT offers second and third level trainings, and as we shall see in a moment, most schools eventually incorporate in-service trainings as a part of the program. If experienced facilitators outside the school community are to be an integral part of a new program (as is usually the case), then, ideally, at least a few of these individuals should be part of the training process. We have found that an excellent way to begin a program is to have the CCT program leaders/mentors also be the trainers for teachers, administrators and others who will be the primary facilitators in the program.

FITTING COUNCIL INTO THE CURRICULUM AND SCHEDULE

There are few puzzles more challenging than creating a school schedule that includes the desired gamut of academic and other activities. Fitting a council program into an already full school program can be a major obstacle in starting up. Generally, it is desirable for councils to take place on a weekly basis, although some programs begin on a bi-monthly schedule and in a few situations (Palms Middle School the first year) we managed to schedule council on a twice-a-week basis. If council is being incorporated in a new school, say a charter school or small private institution, it can often be built into the schedule organically from the beginning.

When class periods are 50-60 minutes long, then in most public school situations where class size can be as large as 35, the group has to be divided into two circles in order that each student has enough time to participate. In these situations, it is often desirable to bring the entire class together once every six weeks or even monthly to build group cohesion. When the class size is less that 20, no division is usually necessary, although it may be desirable. Sometimes the availability of trained facilitators or financial factors determines the size of the council circles. When this results in ongoing circles larger than 20, various forms of council can be used, such as the spiral or fishbowl, to have the program work more effectively.

Finding the right place in the schedule each week for council sometimes depends on who on the faculty are willing to "give up" academic time for the process. As we have emphasized in Chapter 7 and elsewhere, we believe that council can be a "time-efficient" part of the academic curriculum in any school and well worth setting aside one period a week. As an enthusiastic English teacher at Palms said years ago,

> "Having my students in council on a weekly basis improves their literary and writing skills, not to mention all the other developmental benefits of the process. All of these benefits more than justify using one English period a week to sit in circle. So we don't read another short story by an American author or write another expository essay during the year. In the long run, the councils are more valuable to the English Curriculum."

Of course, not all teachers, of English or any other subject, are going to feel this way, particular at first. It takes time for educators to feel comfortable "covering" a little less in their curriculum in order to make room for the less familiar benefits of council.

Here are the ways we have found for including a new council program in a school's schedule, more or less in order of their efficacy in supporting the council experience:

- Council is built into the basic schedule as an integral part of the curriculum, once a week, just as for other weekly activities such as Art, Music, Science Lab, etc. The twenty-five year-old Council Program at the Crossroads School in Santa Monica schedules its council-based "Mysteries Program" in this way. In some private schools (rarely in the public domain), the class length is set at 75 or even 90 minutes, which allows for greater flexibility in the council program and handling larger circles. This approach is more common at the high school level, where schedules are generally more flexible and include a few weekly "activity periods." At the elementary level, where the schedule revolves around "homeroom," greater scheduling flexibility is usually possible.

• Council is introduced to the school through a "Leadership Class" which meets several times a week, one of which is devoted to council. We have found this an excellent way to begin a program, since leadership students usually have a strong influence in the school community and can spread the word about the value of council. We began this way at Palms, meeting twice a week in a Leadership Class that included seventh- Eighth and Ninth-Graders. (This was before Palms made the transition from a junior high school to a middle school.).

• Council is scheduled in place of one of the five-times-a-week class meetings of a core course in the curriculum, such as English or Social Studies. That was the custom at Palms for many years, where it was the English Department that generally embraced council. In the early years at Palms we also experimented with alternating using an English/Social Studies period one semester and a Math/Science period the next. This approach works particularly well at the middle school level, assuming enough teachers are convinced of council's benefits to their standard curriculum.

• Council is scheduled as part of the school-wide advisory period where it is integrated with communicating important information to the students. When such advisory periods are the same length (or longer) as regular classes, this approach can be effective. When the advisory period is shorter and there is a lot of information to communicate to students, trying to do council in the short time remaining can be frustrating.

• Council is scheduled as an optional program to be chosen for a semester by students from a list of offerings. Obviously, this approach reaches fewer students and usually for shorter periods of time but sometimes is the only way to maintain some "council continuity" for those particular drawn to the process.

• Council is scheduled during lunch hour as an optional, drop-in activity. This is the "when everything else fails option" that a few schools have used. In the case of Daniel Webster Middle School (LAUSD) some years back, this approach worked remarkably well for a while, mostly because there was a core group of kids (who had enjoyed regularly scheduled council the year before) that showed up almost every week and ate their lunch as they sat in circle. In a school that has built a tradition of council such optional opportunities are much more likely to work. The "lunch hour" option is not recommended as a way to start a program.

LIMITS OF CONFIDENTIALITY AND ASSOCIATED LEGAL REQUIREMENTS

We have already spoken about the importance of confidentiality agreements in council and alluded to related legal obligations that educators must fulfill in many schools districts (see Chapter 7). To summarize: in starting a council program it is extremely important for the program coordinators to have fully researched state and local laws related to the need to report certain observed behaviors or information received from students. These usually include:

- Statements about abuse in the home from parents, relatives or (in some states) siblings.

- Statements or behaviors that indicate the student is self-destructive.

- Statements or behaviors that indicate the student is seriously planning acts of violence against others.

- Statements or behaviors that indicate the student is involved with illegal drugs, alcohol or misuse of prescription medications.

Since council often creates enough of a trusting environment for students to reveal things about themselves and their home lives that are normally hidden or spoken of to only a few friends, the issue of legal obligations on the part of council facilitators must be addressed. Even though teachers are supposed to be familiar with local reporting requirements, the existence of council in their school enhances the chances that they will hear the kind of information that they must report. Council program coordinators and each facilitator have the responsibility to know these legal obligations and make sure they have dealt with these laws in establishing limits of confidentiality in their circles at the very beginning of the program.

We suggest that facilitators review the local laws briefly with their circle and make clear that they will have to "report" certain situations if they hear of them during council. The following statement is typical:

"Our confidentiality agreement—what is said in council stays in the circle—has its limits. The limits arise when any of you tells us about abuse at home or that you plan to be self-destructive or are seriously contemplating violence against another person. So if you share a story that falls into one of these categories, I am obligated to report it to your school counselor who in turn may contact your parents."

The facilitator may go on to say that exaggerated, dramatic or fabricated stories about abuse or violence are obviously not in the best interests of anyone in the circle and can cause a lot of confusion and unnecessary reaction. In our experience over thirty years, these kinds of situations arise rarely in a council program, since most students either consciously or unconsciously speak of such matters in order to get help, or tend to keep such information to themselves once they hear of the consequences. But, no matter how rare, situations do arise and facilitators must be prepared. We suggest that a plan of action be worked out with the school's counseling staff or administration should a report be necessary. A typical plan looks something like this:

- First, speak to the student after council and make sure you heard correctly what was shared. If you suspect the student is under the influence of some illegal substance, reaffirm that suspicion directly with the student after council before taking the next step.

- If you believe you have to make a report, inform the student that you are planning to do so at the earliest possible moment. This usually produces one of three reactions: relief (he or she has wanted to seek help and was afraid or didn't know how to do it directly); upset, confusion and then a confession that the story wasn't really true (the student was "performing" in council); or anger, resistance and a refusal to either own the statement again or "be reported." In the first case, the facilitator makes arrangements for a consultation with a school counselor *who is already aware of how council might reveal such reportable information and is set up to take the next pre-established step.* This is one of the reasons for having one or more school counselors involved in the formation of a council program right from the start. The same action may be prudent in the second instance as well, since the student was clearly getting attention by touching on issues that may be at an early stage of development and best dealt with immediately. It's a judgment call on the part of the facilitator, who may want to talk to the school counselor in any event to see if there is a history that suggests follow-up is required. If you decide that no further action on your part is necessary, you may still want to suggest to the student that he or she talk about what happened at the next council, so that the rest of the circle has the corrected information. Obviously, the third situation is the most difficult—and fortunately in our experience extremely rare. The facilitator has no choice but to report the information to school authorities immediately whether the student accompanies the facilitator or not.

• Follow up the situation with the circle—at the next session if possible—informing everyone that you made the necessary report, if that was your action, without going into any details. As suggested above, if the student in question confessed that he or she had been less than truthful and you have decided not to pursue the matter further with school authorities, it might be a good idea to have the next council deal with the issue *generally* under the theme of "integrity" or "ways people try to get attention." Encouraging students to be authentic in council rather than performing or making contributions that will be seen as "exciting" is an important part of deepening the process.

Guidelines for Starting a Council Program

Although every school council program is unique, there are several guidelines to consider that may save program initiators a little grief. We learned these mostly the hard way, although in retrospect these suggestions all seem quite reasonable.

Start Small. When there is a lot of enthusiasm for council, there can be a temptation to launch a large program during the first year. Typically, this urge is motivated by wanting all the students at a certain grade level to have the opportunity to sit in circle rather than just a few, or wanting to start an entire new school—say a start-up charter school—with council in the curriculum. While these are worthy goals, it is usually more productive in the long run to start with a pilot program that gives the school a chance to get used to council on a smaller scale and not stretch the number of trained facilitators too thin. We have experienced more than a few times having to shore up a "too-large" new program struggling with fewer experienced facilitators than were really needed, the program leaders becoming overwhelmed or insufficient funding. There are no fixed rules. A small school of 60 or even 80 students, just beginning might very well incorporate council successfully into its program, if the faculty is trained in advance and these teachers are supported by a number of experienced outside facilitators as in-service trainers and mentors for a year or two. On the other hand, in a long established large school, it is often better to break-in the community slowly to the rich harvest of council by starting off with one or a few classes whose teachers are particularly enthusiastic (and well-trained) in council. To summarize, the factors to evaluate in decided on the size of an initial program include:

- The number of successfully trained facilitators

- The strength of the "buy-in" on the part of the faculty, administration and parents—and, of course, students, particularly at the high school level

- The availability of experienced program leadership and mentoring

- The availability of funding to support the training of teachers and the need for experienced support from outside the school.

Guidelines for Expansion. Assuming the pilot program was successful, the rush to expand a program significantly in its second year might become the temptation to resist. We started the council program at Palms with a single Leadership Class divided into two circles— a great model for beginning as we have mentioned before—but then the school's enthusiasm was so intoxicating that we agreed to expand the program into the entire Sixth-Grade the second year. Since that involved over 300 students (20 councils every week) we were working hard right up to the last minute (and long after that!) to make sure all the circles were led by people in whom we had full trust and that the whole faculty felt comfortable with what council was bringing to their school. We pulled it off quite well—with a few bumps in the road to be sure—but it took the whole year to feel satisfied with how everything was going. In 2004-2005—the twelfth year of the program—there were over 100 councils a week a Palms, facilitated by a few teachers and a team of twenty-five outside facilitators. The program was coordinated by a Leadership Circle of five highly experienced council carriers, most of whom were also council trainers. Several members of this leadership group are now playing a central role in LAUSD's Council Practitioners Center. It can take several years for a council program to mature in a healthy way depending on the challenges the school faces in terms of student body fragmentation, teacher and administration acceptance, faculty turnover, and the steadiness of funding.

The program at Palms, which had an annual budget of over $100,000 at its peak (not including the school's "in-kind support"), worked smoothly for many years because of the long experience and competence of its leaders and facilitators, and because the program was supported by a committed administration and a few dedicated teachers. However, the large number of outside facilitators required generating this level of funding annually, which clearly was not sustainable in the long run. Our attempts to train a larger fraction of the faculty in council were ultimately not successful and so, when the school administration went through a major change, the devotion to council lost momentum and we came to realize that a different model—relying much less on outside support—was needed. What evolved from this experience was the "mentor model" which involves an intensive first year of teacher training/mentoring followed by a second transitional year in which the outside facilitators serve mostly as mentors. The mentor model is described in greater detail below. Palms now has a smaller council program, supported almost exclusively by a core of well-trained and experienced teachers.

The expansion of the program in the second and subsequent years is unique to each school and depends on factors similar to these discussed above. The following is a summary of what we have learned over the years:

- A modest increase in the size of a program usually works well—for example, from a program involving 30 students to one involving 60 or even 75. Jumping from 30 to 300, as we just noted can produce definite growing pains.

- If expansion during the second year is to include students at a different developmental level than those in the pilot program, be aware that this is somewhat like starting a new program. The facilitators may need additional training or new facilitators may have to be added to the staff who are knowledgeable about the new students entering the program.

- Be sure to include a careful evaluation of the program at the end of the first year so that the expansion can be planned on the basis of what is learned during the pilot program. We have found that written evaluations are important, although it is always important to also

have councils at the end of the year during which
verbal comments about the program and suggestions
for the future are solicited. The written evaluations
should include: all students who participated in the
pilot program, teachers who were directly involved
in the councils as first year facilitators, at least a few
teachers only indirectly involved with the program
who are closely connected to the students, and
appropriate administrators and school counselors. We
have asked parents on occasion to fill out evaluations,
although parent feedback can also be received during
parent councils that meet several times each year (see
below). Typical evaluation questions might explore
the appropriateness of the council topics chosen, the
skill of the facilitators, the changes in relationships
at school and home that can be attributed to council
and the effect of council on academic performance.[1]
The extent and nature of the expansion during the
second year emerges from the evaluations, particularly if
suggestions for changes are included. For example, the
need for additional training for facilitators and/or more
involvement of parents might become apparent. Taking
the evaluations seriously, summarizing the results and
reporting back to students, teachers and administrators
are very much in the spirit of council.

- The goal is to have the second year of the program
depend significantly less on outside facilitators than was
necessary during the first year. Again, we have learned to
go slow and make sure the teachers involved feel strong
as facilitators before turning them completely loose from
co-leading with, and being mentored by, experienced
leaders.

[1] See "Palms Council Project Evaluation—Final Report" WestEd, by Barbara Dietsch, August
31, 2001

- Assuming teachers feel ready, it is important that the school leadership include strong support for the council program during the faculty meetings before the second year begins. A good way to show this support is to actually use council as part of the start-up process with the faculty. For years at Palms, start-up days often included breaking up the whole faculty into small groups who counciled on issues that were "up" for them as they began the new year.

Making Decisions About the Program

We have heard ourselves say again and again as a program matures and enters the school's mainstream that "council is not just something we do with the kids; it's also a process we use ourselves." The "we" in this statement means the school faculty and administration, as well as the outside program facilitators and leadership. For example, whenever possible, council should be used when soliciting information or make decisions about the program—during faculty, administrative and parent meetings, for example. Adults in the school community "walking their talk" in this way is one of the best affirmations of the program. Students know when advocacy of a program is authentic rather than superficial—and they respond accordingly. An essential part of any school program is regular meetings—including council—preferably at least twice a month that involve all the facilitators and program leadership. This creates a "support group environment" for dealing with the many challenges of facilitation and provides the opportunity for often much-needed ongoing in-service training.

DEALING WITH STUDENTS WHO DON'T SEEM READY FOR COUNCIL

Occasionally, one encounters students who seem clearly unable to keep up with their peers in embracing what is happening in council. For example, they may not be able to follow the basic intentions of council and instead speak frequently out of turn. Or they may have difficulty sitting still for any length of time and be innately uncomfortable with the process. Even some of the ice-breaking activities that are used to ease kids into council may not help some students. There may be indications of ADD or ADHD symptoms that suggest neurological issues are at play.

The basic problem in such situations is the gap between the abilities of the distracted (and thus distracting) child and the rest of the circle. The whole group suffers the effects of his or her discomfort, which increases the tension and, in turn, increases the child's discomfort. More often than not the behavioral problems are psychological, related to troubles at home or some traumatic event. The roots of the difficulties may be as yet undiagnosed neurological disorders. Sometimes it is hard to tell what is behavior and what is neurology.

When we work with circles of special needs kids, everyone is more or less struggling with similar issues and such gaps are smaller. We find ways to help the special needs kids through different kinds of exercises and specially designed council themes. Facilitators of special needs circles develop particular skills in building a container so that council can take place in a productive fashion. We have had many remarkable experiences in recent years as we deepen our understanding of the power of council to actually support the healing process for special needs children. We have also learned that, with the proper leadership, inclusive councils made up of a mix of special needs students and neurologically typical students can offer the latter a chance to deepen their sensitivity, compassion and tolerance, while the special needs kids are stimulated by the inclusive environment to deepen their ability to communicate.

When the behavior of a child stands out in a group, whatever the reasons, and efforts to integrate him or her prove unsuccessful, it is sometimes better to shift them to another circle in which the "gap" will be smaller or place them in a special circle for students who needed extra support in preparing to sit in council. Curricula for such council preparation students and special needs students are available through the Council Practitioners Center at LAUSD.

VISITORS

During a pilot program (and, of course, subsequently as the program matures), teachers, administrators, parents, as well as educators from other schools and potential funders, who are not directly involved in the program, want to sit in on a council to "see what it's like." Obviously, there is no better way to have someone understand the potential of council than to witness it in action. Sometimes, even the most eloquent descriptions cannot do justice to what happens in a council circle. As we have said, council is often seeded in a new school as a result of a visitor's experience in a circle at another. So, being able to have guests visit an ongoing council can be very valuable. On the other hand, when a circle is just beginning to integrate the four intentions and build mutual trust, having a visitor present can significantly influence what takes place in the council—particularly if the visitor is an authority figure for the students.

Whether this influence is productive or not from the facilitator's or students' points of view, facilitators eventually want to be able to welcome guests to their councils, knowing that everyone will learn a lot from the experience. The "guest" has great significance in many traditions and we have found that to be the case for the practice of council as well. There are a few useful guidelines in helping this experience be a positive one all around.

- The visit should be set up in advance in order to have time for the circle to consider both the visitor's and the teacher' motivations in setting up the visitation. It is good council protocol for the facilitator(s) to ask the whole circle's permission for the visitor to join the circle. The more the students understand the purpose for the visit and have had a chance to express their views about it, the more likely the guest will have a good experience of council and the students will learn something from having someone new take a seat in the circle.

- The visitor should always be introduced, welcomed and, whenever possible, asked to say a few words to the circle at the start of council—for example, where she or he is from and the purpose of the visit. This is particularly important when the visit is connected with the topic or focus of the council. If the visitor is there in any way to observe how the facilitator handles the circle (for example, if the visitor is the facilitator's mentor), it is essential to make that purpose known to the circle of students.

- Whatever the purpose of the visit, it is good council protocol to ask the visitor to comment on his or her experience at the end of the council, in the spirit of the "witness/guest." It may also be appropriate for the facilitator to ask if there are comments from the circle about the visit, using either the "pop corn" form of council with the piece in the center or by passing the piece all the way around.

- If the visit stirred the circle in a significant way, it may be useful to have a brief council about the experience when the circle next meets. The focus can be on the specifics of the experience, visitors in general—or both.

PARENT COUNCILS

As mentioned before, we have found it good practice to initiate parent councils during the first year of a program in order to give parents a chance to ask questions about the new program, express concerns and, most important, to experience council themselves directly. Two a semester seems to be a good balance between offering enough opportunities for parents without burdening them with too many "meetings." At least one each semester is essential in most situations. Even though only a small fraction of the parent body may attend, providing the opportunity builds trust in the parent community. As the program evolves, more frequent councils can be offered which focus on parenting and current school issues rather than just finding out what the kids are doing in the council program. At Palms, for example, parent councils were offered regularly for many years. During one two-year period, the parent councils were independently sponsored by a foundation particularly interested in expanding parenting skills. As a result of this program, we saw clearly how effective parent councils can be in building a stronger school community.

For program continuity, parent councils usually are led by some of the same people who are facilitating the student councils. We always urge all the facilitators to attend, particularly the one or two meetings each semester that are focused on talking about the program itself. If many parents show up, then either the spiral form of council can be used or, preferably, the group can be broken up into smaller circles of 15 or so, in order to encourage more intimate sharing. We have found that it's best to not let the parental councils drift into making comments to individual parents about how their kids are "doing in council."

There is never a problem finding themes for parent councils, once parents understand what the program is about and why the school has embraced it. Parenting continues to provide most of us at least as many challenges as we can handle. When parents have an opportunity to sit in council a few of them get so deeply moved by the process that they want to become facilitators themselves. Some of our best facilitators started out as parents!

FUNDING COUNCIL PROGRAMS

The financial state of most American Public School Districts in this first part of the new millennium is stressed at best. Some schools (and even districts) have been taken over by their State Departments of Education or a private educational organization in order to improve academic performance or establish fiscal stability—or both. The increasing intense emphasis on testing over the last several years—and, therefore, on improving student test scores—has tended to shift priorities away from programs such as council. What all this means is that—with some notable exceptions—most districts and individual schools have limited or no funds with which to support a new council program. That means starting a council program usually involves a lot of fund raising effort on the part of both those from the school who want the program and those interested in delivering it. Our good fortune in being able to establish the Council Practitioners Center was based on a three-year initiating grant from the Herb Alpert Foundation, as well as the District's willingness to provide additional support. Our hope, of course, is that the success of the CPC will inspire other school districts to establish similar centers of council activity.

In the present financial environment, it is obviously prudent to obtain funding that has long-range possibilities and for which the school itself takes a major share of the responsibility. Even when seed grants are available to support the program in the first year, ultimately the school has to take over a major share of funding responsibility if the program is to prosper. Furthermore, as we have already mentioned, it is better to train the teachers and other members of the school community to lead councils on their own, as soon as that becomes feasible, rather than relying heavily on outside facilitators year after year as we did at Palms. The basic model we recommend now—the "Mentor-Based Council Program"—brings in an experienced team of facilitators, mentors and leaders with the intention of providing both an initial and then in-service training for enough members of the school community during the first year of the program to allow the school to take over major responsibility for the program in the following year (with perhaps continuing guidance from a smaller staff of experienced council leaders). In a few cases, when funding is limited, we might aspire to achieve this goal in one semester, but it almost all cases a year is required for a program to become viable.

We will describe this model in more detail in the next section. Not only is the mentor model less expensive after the first year but council becomes much more a part of the life-blood of a school when the community takes a greater share of the responsibility for facilitation—and funding. Here are a few suggestions for funding that arise from the numerous juggling acts we have been through trying to support school council programs during the past thirty years.

- The ideal way to fund a council pilot program in the public domain is to get the district involved at the highest administrative level—and for the right reasons: council improves the quality of relationships in a school, reduces violence and fragmentation in the student body, and improves students' self confidence, communication skills and academic performance. In other words, council helps a school truly become a vital educational community. This was the basis for the creation of LAUSD's Council Practitioners Center. If the powers that be see this and find the funds to start a pilot program (perhaps with the assistance of a start-up grant from a foundation), prospects for the long term are about as rosy as they can be in this age of economic uncertainty. In some states there are Federal and/or State funds available for district level funding and, although there are many good programs competing for them, council is becoming better known all the time and can be a viable candidate for support from such sources. In California, several years ago, we were blessed with a two-year

State Grant as part of its "Teaching Tolerance Program" that allowed us to start two new middle school programs and provide partial support for the ongoing program at Palms. Some schools have used Title One funds to start a school program by arguing that council for students is like providing them with "curriculum materials" that they lack in pursuing their academic classes. For us this point of view is not a stretch at all. Being able to listen attentively and express oneself more coherently are among the most basic "materials" for learning.

- Generally we have found that council programs have to find sources of support other than from district level for several years until the district takes notice, decides it's a good program and then finally finds a way to support it either directly, in collaboration with a foundation, or through Federal and/or State funding.

- Sometimes a school can cover a portion of the cost of a council program through "in-kind" contributions. For many years Palms supported its council program by paying for teacher replacements during the student leadership retreats at the Ojai Foundation, providing school buses for these retreats and by petitioning the district for the relief of a key teacher from one or more class responsibilities so he could participate in the program's leadership circle. Funding of this sort obviously depends on the school administration being willing to manifest their enthusiasm in a strong way. Lip-service support obviously won't do in today's financial environment. Picking up the tab for the initial council training of teachers is the most common form of school support that we have experienced.

- If the school's parent organization is fully aware of the virtues of council, it can be an excellent source of

on-going funding. The "Friends of Palms" supported
the schools council program for many years, providing
from about 8 to 15 percent of program costs on
an annual basis. Clearly, offering periodic parent
councils as an integral part of the program increases
the likelihood of the parents' willingness to make this
kind of commitment. Often funding from the parent
organization is generated by bake sales, magazine
subscription drives and other money-generating activities
in which the students can play a major role.

• When a school is well connected to its surrounding
community, local business organizations that have
discretionary funds available for "community service"
can play a role in seeding and keeping a council program
going. Some supermarkets have programs in which a
small percentage of each sale—typically 0.5 percent—can
be assigned to a local school of the buyer's choice.
A major electronics company and a major local mall
developer supported the Palms Program for many
years. This kind of support is obviously more likely to
be available in a school that has a student community
service program and a faculty that is engaged in local
community activities. In some situations it is even
possible to enlist local business people as facilitators.
Palms offered a community council intern program
for several years in which people who live in the
neighborhood sat in on councils as participants. The
CPC is establishing a similar program in some school
communities in LA. Over a period of time some of
these people get sufficiently interested to get trained and
become part of the facilitation team.

• By far the largest source of support for starting and
sustaining council programs have been foundations
and individual donors who want to see programs like

council flourish. Both local and national foundations
have provided grants, some over a period of many years.
The New Visions Foundation in Santa Monica, led
by Paul Cummins, has supported council programs
in several of the charter schools they have sponsored.
One of the most important capabilities for a Council
Program Leadership Circle to have is grant writing.
Some foundations prefer to support the expansion of
an existing program and others are more attracted to
seeding new programs. On occasion, the district may
have a grant from a foundation that can be used to
start or sustain a program. Individual donors fall into
several categories: "friends" of the program leadership
or of key figures in the school community who want to
see programs like council get established in the school;
people who know of council from direct experience and
want to see it spread into public education generally;
and, of course, alumni of the school, the younger of
whom may have even experienced council for the first
time when they were students. Individual donors played
a significant role in the early years of the Palms Program,
accounting for the majority of support until foundation
grants were obtained.

Ultimately, the dream is to have council become an integrated
part of the standard school curriculum, as it is recognized to be as
fundamental to the education of young people as the "Three R's" and
its role in building a school community is fully appreciated. When
that happens, funding council programs will not require the many
challenges we experience now. The light at the end of the tunnel is
coming from charter and magnet schools, as well as innovative independent schools that have started up in recent years with visions
that are grounded in the benefits of open and spirited relationships
among all members of the school community. A few schools in this
group have embraced council in their first few years of existence and

trained their entire faculty. The overall educational experience at the school becomes inseparable from the benefits of deep, attentive listening and authentic communication.

THE MENTOR-BASED COUNCIL PROGRAM MODEL

We call the approach that has emerged over the past five years the "Mentor-Based Council Program" (MBCP) because it relies more on experienced council leaders mentoring a school's faculty than it does on the outside facilitators implementing the program themselves. In most cases, the goal is to have experienced council facilitators mentor the teachers (and possibly others in the school community) for a year. The program coordinator and possibly a few other experienced facilitators, working closely with one or more school program coordinators may need to be involved for a second year in some situations. This is the basic approach being taken by the CPC in the Los Angeles District. The template for a MBCP looks like this:

- An experienced CCT council leader is selected to oversee the program, coordinate all the activities and help the school become self-sufficient for a period of from one to two years. We refer to this person as the "Trainer/Mentor" (TM).

- The TM is assisted by other experienced council facilitators, who are not part of the school community, and who will be involved primarily during the program start-up phase—in most cases, the first year.

- The facilitators being trained are teachers, administrators, counselors, parents (past and present) and possibly other members of the school community (grandparents, local business people, etc.)—all of whom undergo an intensive CCT or CPC "Introduction to Council" training before the program starts. In most cases, these members of the school community are trained together as a group, with the TM as one of the trainers.

• The program begins with each trainee paired with an experienced facilitator (including the TM), assuming funding and availability permit, or, when this is not the case, each of the experienced facilitators take on a small group of trainees each one of which they will mentor by periodically co-leading their councils in rotation. The trainees lead the councils by themselves at other times. The TM is responsible for coordinating all the mentors, which includes bi-monthly meetings of the teacher/trainees plus all the mentors. These meetings constitute an important part of the in-service training, act as a support group and also provide a context for council curriculum development.

• If funding permits and each trainee becomes ready to lead council on her or his own (guided by their mentor), they do so until the whole group is working independently. If this not possible, a time is set during the second semester for the mentors to complete their training and the TM (or a designate) takes over the mentoring process, rotating through all the trainee's councils observing and offering feedback. The bimonthly meetings continue until the TM feels the group of trainees is ready to take over completely and several members of the group have been selected to form a school-based "Program Leadership Group." The TM then mentors this group for the duration of the pilot program. Hopefully, this can all happen during the first year.

- If further mentoring and training becomes necessary, either of the Program Leadership Group or individual teacher/facilitators, the second year of the program will reflect these needs. This additional support from CCT facilitators may be necessary due to teacher turnover, expansion of the program to a new (and different) group of students, dealing with a particularly challenging student body, etc. Ideally, the TM stays with the program until there is strong evidence that the transfer of full responsibility to the school-based Program Leadership Group will lead to a viable and productive ongoing experience for students, teachers and the wider school community. If funding permits the program to expand each year, it may take several years to reach that goal.

OTHER MODELS FOR INITIATING COUNCIL PROGRAMS

A model being pursued now enthusiastically involves collaboration between a district wide council center, such as the CPC (all of whose members can function as TM's) and the larger pool of CCT facilitators in the area. The district center has the assignment to train teachers and initiate council programs in district's schools. When a school indicates an interest in starting a program, the center reaches out to CCT facilitators in its area to fill out the team that will initiate the MBCP's at that school. The funds needed to support the first year (and perhaps part of the second year) of each program are provided either by the district or any of the other sources described above. We feel these hybrid models, in which district leaders and non-district facilitators work together to train teachers and start programs in the district, are a realistic path to having council become an integral part of our educational system.

)((

Appendix II
Council
Training

[*Out of breath and speaking fast*] "Is this the Ojai Foundation?
I'm supposed to be in a council training this weekend . . . I'm
late. The traffic getting out of L.A. was miserable. I thought
I'd never get here. On top of all that, I missed the turnoff."

"You've found us. Welcome! The training starts after supper. We'll be meeting over there in the community yurt. Why
don't you catch your breath and clean up. We'll help you get
settled after you eat."

[*After supper, somewhat slower*] "I assume this is the community nurt, or whatever it's called."

"You're in the right place. Come in and take a drum or a
rattle from the big basket. We're going to make a little music
as people gather."

"*Drum?*"

Teachers, business men and women, members of other communities, therapists, artists, and a few "wild cards" drum and rattle together. Soon nervousness and the tensions of the road subside.

"This training may be a little different than others you've taken," one of the two facilitators says into the silence after the drumming. "The process will be primarily experiential rather than didactic, although there will be several hours set aside for discussing specific challenges in using council in a business organization, classroom, intentional community, or family.

"We will meet together in council several times a day, telling stories about the challenges we face in our work and personal lives. We'll experiment with different forms of council and talk about the times when each form can be useful. We'll tell you a little about our experience with council and ask you to share your own insights. Some of you may know a lot about the process; some may be new to it. We urge those of you who know council to enter this training with a beginner's mind. Every circle brings new teachings.

"You are all invited to join the community meditation before breakfast. We sit in silence together, each doing our own practice, although we'll be glad to offer a little basic meditation instruction on request. We'll have a chance to share dreams tomorrow and Sunday morning, in the spirit of council, as stories of the night.

"Together, we will explore the art of council leadership, including the use of different forms, becoming an exemplary practitioner of the intentions of council, finding personal authenticity, and learning how to see what's going on in the circle. Hopefully we will experience how council can become a practice, a way of being together, that awakens and refreshes our spirits.

"We will explore 'turning into the skid'—that is, facing the shadow side of what's happening in the circle and with ourselves. We'll discuss letting go of expectations about what constitutes a 'good' council and releasing the need to have issues resolved when the truth of the circle is otherwise. All of this should be a lot clearer by Sunday afternoon.

"Each of these trainings is unique. We never know exactly what's going to happen, although we have an overall format and intention. We invariably discover new ways to talk about council and sometimes even new refinements of form emerge from our time together.

"We hope the training will mark the beginning of a personal relationship with this land for each of you. The council process has been seeded and nourished here by hundreds of children and adults over the years, just as it has in a number of other communities, schools and business organizations around the country and abroad. By bringing your personal experience to the circle, our knowledge about council grows. We hope what you learn here will strengthen the spirit of council in your own circles.

"Now it's time to discuss the four main intentions of council, and then we'll set the theme for tonight's opening circle . . . "

Several CCT introductory and intermediate trainings for prospective and experienced council leaders, respectively, are offered annually at the Ojai Foundation and LAUSD's Council Practitioners Center (CPC) in Los Angeles. In addition, an annual "Gathering of Council Leaders" takes place at the Foundation to give CCT trainers from all over the world an opportunity to gather and share mutual concerns. At the Gathering, training standards and curricula are discussed, standards set, ways in which trainers in the international CCT network can support each other are explored, and new trainers are initiated. The leadership of the Gathering changes each year, now that Gigi and I have passed the baton to the entire circle of some forty trainers, more than a half-dozen of whom live outside of the US.

There is also a third level of CCT council training that Gigi and I used to lead regularly for senior facilitators and trainers in training, usually at the Foundation. This level of training is focused on "living the way of council" and preparing seasoned facilitators to be trainers. It is planned to carry on this third level in several ways in the future: through the seven-day Nature of Council leadership training in Big Pine and also through shorter advanced trainings at Ojai and the CPC in Los Angeles.

CCT trainers also offer preparatory, intermediate and advanced trainings designed specifically for business organizations, communities and schools, at their locations both in the US and abroad. In recent years trainings have been offered in Europe, Israel and Africa.

In order to support the council in nature aspect of school council program, a limited number of student retreat internships for educators are available each fall and spring at the Foundation. Interns work directly with groups of children from public and independent schools, co-facilitating council and participating in other community activities on the land. Those interested in youth retreat internships should contact Trisha Graham at the Foundation: 805 646-8343. Internships are also available at the School of Lost Borders: PO Box 796, Big Pine, CA 93513.

Internships for council facilitation in schools are also available, primarily at Crossroads School. The CPC is now implementing plans to establish a school-based internship program at LAUSD. Those interested in classroom apprenticeships in council should contact Trisha Graham at The Ojai Foundation: 805 646-8343.

The implementation of council programs in Los Angeles public schools is now the responsibility of the CPC in partnership with the Ojai Foundation. Independent school programs are led and staffed by CCT trainers and program leaders that work closely with the CPC and the Foundation. All school program leaders are invited to the annual gathering of trainers at the Foundation.

A group of criminal justice specialists and CCT trainers have been working since 2002 to create a council-based initiative called the "One Thousand Days Program" (OTDP). This multi-faceted project includes bringing council into the California Prison System, as well as working with the prisoners' families and community support organizations in the locations to which released inmates return. The OTDP offers a sequence of council (and related) trainings for those individuals who are interested in doing council with prison inmates, their families and community support organizations. Further information about the OTDP can be found on The Ojai Foundation web site: www.ojaifoundation.org or by contacting Alan Mobley at: alan.mobley@sdsu.edu.

The CCT network is by no means the only group offering training in council and related practices. There are a number of initiatives, organizations and now even universities that offer opportunities to be trained in a variety of circle processes. One we would like to mention in particular, because of our long association, is the PeerSpirt circle, led by Christina Baldwin and Ann Linnea and others. PeerSpirit is based in Langley Washington.

We are greatly encouraged by how the "Field of Council" is growing in its many forms. Talking circles are happening in more and more places throughout the world. The essence of this Field is simple and graceful . . . In any given moment, one person is speaking and the rest of the circle is listening.

)(

APPENDIX III
BIBLIOGRAPHY

Books

Flesh and Spirit: The Mystery of Intimate Relationship, by Jack Zimmerman & Jaquelyn McCandless, Bramble Books, Las Vegas, 1998.

Peacemaking Circles: From Crime to Community, by Kay Pranis, Barry Stuart, & Mark Wedge, Living Justice Press, 2003.

The Little Book of Circle Processes: New/Old Approaches to Peacemaking, by Kay Pranis, Good Books Press, Intercourse, PA, 2005.

Calling the Circle: The First and Future Culture, by Christina Baldwin, Bantam Doubleday Dell Publishers, New York, 1998.

Dreaming the Council Ways: True Native Teachings from the Red Lodge, by Ohkey Simine Forest, Samuel Weiser Inc., York Beach Maine, 2000.

The Earth Shall Weep: A History of Native America, by James Wilson, Grove Press, New York, 1999.

Secret Teachings of Plants: The Intelligence of the Heart in the Direct Perception of Nature, by Stephen Harrod Buhner, Bear & Company, 2004.

Emotional Intelligence, by Daniel Goleman, Bantam Books, New York, 1995.

Flow: The Psychology of Optimal Experience, by Mihaly Csikszentmihalyi, Harper & Row, New York, 1990.

Owning Your Own Shadow, by Robert A. Johnson, HarperSan Francisco, 1991.

The Magic of Conflict: Turning a Life of Work into a Work of Art, by Thomas F. Crum, Touchstone/Simon & Schuster, New York, 1987.

Proceed with Passion: Engaging Students in Meaningful Education, Paul F. Cummins, Anna Cummins, & Emily Cummins, Red Hen Press, Los Angeles, 2004.

The Practice of the Wild, by Gary Snyder, North Point Press, San Francisco, 1990.

The Soul of Education: Helping Students Find Connection, Compassion and Character at School, by Rachael Kessler, Association for Supervision and Curriculum Development, April 2000.

Examplar of Liberty: Native America and the Evolution of Democracy, by Donald A. Grinde & Bruce E. Johnson, University of California, American Indian Studies, 1991.

Storycatcher: Making Sense of Our Lives through the Power and Practice of Story, by Christina Baldwin, New World Library, 2005.

The Box: Remembering the Gift by the Terma Company , Santa Fe, New Mexico , 1990. Contact Gigi Coyle at: gigicoyle@earthlink.net.

The Tao of Democracy: Using Co-Intelligence to Create a World that Works for All, by Tom Atlee, World Works Press, 2002.

Listening: A Way of Hearing in a Silent World, by Hannah Merker and Henry Kisor, Southern Methodist University Press, 2000. A poetic book about working with the hearing impaired that speaks deeply about the nature of listening.

Original Instructions: Indigenous Teachings for a Sustainable Future, Edited by Melissa K. Nelson, Bear & Company, 2008.

Web Sites

www.ojaifoundation.org The Ojai Foundation website: information, council trainings and retreat schedule,

www.artforthesky.com Daniel Dancer, large-scale earth art

www.boulderinstitute.org The Boulder Institute for Nature and the Human Spirit, Elias Amidon and Elizabeth Roberts. Especially note their on-going pilgrimage memoirs: "Letters from the Road."

www.schooloflostborders.net The Nature of Council: learning its roots and what it means to live council, leadership trainings and initiations as a council leader, council application in many settings including rites of passage.

www.ldnafricaaids.org A web site that describes both the medical research being done in Mali, Africa with Low Dose Naltrexone to prevent HIV positive individuals from developing AIDS, and a concurrent council-based program for men and women to improve inter- and intra-gender communication and support the empowerment of women.

Link TV

"A Council of 13 Indigenous Grandmothers." An hour-long feature tentatively titled: *Prayer & Action.*